STATES IN CRISIS

BY JAMES REICHLEY

WITH

EARL BEHRENS (CALIFORNIA)
San Francisco Chronicle

JAMES COOPER (ARIZONA)
Tucson Daily Citizen

LEO EGAN (NEW YORK)
New York Times

JOHN HARRIS
(MASSACHUSETTS)
Boston Globe

JAMES LATIMER (VIRGINIA)
Richmond Times-Dispatch

MICHAEL MALONEY (OHIO)
Formerly with the
Cincinnati Enquirer

JOHN MC CULLOUGH
(PENNSYLVANIA)
Philadelphia Bulletin

RICHARD MILLIMAN
(MICHIGAN)
Formerly with the
Lansing State Journal

RICHARD MOREHEAD (TEXAS)
Dallas Morning News

FRANK RALL (NEBRASKA)
Lincoln Journal

STATES
IN
CRISIS

POLITICS IN TEN AMERICAN
STATES | 1950-1962

THE UNIVERSITY OF NORTH CAROLINA PRESS
CHAPEL HILL

Copyright © *1964 by*

THE UNIVERSITY OF NORTH CAROLINA PRESS

Library of Congress Catalog Card Number 64-13557

PRINTED BY VAIL-BALLOU PRESS, INC., BINGHAMTON, NEW YORK

Manufactured in the United States of America

FOR MARY

PREFACE

From the moment in 1787 when James Madison laid down his pen and the weary delegates to the Constitutional Convention departed from Philadelphia, there has existed in the United States a natural tension between the national government of the federal union and the still partially sovereign governments of the several states. Almost two centuries after the federal experiment began, the surprising fact is not that power has gradually shifted toward the national end of the balance, but that the states have succeeded in maintaining very considerable measures of independence and authority.

The persistent vitality of the states is derived not only from their roles in the functional work of government (which in recent years have fallen more and more under the influence of the federal bureaucracy) but also from their importance in the national political structure. In an age when armies, economies, religions, cultures, and almost everything else are organized on a national or international basis, the states remain the fundamental units of American politics.

This political significance is due in part to the nature of the federal Constitution. The members of the legislative branch of the national government—particularly the senators, but also to a great extent the members of the House of Representatives—are elected to represent states, and trace their political interests and loyalties to the state level. Moreover, the institutions of the electoral college and the national party convention make it necessary for every presidential campaign to be built, first and last, around the states. The state house has been a great steppingstone to the White House, and even those presidential candidates who have not launched their campaigns from governors' chairs have usually formed their personal organizations from the party structures of their native states.

Of course, what has been is not necessarily a pattern for what will be. The states, as politically powerful units of government, will hardly survive indefinitely if they prove to be of no permanent value to American society. Having assumed a degree of responsibility for most traditional state functions—such as education, welfare, and public health—the federal government, led by the Supreme Court, has during the past decade begun to deal with a number of problems which are organic to the states themselves. Racial segregation, religious observances in the public schools, malapportionment of state legislatures, all of which have been the subjects for federal court edicts, are not, theoretically at least, problems on which the states are physically incapable of acting. Federal interference on these matters has occurred precisely because of the apparent lethargy of the states.

If both the traditional services and the traditional authority of the states are continually superseded and eroded, the state governments will inevitably be reduced to mere shadows of their former importance. Governmental function and political power, though by no means identical, are certainly not unrelated. The latter, of necessity, will eventually follow the former—as the British aristocracy gradually lost power once it had ceded responsibility for the business of government to a democratically elected House of Commons, and as the League of Nations finally collapsed when it failed to take over any significant governmental functions from its member nations.

The course of state politics, as a general phenomenon, is therefore of great importance to every American, both for its immediate influence on the practical activities of the federal government and for the decisive part which it will play in determining the future nature of the national political system. In addition, of course, every citizen has reason to be concerned with the powerful effect the government of his own state continues to exert over the schools in which his children are educated, the roads on which he drives his car, the civil and criminal courts through which most of his rights are protected, and the social atmosphere in which he must live a large part of his daily life.

There can be no doubt that state governments today face severe problems—constitutional, financial, and even psychological. These problems will be either met or permitted to become unsolvable through the operations of state politics.

The study reported in the following pages was undertaken, through the sponsorship of the American Political Science Association and on a grant from the Stern Family Fund, as a kind of progress report on the politics of ten states which were judged for one reason or another to be crucial, typical, or otherwise important.

The first section of the study is composed of case histories of political activity in Virginia, Michigan, Arizona, Pennsylvania, Nebraska, New York, Texas, Ohio, Massachusetts, and California since approximately 1950. The second section contains a review of certain general characteristics—organization, finance, influence of ethnic and economic factors, and the like—as they are represented in the states previously mentioned. A final chapter applies all of this material to the question of the future of the states as agencies of creative and progressive government, functioning as parts of the federal system.

A great deal of the credit for whatever value this study may have must go to the ten journalists who participated in its preparation by submitting reports on what happened in politics in their states from 1950 to 1962. They supplied most of the data, wrote drafts for the state chapters, and went over the final product. However, opinions expressed, particularly in the general sections that follow the case histories, are the responsibility of the project director alone.

Literally hundreds of people contributed information and advice during the course of the study. I give to all my heartfelt thanks. Special gratitude goes to my ten excellent collaborators; to Warren

Weaver, Jr., of the *New York Times* who graciously went over the chapter on New York State; to Richard Scammon, who made available materials gathered for his highly useful *America Votes* volumes; to the American Political Science Association and its advisory committee for the state politics project; to the consistently generous trustees of the Stern Family Fund; to Dr. Evron M. Kirkpatrick, director of the American Political Science Association, and Mrs. Helen Hill Miller, executive secretary of the Stern Family Fund, both of whom offered invaluable counsel and encouragement; to Jeanne Benson, who prepared the maps and figures; and to my wife, for unfailing assistance and support.

Shortly before the completion of work on *States in Crisis,* Leo Egan, who prepared the material on New York, suffered a fatal heart attack. His passing removed from the profession of journalism a reporter with acute judgment, enormous factual knowledge, and warm appreciation for the human drama of politics. His generous and scrupulously factual responses to my questions provided one of the principal pillars on which this study is built.

A. J. R.
Pottsville, Pennsylvania
September 2, 1963

CONTENTS

PART II | PATTERNS OF STATE POLITICS

PART ONE

TEN CASE HISTORIES

VIRGINIA

A SENSE OF THE PAST

It is an anomalous fact that Virginia, once a principal source of liberal inspiration and leadership in the United States, has in the twentieth century come to be regarded as the stronghold of an extreme form of conservatism. The reasons for this apparent reversal reach far back into American history—at least as far as 1619, when the Jamestown colony, the first permanent English-speaking settlement in the New World, was only twelve years old. In the summer of that year two epoch-making events occurred: a pirate ship, disguised as a Dutch man-of-war, arrived at the mouth of the James River bearing a cargo of twenty Negro slaves; and a few weeks later the House of Burgesses, the first freely elected representative legislature in the Western Hemisphere, met in the colony's small Anglican church. Although the initial effort at self-government was abandoned after only six days, due to "the intemperature of the weather, and the falling sicke of diverse of the Burgesses," the seeds of democracy and slavery had been planted, side by side, among the roots from which American society was to spring.

A century and one-half later the experiment with self-government, begun at Jamestown and carried on at the colonial capital at Wil-

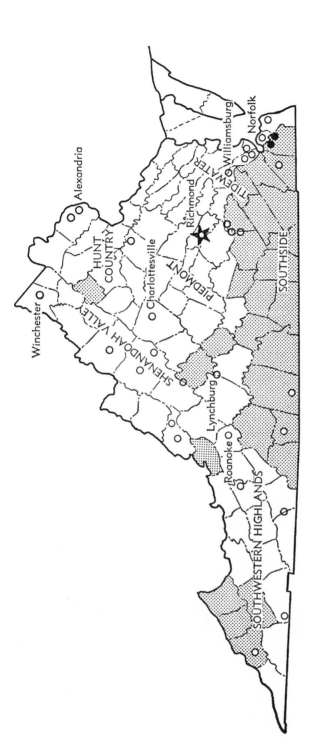

Counties Carried by Democratic Candidate for President, 1956

● Independent Cities Carried by Democratic Candidate for President, 1956

○ Independent Cities Carried by Republican Candidate for President, 1956

VIRGINIA

liamsburg, produced the remarkable flowering of political leadership —on whose roster the names of George Washington, Patrick Henry, Thomas Jefferson, James Madison, and John Marshall were only a few of the most illustrious—which in large measure was responsible for the design, creation, and early administration of republican government in the United States. But within less than one hundred years, the seeds of slavery bore their own bitter fruit in the short-lived Southern Confederacy; in this experiment, too, Virginia played the leading part.

Slavery was one, but by no means the only, cause for the underlying conservatism of Virginia (which left its mark on Jefferson and Madison, as well as on Washington and Marshall). The tobacco economy of the colony had early led to a decentralized society and an oligarchic form of government. As the tobacco crops exhausted the soil, the planters were driven to acquire more land, more power, and more slaves. In the Tidewater, the fertile plain between the seacoast and the fall line of the slim rivers—Potomac, Rappahannock, Mattaponi, James, Appomattox—that race east from the Appalachian hills, the owners of the big plantations achieved particular dominance. The Piedmont, the belt of foothills extending from the fall line to the Blue Ridge, was settled more slowly and did not at first mold its society along quite so aristocratic a model. (According to an old Virginia adage, "Gentlemen and clams end at the fall line.") Here too, however, the big planters generally were in control. In the area beyond the Blue Ridge, an entirely different kind of society began to come into existence during the second quarter of the eighteenth century.

The Shenandoah Valley was settled originally by Scotch-Irish, German Protestants, and Quakers, who moved down from Pennsylvania, rather than by the planters and their dependents who inhabited the Tidewater and the Piedmont. The Valley, as it has always been known in Virginia, became the site of a relatively democratic society based on a small-farm economy, with few slaves and little aristocratic fluffery. The differences in culture and economy between the areas east and west of the Blue Ridge have had an enduring influence on the state's politics.

Two other regions and three metropolitan areas complete the

major geographic divisions of present-day Virginia. The Southside, including portions of both Tidewater and Piedmont, is composed, generally speaking, of those counties south of the James River. Rich tobacco country, it has remained rigidly conservative in its politics. Of the state's fifteen counties having a majority of Negroes in their populations in 1960, eight were located in the Southside. Only two of the region's seventeen counties were less than 25 per cent Negro.

The Southwestern Highland region, variously known as the "Fightin' Ninth" (after the congressional district that includes much of its area) and the "Mountain Empire," covers the narrow neck of the state that stretches into the Alleghenies. It is a region of small-farm agriculture and coal mining. In 1960, nine of its eighteen counties suffered from serious unemployment (more than 7 per cent of the work force). Historically, it has been the citadel of Virginia Republicanism and, at the same time, a breeding ground for political radicalism. It is the only part of the state in which election fraud or charge of election fraud are at all common and in which campaign expenditures (frequently for purposes more or less illegal) reach startling heights.

These five regions, along with the metropolitan areas of Richmond, the state capital; Norfolk, a major Atlantic Coast port; and Alexandria-Arlington-Fairfax, suburbs of Washington, D.C., form the geographic stage on which Virginia's politics are performed. No one city or region has succeeded, at least since colonial times, in gaining dominance; nor is there a clear-cut rivalry between a single metropolitan area and the rest of the state, as is found in New York, Michigan, and Illinois. The state's regional divisions, though not without significance, are bound together by strong ties of common ethnic background and religion. Outside of the Washington suburbs, only one county, Prince George, near Richmond, in 1960 had a population including more than 10 per cent foreign stock (immigrants, and natives with at least one immigrant parent). A survey by the National Council of Churches conducted in 1957 found only one county, Fairfax, with a population more than 10 per cent Roman Catholic. The state's total population was less than 3 per cent Catholic and less than 1 per cent Jewish. Aside from the Negroes, the Washington suburbanites, and a sprinkling of refugees from New

York State tax laws in northern Virginia's so-called hunt country, the state's inhabitants are overwhelmingly Protestant and Anglo-Saxon in origin. The influence of Old England remains strong in common law and social custom. In part because of this homogeneity, Virginians exhibit an unusual degree of cohesion and state pride. Even Virginia Negroes tend to view their racial brethren farther south with considerable condescension.

Virginia's predilection for conservatism was mightily re-enforced by the Civil War and, even more intensely, by the events of Reconstruction that followed. Although at first inclined to take moderate positions on the issues of slavery and secession, the state, pressed on by its straitened economy and a nagging compulsion to maintain its leadership of the South, eventually threw itself into the Confederacy with dedicated resolve. At the end of the war, beside having become a conquered province, Virginia found itself bowed beneath a debt of $45 million. Moreover, the northwestern hill country that had remained loyal to the Union as West Virginia, containing most of the mineral resources formerly within the boundaries of the Commonwealth, had become a separate state and declined to assume any part of the prewar debt. With characteristic honor and fiscal conservatism, the Virginia legislature affirmed in 1866 that the debt would be paid in full, thereby assuring the impoverishment of the state government during the remainder of the nineteenth century.

Funding, as the payment-in-full position was called, enjoyed much less than universal approval. Even after the withdrawal of Federal troops, the Republican party, by advocating a scaling down of the debt, managed to maintain a political popularity that it did not enjoy elsewhere in the South. After a brief period in the 1880's of Republican rule, with Negro support, the funders, who had adopted the Democratic party as their vehicle, won conclusive victory, and the institution commonly known as the Organization began to assume the control of state politics that it has maintained ever since.

Somewhat contrary to legend, the Organization at its inception was not the political instrument of the old planter aristocracy. Its first leader, Thomas Staples Martin, a shrewd railroad lawyer, won election to the United States Senate over an authentic aristocrat, General

Fitzhugh Lee, in a contest marked by charges of bribery and lavish expenditure of railroad funds. Martin served in the Senate from 1894 until his death in 1919, a period during which the Organization acquired many of the characteristics which have persisted to the present day.

Among the Organization's first accomplishments was the Virginia constitution of 1902, which sought to reverse the results of the Civil War and the Fourteenth Amendment through such devices as the poll tax, literacy tests for voter registration, and racially segregated schools. The desired ends, at least temporarily, were almost completely achieved. The number of Negroes qualified to vote shrank immediately from 147,000 to 21,000. As an incidental effect, many white voters were also disfranchised. The number of votes cast in Virginia in the presidential election of 1904 was slightly more than half the total that had been cast four years earlier.

Beside reducing the electorate to manageable size, Martin and his associates concluded a working alliance with Bishop James Cannon, Jr., the renowned Methodist prohibitionist. Martin and Cannon fell out in 1917, leading to the election of an insurgent candidate as governor. Otherwise, the Organization enjoyed a period of unchallenged control.

After Martin's death, state politics drifted through a period of collective leadership. In 1923, a referendum authorizing a $50 million bond issue for construction of state highways was placed before the electorate. Opposition to this proposal was led by an economy-minded young apple grower and state senator from Frederick County, the northeastern corner of the Shenandoah Valley. For the first time —but hardly for the last—the slogan "pay as you go" was identified with the name Harry Flood Byrd.

A direct descendant of William Byrd, founder of the city of Richmond, Harry Byrd had grown up during a period of hard times for both his state and his family. Leaving school in 1902 at the age of fifteen, he took over management of his father's nearly bankrupt newspaper, the *Winchester Star,* and within a few years built it into a paying property. At about the same time, he rented part interest in an apple orchard, thereby initiating an enterprise which by 1956 made him the largest individual apple producer in the world. With his two brothers, Admiral Richard Evelyn, explorer of the Antarctic, and Tom, a partner in the apple business, he was to raise the Byrd family from near poverty to a position exceeding even its old eminence.

After leading the successful fight against the bond issue, Byrd sought new tests for his political skill. Encountering Bishop Cannon at the Democratic national convention in 1924, he was favored with an oblique warning from the celebrated Dry to stay out of the governorship race the following year. Although he had not intended to seek the state's top executive office until 1929, this edict, according to Byrd, "got his dander up." He entered the Democratic primary and defeated Cannon's candidate by 40,000 votes.* In November of 1925 he was elected governor of the Commonwealth, receiving almost 75 per cent of the votes cast.

Byrd's term as governor is generally conceded to have been "one of the most fruitful . . . in Virginia history." He converted a million dollar deficit into a $2.5 million surplus, sponsored the first state law making all members of a lynch mob subject to murder charges (Virginia has had no lynching since), feuded successfully with the oil companies and the telephone utility, modernized the state administration, and secured passage of a constitutional amendment making most state executive officers appointive by the governor. This last reform, vainly promoted in many states by liberals and political scientists, has been described by some critics in Virginia as a constitutional pillar of the Byrd machine, which the Organization came to be called in unsympathetic circles.

But a far more important support for the machine was established four years after Byrd himself had left the governorship. The State Compensation Board, instituted in 1934, holds authority to determine annual salaries and expense budgets for a number of county and city officials, including Commonwealth attorneys, sheriffs, and tax collectors. The Board, whose decisions may be appealed in the courts, provides an efficient means for controlling the salaries of officials who serve both state and local functions. At the same time,

---

* Both election statistics (other than percentages) and dollar amounts will be rounded off to the nearest thousand, except where exact figures are essential to meaning.

there can be no doubt that the Board's authority has helped cement bonds of loyalty reaching upward from county officeholders to the state administration, normally controlled by the Organization.

This was particularly true during the many years that E. R. Combs, Byrd's most powerful associate and known within the Organization simply as "the Chief," was chairman of the Board. A graduate of the tough school of politics practiced in the Southwestern Highlands' "Fightin' Ninth," Combs first teamed up with Byrd in the fight against the highway bond issue. When the office of state comptroller was created as one of the "Byrd reforms" in 1927, Combs was named to the new job. He was chairman of the Compensation Board from the time it was set up—except during one term in the late thirties when a governor unfriendly to Byrd was temporarily in power—until his retirement in 1950. During his years in Richmond, Combs was known as the man to see. Young Democrats anxious for political advancement dutifully traveled to his office to talk things over. No one has succeeded to his role—something between chancellor and high priest—within the Organization, but the Compensation Board retains its disciplinary influence over the courthouse politicians. Although a firm advocate of decentralization on the federal level, Byrd paradoxically contributed to the establishment in Virginia of one of the nation's most centralized political systems.

The Organization survived the New Deal years with little difficulty, despite growing estrangement from the Roosevelt administration and the national Democratic party. In 1933 Byrd went to the Senate, where in his view he has ever since sought to put into effect the 1932 national Democratic platform. Describing himself in an interview for *Human Events* magazine in 1957 as "one of the last of the old New Dealers," Byrd observed that Franklin Roosevelt came into office on a platform pledging reduced federal spending, economy in government, and renewed dedication to states' rights. "I'm still standing on it," the senator concluded, not without a touch of irony, no doubt.

The first serious challenge to the reign of the Organization occurred in 1949, when Francis Pickens Miller, recently returned from service as a colonel in Army intelligence during World War II, entered the Democratic primary for governor against the Byrd candidate, state Senator John S. Battle of Charlottesville. The year before, Byrd, increasingly at odds with the Truman administration, had given his support to a clumsily drawn piece of state legislation freeing Virginia's Democratic presidential electors of their obligation to vote for the national Democratic ticket. Although the bill was eventually modified to permit electors pledged to the national Democratic ticket to appear on the presidential ballot, many party regulars were disturbed by the independent course being pursued by the Organization. At the same time a tax increase was voted, perhaps without Byrd's approval, which almost doubled the state's bite on the incomes of both corporations and individuals. Scenting the winds of discontent, two formerly loyal Organization stalwarts, ignoring the fact that they had failed to receive the nod, jumped into the primary with Battle and Miller. As Virginia at that time had no runoff primary law, it seemed possible that the anti-Byrd candidate might slip through between the divided Organization forces.

Miller waged a vigorous campaign, describing the Organization leaders as a "political clique of backward looking men," and terming

Figure 1. Virginia Battle Graph, 1948-61

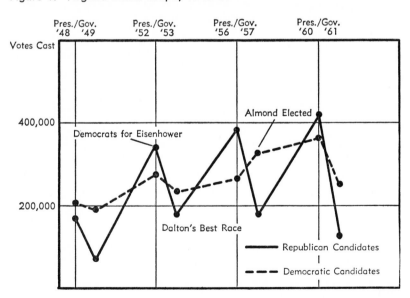

Byrd himself "the absentee landlord" of Virginia politics. Byrd responded by labeling Miller "the CIO supported candidate." As the primary date approached—and the Organization's anxiety increased —the state's former Republican national committeeman, a conservative, suddenly urged Republicans to enter the Democratic primary to cast votes in support of Battle.

The result of the August 2 primary was victory for Battle, though by less than an absolute majority. Norfolk, Richmond, the suburban counties around Washington, the Southwestern Highlands, and one county (his own) in the Shenandoah Valley returned pluralities for Miller. The defeated insurgent estimated that some 50,000 Republicans, a considerably larger figure than Battle's winning plurality, had voted in the Democratic primary. Ted Dalton, a county lawyer from the Highlands, who at that time was assuming the leadership of the state Republican party, concurred: "The Byrd organization may deny that it owes its political neck in the state government to the Republicans . . . but the county and precinct workers know otherwise." On the other hand, Organization leaders pointed out that Miller's share of the vote, 35 per cent, was no more than had been received in prior elections by anti-Byrd candidates. Battle's total, they argued, was reduced by the vote for the other two regulars, which would normally have gone to the Organization's man. Nevertheless, a mood of crisis and impending change had been created by the unusually hard-fought primary.

Three years later, with the preliminary stages of the 1952 presidential campaign already underway, Miller took on Byrd himself in the Democratic primary for United States senator. Directing his campaign against President Harry Truman and the CIO, Byrd rolled up an easy victory. Although Miller's total vote increased slightly over 1949, he failed to carry Norfolk, Richmond, or the Washington suburbs. Only the "Fightin' Ninth" remained loyal to the insurgent cause.

A few days after the primary, the Democratic national convention met in Chicago. Many members of the Virginia delegation, composed of Organization stalwarts still savoring their recent victory, were clearly itching for an opportunity to display their contempt for liberalism and all its works before a national audience. Byrd himself was prepared and perhaps eager to have the delegation either bolt or be thrown out of the convention. Governor Battle, on the other hand, while sharing Byrd's determination that the South should not be humbled within the Democratic party, was anxious to preserve peace if at all possible. On the fourth day of the convention, as the roll call of states for nominations for president began, Battle requested a ruling from the chair on the status of the three Southern delegations, including Virginia, that had refused to take an oath of loyalty to the national Democratic ticket. Sam Rayburn, speaker of the United States House of Representatives and permanent chairman of the convention, ruled that the three delegations could not be seated until they had taken the oath.

In the uproar that followed, both Battle and former-Governor William M. Tuck, a Southside fire-eater, started toward the speakers' platform. Tuck carried with him a scorching speech of defiance, evidently approved by Byrd, which in all probability would have led to the delegation's expulsion from the convention. Before the former governor could reach the speakers' stand, however, Battle had won "the great foot race"—as it was called by journalists observing the event—and made a conciliatory speech. A successful appeal against Rayburn's ruling followed, and the Virginia delegation, unoathed and unpledged, was seated.

In the presidential campaign, Byrd remained silent until mid-October, at which time he announced that he would discuss the issues over an eleven-station Virginia radio network. He gave in advance no clue to his position. His address, delivered on October 17 from the studio of WINC in Winchester, turned out to be a ringing indictment of Adlai Stevenson, the Democratic candidate for president, for the crime of "Trumanism." Having won his own primary fight in July as an opponent of "Trumanism," Byrd said he felt compelled to keep up the struggle. Although he stopped short of endorsing the Republican ticket, the message was clear to most Virginians. Virginia Democrats for Eisenhower, led by Richmond businessmen, powerfully supplemented the Republican statewide effort. On election day, Dwight Eisenhower swept the state, the first Republican to receive Virginia's electoral votes for president since Herbert Hoover in 1928. All sections of the state went Republican except Norfolk and the Southside. Byrd's own Winchester bailiwick gave Eisenhower 69 per cent of its vote (as compared to 19 per cent for the Republican candidate for governor the following year, when the senator was back on the reservation).

The Republican victory in the presidential election had a sobering effect on the state's Democrats. Insurgents and Organization men, forgetting old differences, sought to make common cause against the expected Republican thrust for control of the state government. A half-hearted insurgent effort in the 1953 gubernatorial primary against Thomas B. Stanley, the Organization candidate, carried little beyond the Washington suburbs, which were represented by the insurgent candidate in the state Senate. The primary vote was small, and Democrats were further chilled by the comparatively close race made by an unknown Republican against former-Governor Tuck, who on primary day was being elected to Congress from his normally overwhelmingly Democratic Southside district.

The Republicans, meanwhile, were putting forward a strong ticket, led by Ted Dalton, state senator from Radford in the Southwestern Highlands. Dalton, a drawling, eloquent speaker with great personal charm, announced a program that included poll tax repeal, election law reform, and an expanded state effort for schools and hospitals. Stanley, counting on the Organization to pull him through, ran on a program of sound business administration and no increase in taxes. The Republican campaign was initially aided, though perhaps ultimately damaged, by the indictment for income tax evasion of Stanley's campaign manager, Sidney Kellam, boss of Princess Anne County, which surrounds Virginia Beach in the state's southeastern corner. This breath of scandal at first seemed to hurt Stanley, but in the long run, by shocking previously lethargic local Democratic leaders, it may actually have contributed to his victory. (Kellam was exonerated and acquitted of all charges after the election.)

Whatever chance Dalton may have had was effectively ended by a proposal he made in Staunton in the middle of October for a $50 million bond issue to expand and improve the state's highway system. Byrd, reacting like an old firehorse who has heard the alarm, swung happily into the campaign with the charge that Dalton "wants to junk the pay-as-you-go plan." Despite an ambiguous endorsement from Francis Pickens Miller (who wished to keep his own record of party regularity clean), Dalton went down to defeat with 45 per cent of the vote. It was the best showing made by a Republican candidate for governor in the twentieth century. The Washington suburbs, the Highlands, and Henrico County (surrounding Richmond) produced Dalton majorities. The conclusion was widespread, however, that the Republicans had shot their bolt. Further opposition to the Organization would have to come from within the Democratic party.

Governor Stanley had been in office only a few minutes when he succeeded in destroying the relative harmony that had been achieved among the Democrats during the campaign. Midway through his inaugural address, he recommended a one cent increase in the state gas tax, thereby violating his oft repeated pledge of "no increase in taxes." This reversal of position, he contended, was necessary due to the pressing need for improvement of Virginia's highways. Unimpressed, the leaders of the legislature, who were, among other things, annoyed that they had not been notified of the recommendation in advance, quickly consigned the gas tax rise to oblivion.

Somewhat shorn of prestige by this early defeat, Stanley soon found himself faced with a full-scale revolt in the House of Delegates. Discovering that the state general fund showed a surplus of $7 million, several younger delegates, most of whom had reached the Assembly with Organization support, moved to amend the budget so this sum could be appropriated for public purposes. To do this, it was first necessary to suspend a law passed four years before, under the sponsorship of state Senator Harry Byrd, Jr., which provided for automatic repayment of unexpended surpluses to the taxpayers. Both measures were enacted by the lower house but, under opposition from Governor Stanley and the younger Byrd, were rejected by the Senate. A deadlock developed, which remained unresolved at midnight on the Saturday set for adjournment. With clocks stopped in the legislative chambers, the wrangle continued until 10:30 Sunday evening, when it was agreed that one-third of the surplus would be appropriated and the other two-thirds paid back to the taxpayers.

This compromise represented the first major frustration suffered by the Organization in the legislative halls at Richmond for many years. Newspapers throughout the state predicted the decline and possible overthrow of the Byrd machine. A "political revolution now in the making" was sensed by the *Staunton News Leader,* while "a political ferment . . . sweeping the state" was reported by the *Richmond Times-Dispatch.*

The soundness of these predictions was never to receive a fair test due to the unexpected introduction of a new and explosive issue into state politics a few weeks after the legislature adjourned. On May 17, 1954, the United States Supreme Court unanimously decreed racial segregation in public school systems to be unconstitutional. Reaction in Virginia was at first restrained. Governor Stanley announced that he would appoint a citizens commission, including members of both races, to study the problems posed by the court's decision. Even as Stanley spoke, however, quiet discussions of the impact of the Supreme Court decision were taking place within the high command of the Organization. The exact role of Senator Byrd in these discussions has never been certainly determined. There is no doubt, however, that the eventual decisions to which they led had his endorsement; and there is wide belief that many of these decisions originated in the complex imagination of the senator himself.

The importance of the segregation issue to the Organization is shown by the fact that almost all of the state's 54 counties and independent cities with populations more than 25 per cent Negro have traditionally been bulwarks of strength for Byrd-supported candidates. In 1953, for instance, Ted Dalton, Republican candidate for governor, carried 29 of the state's 129 counties and independent cities—but only 2 of the 54 more than 25 per cent Negro. In 10 of the 15 counties more than 50 per cent Negro, Dalton received less than 25 per cent of the vote—compared with 45 per cent statewide. In the hard-fought Democratic primary of 1949, anti-Byrd candidates carried 32 of 125 constituencies—but only one of the 15 constituencies more than 50 per cent Negro. As the Negro vote itself was slight, except in a few cities, it may be assumed that racial fear contributed to the strong showings made by Organization candidates in biracial counties. Not surprisingly, with both Republicans and insurgents gaining strength, the Organization leaders were tempted to make political capital out of the threatened integration of schools. (Voting among Negroes themselves, on the other hand, steadily increased during the fifties. By 1960, Negroes comprised about one-tenth of the state's registered voters, as compared to about one-fifth of the total population. Although not well organized, the Negro vote was becoming a factor to be reckoned with in municipal elections in Richmond and Norfolk. Generally, it was cast against Byrd-sponsored candidates.)

The first clear indication of the direction in which the Organization intended to move came with Governor Stanley's appointment of an all-white study commission, under the chairmanship of state Senator Garland Gray, an uncompromising segregationist from Sussex County, in the heart of the Southside. After more than a year of deliberation, the Gray Commission recommended a plan that would permit some integration, on a local-option basis, but would also provide tuition grants for children whose parents declined to send them to integrated schools. As this provision required an amendment to the Virginia constitution, the issue was presented to the voters in a referendum on January 1, 1956. Despite the opposition of many clergymen and denominational publications, including the *Baptist Religious Herald,* the *Virginia Methodist Advocate,* and the *Presbyterian Outlook,* the referendum was carried by a margin of better than two to one. Encouraged by the overwhelming size of their victory, the Organization leaders prepared to substitute stronger medicine for the relative moderation of the Gray plan.

At his annual apple orchard picnic in the summer of 1956, Senator Byrd announced to his neighbors and political associates that Virginia must fight the Supreme Court decision "with every ounce of energy and capacity." He warned, "If Virginia surrenders, if Virginia's line is broken, the rest of the South will go down, too;" and added that if the public schools were destroyed in the coming struggle, it would be the responsibility of "those who try to force mixed schools upon us—something a large part of Virginia will never take." Two days later in Richmond, an extra session of the assembly convened to act on Governor Stanley's recommendation that state school funds be cut off to any city or county in which a public school became integrated. This and companion proposals were passed, easily in the House of Delegates and by fairly narrow majorities in the Senate.

In the same speech in which he urged unyielding opposition to school integration, Senator Byrd directed a number of critical remarks at the civil rights and fiscal policies of the Eisenhower administration. However, he refrained from endorsing Adlai Stevenson, again the Democratic presidential candidate, and in November President Eisenhower carried Virginia by a larger margin than he had received in 1952.

A few days after the 1956 election, state Attorney General J. Lindsay Almond, who, though a product of the Organization, had succeeded in causing Senator Byrd irritation on one or two occasions, announced his candidacy for governor. Almond had given up his seat in the United States Congress, representing the Roanoke district, to become attorney general in 1948. Since that time, he had worked tirelessly at building a following throughout Virginia at the grass-roots level. His announcement was received with limited enthusiasm within the high command but, no other strong candidate being available, two Organization stalwarts were in due course authorized to bestow the nod. On December 7, 1956, the *Richmond News Leader* reported, "Yesterday afternoon there came a knock at the door of Attorney General J. Lindsay Almond . . . Our silvermaned friend peered through a crack, thinking for an awful moment that it might be a process server or a delegation from the NAACP, but what to his wondering eyes should appear? It was State Treasurer Jesse W. Dillon and the Hon. Sidney S. Kellam of Princess Anne County . . . They embraced, the three statesmen, and copious tears were shed by all—especially by Messrs. Dillon and Kellam, who might have wished that Judge Almond had come knocking at their doors. And what this mystic rite symbolized, to be sure, was that the Byrd Organization will back Judge Almond for the Governorship next year. In the present state of Virginia politics, that is all that is required."

Campaigning as an outspoken advocate of massive resistance— as Byrd's campaign against integration had come to be called— Almond had little difficulty overwhelming an insurgent opponent in the primary and defeating Ted Dalton, drafted by the Republicans, in the general election. A pink-faced, white-maned orator of the old school, Almond stumped the state, promising to fight the Supreme Court's iniquitous edict "from here to eternity." After President Eisenhower dispatched troops to enforce integration of schools in Little Rock, Arkansas, in September, Dalton, who had announced himself a moderate segregationist, became the target for widespread ire against the Republicans. "Little Rock knocked me down to nothing," he later said. "From then on, I couldn't do a thing."

Early in 1958 Senator Byrd created a mild sensation by announcing that he would not be a candidate for re-election that autumn. Former-Governors Tuck and Battle—contestants in 1952's "great foot race"—immediately began to maneuver for their leader's Senate seat. Whether disturbed by this threatened split within the Organization or impressed by the nationwide outcry from fiscal conservatives, Byrd eventually acceded to a resolution from the Virginia Assembly urging that he change his mind and run again.

Almond meanwhile had set about implementing his pledge to put massive resistance into effect. "Integration anywhere means destruction everywhere," he declared in his inaugural address. "I find no area of compromise that might be usefully explored." The following September, nine schools, under court order to integrate, were closed by the new governor.

On January 19, 1959—Robert E. Lee's birthday and a legal holiday in Virginia—the state Supreme Court of Appeals declared that the massive resistance laws violated the state constitution. On the same day, a federal court in Norfolk found massive resistance to be in violation of the United States Constitution as well. That evening in Richmond, reporters passed the word: "Old Massa Massive's in de col', col' ground."

On January 20, Almond took to the radio to proclaim, "I will not yield to that which I know to be wrong . . . We have just begun to fight." Eight days later, calm but still determined, the governor asked the General Assembly to repeal the compulsory school attendance laws, strengthen state laws against violence, and pass other measures to deal with the "emergency." Finding nothing in Almond's program to prevent immediate integration, some Assembly members offered amendments that would have, in effect, re-enacted massive resistance. These were rejected by Assembly moderates, following Almond's leadership. On February 2, school integration was achieved in Norfolk and Arlington County, without hint of violence or disorder. Whatever political fuel it had drained from the segregation issue in the past, the Organization, with the support of both Byrd and Almond, had made clear that hooliganism would not be tolerated.

The following winter Almond explained, in an interview with Virginius Dabney for *U.S. News and World Report,* that he had been "tired, harassed and under strain" when he made his broadcast of defiance on January 20. "My words," he said, "inadvertently gave the impression that I knew of some way to prevent any mixing of the races in the public schools, when nothing of the sort was possible." The 1959 special session of the Assembly eventually enacted, against the bitter opposition of Harry Byrd, Jr., a return to the local-option approach of the Gray plan (although Gray himself had joined the last ditch proponents of massive resistance).

Almond encountered further difficulties with the younger Byrd, Gray, and other Organization leaders when he proposed a 3 per cent general sales tax to the Assembly in 1960. Although the sales tax was killed in both houses in committee—"stacked and packed," according to Almond, by his opponents—most of the governor's recommended expenditures were approved, making necessary the enactment of temporary taxes on liquor, beer, and—for the first time in Virginia—cigarettes. The gulf between Almond and the Organization began to widen. "If these gentlemen want to play it rough," the governor said, referring to the Organization leaders in the legislature, "that suits me, for the remainder of this administration and for the days to come after the close of this administration."

As the 1960 presidential campaign got underway, Senator Byrd told a chuckling audience at his annual picnic that he often had found that silence is golden in politics. "Democrats for Eisenhower" was re-activated as "Democrats for Nixon-Lodge," and for the third straight time Virginia wound up in the Republican column for president, though by only about one-third the majority Eisenhower had received in 1956. Governor Almond, who had been a vigorous supporter of John F. Kennedy, gained some prestige for having been on the winning side nationally, while at the same time losing face for failure to swing Virginia. (In April, 1962, President Kennedy appointed Almond as judge of the United States Court of Customs and Patent Appeals. The Senate Judiciary Committee, chaired by Harry Byrd's good friend, James Eastland of Mississippi, coolly ignored the appointment, and in mid-1963 Almond had not yet received Senate confirmation.)

Four days after the presidential election, Lieutenant Governor A. E. S. Stephens, evidently hoping to duplicate Almond's coup of four years before, announced that he would run for governor in 1961. Like Almond, Stephens had risen from the ranks of the Organization. Since becoming lieutenant governor, however, his relations wtih such high-command potentates as Senator Gray and former-Governor Tuck had grown cool. Though a native of the Southside, he had sided with Almond and the moderates in the massive resistance controversy of 1959–60.

The Organization was determined that no ally of "Benedict" Almond—as he was by then known in the Southside—should succeed to the governor's chair. To stave off this possibility, it turned, somewhat reluctantly, to Attorney General Albertis S. Harrison, who had avoided close entanglement with Almond or ruction with the leaders of the Organization although he had approved the moderate approach to the segregation issue. Harrison accepted leadership of a ticket otherwise composed of diehard segregationists. Though evidently disappointed by his failure to take the Organization by storm as Almond had done, Stephens decided to stay in the race after state Senator Armistead L. Boothe, leader of the insurgents in the legislature, agreed to run for lieutenant governor on a ticket with him.

In the primary campaign, Stephens launched a series of bitter criticisms at the Byrd machine that, he claimed, was crushing incentive among aspiring young Democrats in Virginia. The effect of these charges was somewhat blunted by Byrd's release of a letter Stephens had written the year before, eagerly seeking the senator's support for his candidacy. The entire Organization slate was victorious, with Harrison running a bit ahead of the rest of the ticket.

This result was generally interpreted as a decisive triumph for the Organization, but in reality Stephens, probably not the strongest imaginable candidate, did remarkably well. His vote was eight percentage points higher than that received in 1947 by Francis Pickins Miller, the last strong insurgent candidate for governor; and he made some inroads in former Organization strongholds in the Tidewater and the Piedmont, as well as carrying Norfolk, the Washington suburbs, and the Southwestern Highlands. The city of Richmond and its suburbs, on the other hand, gave overwhelming majorities to Harrison.

In the general election, Harrison easily polished off the Republican candidate, H. Clyde Pearson of Roanoke. The first year of the new administration was marked by some strain between the governor and the Organization on the perennial tax problem, but by and large harmony was maintained. Harrison agreed to a token reapportionment of the General Assembly which left the rural counties dominant. (The larger cities and their suburbs contain a relatively small proportion of Virginia's population—about one-third—so even completely equal representation would still give the rural counties a majority in the legislature. In November, 1962, a federal court held that the urban and suburban communities of the state were victims of "invidious discrimination" under the new apportionment acts and declared the acts null and void. This decision was stayed by the United States Supreme Court, pending further study of the case.)

After more than a decade of sound and fury, first from the insurgent Democrats, then from the Republicans, then from the insurgents again, the Organization in the summer of 1963 was still firmly established in power. Though Senator Byrd's eventual withdrawal from the political scene is inevitable and may produce a crisis within its structure and though current population trends seem to work to its disadvantage, the powers of the Virginia machine to endure and to prevail remain impressive.

The strength of the Organization rests not merely on its resources for managing state and local politics, nor on the political skill of its leaders, but also on the fact that, unlike its big-city counterparts in the North and West, it has achieved the status of an institution.

For many Virginians, the Organization has come to be one of the many symbols of a past in which they take justifiable pride. To the charge that the practices and attitude of the Organization are in reality a contradiction of the very political philosophy that once made Virginia great, Organization leaders—and many ordinary Virginians—are likely to respond that not Virginia but the world has changed: Harry Byrd, they insist, stands for the position of limited government, strict construction, and rural dominance once developed by Thomas Jefferson.

Underlying this rather abstract argument is a point of view expressed with great charm on a recent summer afternoon by a genteel lady guiding tourists through the reconstructed House of Burgesses at Williamsburg. In a soft, Southside drawl, she briefly lectured her charges at the completion of their tour on the meaning of what they had seen. Why had they come here, those early colonists? Why had they instituted self-government, overthrown the rule of England's King, established the Republic? It had all been done, she said, "to preserve gracious living." And we in our time, she concluded, must do what is possible to preserve gracious living, too.

Unthinkable as this analysis of American history would be in such colonial shrines as Philadelphia or Boston, not to mention the nation's universities, it is one that is shared by many Virginians. The exact meaning of the philosophies of Jefferson and Madison seem less important, one feels, than the fact that they were, after all, gentlemen, and administered the government in a manner of which other gentlemen might approve. In Virginia today, if nowhere else, gentlemen—or reasonable facsimiles thereof—continue to rule. There is little reason to believe that the majority of Virginians do not prefer it that way.

2

MICHIGAN

LABOR'S LOVE LOST

A witticism commonly heard in political circles during the late 1950's had to do with a bitter-tasting Midwestern cocktail known as "Michigan on the rocks." This jibe expressed the conservative opinion that a ruthless, left-wing labor party led by (or, in another version, manipulating) a millionaire fanatic, who mistook himself for a lay reincarnation of Peter the Hermit, had fallen upon the once proud and prosperous state of Michigan, scattering the public weal and driving terrified industrialists to more congenial sovereignties. While not, of course, concurring in the pejorative tone of this description, liberals were inclined to accept the impression that an advanced experiment in share-the-wealth socialism was indeed proceeding in the area bounded by four of the Great Lakes.

In reality, the events in Michigan during the six consecutive administrations (1949–61) of Governor G. Mennen ("Soapy") Williams were neither so simple in execution nor so radical in effect. While Governor Williams clearly was anxious to lead his state down the road to something or other (better schools, better highways, better medical care, in his view; deepest socialism, in that of his opponents), his inability to command a reliable majority in the state legislature at any time during his tenure severely limited the success of his aspirations. However, between 1949 and 1961, Michigan *did* more than triple its annual expenditures on both highways and education, double its outlay for mental health, and spend more than half-again as much on public welfare. The gross state budget rose from less than $500 million in 1949 to almost $1,200 million in 1961. Annual tax revenues during this period rose more than 150 per cent. The need for increasing the state's services during the Williams era are not today seriously debated in Michigan (for one thing, the state's population rose by more than one million during the decade). Whether even greater increases should have been made and whether those that were made were financed with maximum fairness and efficiency are questions contributing to the ferment that now seems to be producing an entirely different kind of political phenomenon in the State of Great Water.

Before the advent of Williams and his associates, Michigan was normally conservative and Republican—"operated much as a company town," in the opinion of one writer. Jackson, sixty miles west of Detroit, claims to be the birthplace of the Republican party, and for almost seventy years following the Civil War, Michiganders regarded Republicanism as being synonymous with patriotism, morality, and sound thinking. During three terms of the state legislature in the early years of the present century, not a single Democrat sat in either the Senate or House of Representatives at Lansing, the state capital. Heavy immigration from Europe (even in 1960, one out of four Michiganders was a first or second generation American) and rapid industrialization, after Detroit had become the center of automobile manufacturing in 1914, did not at first shake Republican rule. In the New Deal years, while the United Auto Workers were battling for recognition of their union, Democrats for a time captured control of the state government. By the middle of the 1940's, however, the Grand Old Party was once more firmly in power. In 1946, Kim Sigler, a Republican, was elected governor with 61 per cent of the vote; Republicans held ninety-five of the one hundred seats in the state Senate; and Senator Arthur Vandenberg, a perennial possibility for the Republican presidential nomination, was re-elected with a two-to-one majority.

This façade of Republican strength was not so solid as it seemed. Sigler had won the gubernatorial primary, against the incumbent lieutenant governor, on the strength of a reputation gained as a prosecutor of graft in the Republican controlled state legislature. Understandably, his party colleagues in the legislative halls did not view him in the warmest possible light. The graft investigations culminated in the murder of a state senator who was about to give

MICHIGAN

testimony. A reform-from-within movement was launched, with the support of the big automobile companies, under the leadership of Arthur Summerfield of Flint, one of the world's most successful Chevrolet dealers. Despite the success of this movement in gaining control of the party machinery, the GOP was badly divided by 1948, and Sigler went down to defeat before an aggressive young Democratic attorney whom he had the year before appointed to the state Liquor Control Commission.

G. Mennen Williams, a member of the family that owns the Mennen's soap industry, began his political career in the early thirties as president of the Princeton Young Republican Club. Soon after leaving college, however, he became convinced that "liberal Republicanism" was an internally contradictory term and transferred his allegiance to the party of the New Deal. In 1948, he won the Democratic nomination for governor by 8,000 votes, due to a split within the regular party organization which at that time had slipped under the domination of the rising young president of the local teamsters' union, James R. Hoffa. In the general election Williams defeated Sigler by a 160,000 vote majority, but professionals in both parties continued to regard his victory as something of a fluke.

Setting out to break Hoffa's hold on the state Democratic organization and to construct what he never tired of calling "a programmatic, participative political party," the new governor received the immediate support of Walter Reuther, president of the United Auto Workers, and Neil Staebler, a wealthy Ann Arbor oil man and former Socialist (almost nobody in Michigan seems to have *begun* as a Democrat). Teamster allies were gradually removed from high party positions, including those of state chairman and national committeeman. In 1950, Staebler, a baggy-pantsed, squeaky-voiced genius at political strategy, became state chairman, a position which he held for the next ten years.

The Republicans meanwhile were renewing their intraparty feuding in the gubernatorial primary of 1950. A popular former governor, Harry F. Kelly, easily defeated Summerfield's candidate, Fred M. Alger, Jr., for the privilege of opposing Williams' bid for a second term. Examining the returns on the night of the general election, Kelly concluded that he had won a narrow victory and headed south for a Florida vacation. Williams and Staebler, however, insisted on a recount. In the weeks that followed, dozens of attorneys, teachers, and other volunteer workers vied with Republican regulars on election boards all across the state. It was discovered that affirmative votes on a referendum permitting the sale of colored oleomargarine, which also appeared on the ballot, had in some districts generously been credited as votes for Kelly. When the recount was at last called off, Williams had edged into a lead of 1,154 votes. Besides winning the election, the Williams-Staebler organization had solidified its ties with the young but energetic amateurs who had served as its agents. Many of these were to play roles of increasing importance in the state government during the coming decade.

Except for the governorship, the Republicans recaptured all state offices in 1950. In the spring election the following year, Republican candidates won sweeping victories. (Several state offices, including superintendent of public instruction and state highway commissioner, were, prior to adoption of the 1963 constitution, regularly elected in the spring of odd-numbered years in Michigan; the governor and other elective state administrative officers were chosen, as in most states, in the fall of even-numbered years.) Approaching the presidential election of 1952, leaders of the GOP felt reason to hope that the Williams era was nearing its end. Summerfield enjoyed a period of national celebrity as leader of the key Michigan delegation to the Republican national convention, and, after the nomination of Dwight Eisenhower, became Republican national chairman. With his support, Fred Alger was victorious in another bitterly fought gubernatorial primary.

At the Democratic national convention, Williams was a leader in the drive to impose a loyalty pledge on the rebellious Southern delegations. In the balloting for president, Michigan first voted for Williams as a favorite son, then shifted to Estes Kefauver, thereby initiating a habit of getting on losing horses at the quadrennial party meetings. (In 1956, Williams at first supported Averell Harriman; then shifted to Stevenson after, according to conflicting stories, either Walter Reuther had changed his mind or Chester Bowles had shown him the light. With great fanfare, Williams in the spring of 1960 announced for John F. Kennedy at a dramatic meeting with the future president on Mackinac Island. This did not prevent the Michigan delegation from falling into its customary role of bewildered intransigence at the convention. Kennedy's decision to award the vice presidential nomination to Lyndon Johnson was interpreted as an almost personal affront by Williams, a reaction which he did not hesitate to communicate to the national television audience.)

Although Eisenhower carried Michigan in the fall of 1952 by 320,000 votes, Williams once more squeezed through. This time the Republicans demanded a recount, but Williams' final majority stood at better than 8,000 votes.

During all of this period, Democratic strength in the state rested largely on overwhelming majorities produced by the city of Detroit and surrounding Wayne County. Almost half of Michigan's population in the 1950's was contained in Wayne County and the adjoining suburban counties of Oakland and Macomb. By 1952, Wayne, about twice the size of the other two combined, was polling majorities of better than 60 per cent for the Democratic ticket. Macomb, with high proportions of industrial laborers, Catholics, and foreign stock in its population, slipped its Republican moorings in the forties and was thereafter reliably Democratic. Even Oakland, the state's high-income county, was tending toward the Democrats in the early fifties.

The remainder of the state, spanning an area of almost 100,000 square miles (about half of it water), can be divided into a southern belt of spick-clean, middle-sized manufacturing cities; a predominantly rural region covering the upper two-thirds of the Lower Peninsula (the land area of the state is composed of two peninsulas, separated by Lake Michigan); and the Upper Peninsula. The southern cities, with few exceptions, remained Republican in state elections in the early fifties (all of Michigan's major cities except Ann Arbor have nonpartisan elections for local offices). Heavily industrialized Genesee County (Flint) and the smaller lakeside counties of Muskegon and Bay were moving toward the Democrats at this time; but such prospering metropolitan areas as the counties of Kent (Grand Rapids), Ingham (Lansing), Washtenaw (Ann Arbor), Jackson, and Kalamazoo continued to produce sizable Republican majorities.

The rural counties of the Lower Peninsula were even stronger in their adherence to the GOP—of the thirty-seven counties north of a line drawn from Bay City on Lake Huron to Muskegon on Lake Michigan, twenty-five went Republican for governor in 1952 by more than 65 per cent. The Upper Peninsula, containing one-third of the state's area but less than one-twentieth of its population, was, on the other hand, tending Democratic. Nine of its fifteen counties polled majorities for Williams in 1952. Once prosperous iron ore country, the Upper Peninsula had fallen into a condition of chronic economic depression. By 1960, unemployment had reached 18 per cent in Mackinac County and was over 7 per cent in all but one Upper Peninsula county.

The real breakthrough for the Democrats occurred in 1954. Michigan was experiencing an economic slump, and unemployment was rising, not only in the Upper Peninsula, but also in Detroit and some rural Lower Peninsula counties as well. Williams was re-elected to a fourth term by more than 250,000 votes and for the first time was able to carry a full slate of Democrats with him into the

Figure 2. Michigan Battle Graph, 1948-62

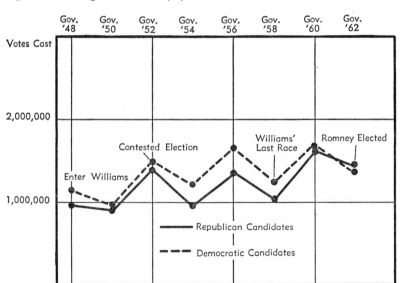

other state offices. The most dramatic turnover occurred in the former Republican citadels north of Bay City, where the Democratic vote for governor increased by more than 10 per cent in twenty-one counties. Also, however, Williams greatly improved his showing in suburban Oakland and the southern cities, and swept all but two counties in the Upper Peninsula.

Along with the economic downturn and the evident response to Williams' personality (according to a friend, he succeeded in shaking the hand, at one time or another, of virtually every voter in the state), the concentrated support of organized labor, particularly the UAW, was given a large share of the credit for the Democratic landslide. Conservatives began to charge—and many disinterested persons began to believe—that something approaching a genuine labor party had won control of the state of Michigan. The extent of labor's dominance (or, in a simplified version, Walter Reuther's dominance) over the state Democratic party has been disputed ever since. Certainly the relationship is intimate. Staebler has explained, with what Republicans regard as calculated understatement, "Labor does a lot of things that have to be done."

As early as 1948, the state CIO Political Action Committee announced in formal resolution, "Progressives and liberals within the Democratic party have often been outnumbered by conservatives and reactionary elements. The PAC is unanimous in its opinion that the best way of supporting liberalism within the Democratic party, to conform to the national CIO policy, and to serve the best interests of Michigan labor is to join the Democratic party . . . We therefore advise CIO members to become active precinct, ward, county and congressional district workers and to attempt to become delegates to Democratic conventions." Many persons who became prominent in state politics under Williams, including the minority leader of the state House of Representatives, the deputy state Democratic chairman, a member of the board of governors of Wayne State University, a trustee of Michigan State University, a supreme court justice, the press secretary to Williams' successor, and the Democratic leader in the 1961 constitutional convention, were UAW officers or staff members. Unions affiliated with the Wayne County AFL-CIO during the fifties contributed two cents a month for each of their dues-paying members to a "citizenship fund," which thereby accumulated more than $70,000 a year. In addition the UAW maintained its own citizenship fund; the Committee on Political Education (COPE) solicited one dollar yearly from all AFL-CIO members (about 15 per cent usually paid); and in 1960 the state AFL-CIO voted approval of a special $108,000 fund for "citizenship education" and registration drives in the still predominantly Republican outstate areas. These sums were not paid directly into Democratic party coffers. Instead, COPE, from behind the modern glass façade of the UAW's Solidarity House in Detroit, directed its own highly effective campaigns of voter education, leadership training, and candidate promotion.

The extent of Walter Reuther's personal involvement in Michigan politics has probably been exaggerated—"It just happens that some of his programs and mine coincide," according to Williams—but through his brother, Roy, and other union leaders, the UAW president has exerted a powerful, if indirect, influence over the Democratic party and state government. At Democratic state nominating conventions, Roy Reuther and his associates regularly organized a labor caucus, which usually produced the slate of candidates that subsequently received the party nominations. Labor made no effort to minimize its role in Democratic party success. Announcing the results of the 1960 elections, the *Michigan AFL-CIO News* reported, "The labor-liberal Democratic party coalition won Michigan's 20 electoral votes for President-Elect John Kennedy and gained all statewide offices contested in Tuesday's election." Labor did not always have its own way, even in the Democratic party, in Michigan during the 1950's, but there can be no question that it was politically better organized and more effective than in any other state in the nation.

Following their 1954 debacle, the Republicans set out with compulsive determination to get Williams. In this endeavor they were twice more to fail; and finally, at the end of the decade, were to fail, as well, to prevent the election of his chosen successor to the governor's chair. In 1955, Summerfield, by now postmaster general in the Eisenhower cabinet, sought to reassert his authority over Michigan Republicans by replacing the state chairman, John Feikens, a young Detroit attorney with moderate views who had led a grass-roots campaign for Eisenhower in 1952. Feikens decided to make a fight of it and, with the support of some executives of the Ford Motor Company, was able to hold onto his job, despite the opposition of Summerfield and the General Motors top brass. Thereafter, Summerfield managed what little federal patronage was available for Republicans in Michigan, and the state organization, with no state jobs after 1954, was permitted to wither.

As a result, the main voice for Republicanism in the state became the conservative majority party leadership in the legislature. Although the Michigan House of Representatives was apportioned during the fifties with relative equality (Wayne County had about one-third of the seats, the same proportion as it contained of the state's population), the distribution of Democratic voters weighed heavily in favor of Republican control. Only once in the decade, during the 1959–60 term, did the Democrats achieve so much as a tie in the lower house. Even then the Republicans held an almost two-to-one majority in the Senate, where representation was determined on the basis of constitutionally designated geographic districts.

The Democratic governor and the Republican legislatures quarreled frequently on a wide variety of subjects, but their main area of dispute was early established in the field of finance. Williams sought enactment of a tax on corporation profits, similar to the levies long in force in industrial states like New York, Pennsylvania, and California, to supplement Michigan's general sales tax, which produced almost 40 per cent of the state's tax revenue. This proposal was annually rejected by the Republican legislatures on the ground that it would drive tax-shy industries beyond the state's borders. In 1953, the legislature enacted a business activities tax, drawn up by lobbyists and economists for the automobile companies, which levied on the value added to products by business in Michigan. Neither this complicated device, which Williams permitted to become law without his signature, nor repeated increases in taxes on cigarettes, liquor, and petroleum, served to meet the state's spiraling expenses.

The legislature then embarked on a series of gimmicks designed to provide the state with temporary financial windfalls: the inventories of the state liquor stores were, in the financial sense, liquidated; bonds being held for military bonuses were cashed; due dates on some business taxes were moved ahead to provide two payments within a single fiscal year; state institutions were authorized to borrow money to help finance their operations. The day of reckoning seemed to have arrived in 1959 when state employees went payless for five days past the regular payday. Breathing deeply, Williams and the legislature agreed to move $50 million in government securities, set aside after World War II to finance veterans' aid programs, into the general treasury.

At last, however, with the state gaining a national reputation for insolvency and the voting public becoming alarmed, both governor and legislature set about finding some release from their impasse. Williams offered to modify his corporate tax proposal into a tax package, including both a tax on corporation profits and a graduated income tax. Relying on public opinion polls that showed voters preferring an increased sales tax over the income tax, Republican legislative leaders rejected the Williams package in favor of a constitutional amendment that would permit the sales tax to be raised from 3 to 4 per cent. Finally capitulating, Williams agreed to a temporary increase in taxes on cigarettes, beer, and whiskey, until the voters had a chance to pass on the sales tax amendment. In 1960 the electorate approved an increase in the sales tax to 4 per cent, and the state's financial woes were, at least temporarily, reduced.

On some occasions, Williams succeeded in winning the support of a sufficient number of Republican legislators to enact specific items in his program. In 1955, for instance, a House committee which had refused to report out a highway construction bill involving an increase in the gas tax was discharged by a coalition of moderate Republicans and Democrats. Later that year, the same coalition, overcoming conservative opposition, enacted a program enlarging state hospital facilities to treat an enormous waiting list of mentally retarded children. Normally, Williams dealt with the legislature as though setting out to whack the snout of a large and obstreperous hog. A favorite device was to appeal directly to the voters to contact their recalcitrant representatives—"bringing the government to the people," as he called it. This tactic worked well with such issues as the mental health bill and a bill to improve traffic safety regulations, but failed dismally in 1959 when the governor attempted to marshal popular enthusiasm for his tax package proposal.

Whether out of discontent with the tax muddle or because of the natural accumulation of resentment against a governor so long in power, Williams' popularity after 1956 began to decline. In 1958 the governor, winning a sixth term, trailed the Democratic state ticket. His personal majority was reduced two percentage points by his Republican opponent, Paul D. Bagwell, a professor of speech at Michigan State University.

When Williams decided to retire from the governorship in 1960 to devote full time to the national campaign, the programmatic, participative party became participative to an almost ruinous degree. Three candidates, including Lieutenant Governor John B. Swainson, who had lost both legs as a result of combat action in World War II; Secretary of State James M. Hare, who had received the largest victory margin in 1958; and Detroit Councilman Edward Connor, announced for the Democratic nomination for governor. Seven more went into the race for lieutenant governor. The contest between Swainson, who had the backing of most of the union leaders, and Hare, an enormously popular campaigner, soon became intense. Staebler held weekly meetings of the competing candidates in an effort to keep intraparty acrimony to a minimum. On primary day, Hare, the betting favorite, carried more than two-thirds of the counties, but went down to defeat before heavy majorities for Swainson in Detroit, the suburbs, and the southern cities. On the same day, however, the AFL-CIO endorsed candidate for lieutenant governor was defeated by T. John Lesinski, a state representative from Detroit.

In the fall elections, the labor-liberal coalition barely succeeded in holding the state for Kennedy and the rest of the Democratic ticket. Bagwell, again the Republican candidate for governor, received 49 per cent of the vote, as compared to 46 per cent two years before. The rural counties of the Lower Peninsula returned emphatically to their Republican allegiances, and sizable Republican majorities were once again produced by suburban Oakland and the manufacturing counties of Ingham, Saginaw, and Kent. Even Genesee and Muskegon Counties, Democratic for a decade, slipped over into the Republican column. Only heavy majorities from Wayne and Macomb Counties saved Kennedy (who, on election night, desperately needed Michigan's twenty electoral votes) and Swainson. Some Democrats blamed the religious issue, which had been injected into the presidential campaign, for their relatively poor showing; but in 1957 the state had more enrolled Catholics (22 per cent of the population) than Protestants (17 per cent). Identification by Catholics in Macomb County and the Upper Peninsula with the Democratic presidential candidate may have counted for more than latent anti-Catholicism in the rural counties of the Lower Peninsula. In any case, on the same day that Kennedy and Swainson were elected, Michigan's voters approved a constitutional amendment making possible a state constitutional convention. The proposal to draft a new basic law had been opposed by Swainson, most of organized labor, and many conservative Republican legislators, but supported by a fresh element in the state's political life, "Citizens for Michigan."

Utilizing the same kind of volunteer effort that had in the early fifties been harnessed for the Democratic party by Williams and Staebler, Citizens for Michigan had set out in 1959 to provide a third force in the state, capable of breaking the deadlock between the Democratic governor and the Republican legislature. Study groups were set up to conduct "nonpartisan" analyses of such problems as taxation, spending, and governmental organization. Among the early leaders of the movement was the Ford Motor Company's Robert McNamara, later secretary of defense in the Kennedy cabinet; but from the start the organization's real drive came from the dynamic president of American Motors, George Romney. An energetic and unconventional businessman, Romney had succeeded in annoying the automobile industry's Big Three (General Motors, Ford, and Chrysler), first by breaking their resistance to producing a small car for the American market, and then by signing a profit-sharing agreement with the UAW.

Citizens for Michigan quickly decided that a new state constitution was a fundamental necessity for more effective government. A referendum drive was launched, in cooperation with the League of Women Voters and the Junior Chamber of Commerce. The constitutional convention ("Con-Con," as it was at once nicknamed) was opposed not only by conservatives, fearful that their control of the legislature might be imperiled, but also by some leaders of the labor-liberal coalition, who argued that delegates to the convention would be chosen on the basis of current apportionment, thereby placing them in a sure minority. Labor-liberal opposition to the referendum turned out to have been a strategic error, as the voters, after approving the convention, elected an overwhelming majority of Republican delegates, even from normally Democratic districts in Wayne County and the Upper Peninsula, evidently on the theory that the Democrats were not in sympathy with the project.

Romney himself was elected on the Republican slate as a delegate from Oakland County. (Although he had earlier identified himself as a Republican, the auto-maker had adopted a nonpartisan status during the two years that he led Citizens for Michigan.) At the convention in Lansing, which got underway in the fall of 1961, he lost some early skirmishes with conservatives. These defeats seemed only to confirm the popular impression that he was free of involvement in the existing party situation. Doing nothing to discourage this view, Romney criticized the Republican party as "too much dominated by business," as the Democrats were "too much dominated by labor." Ultimately, he united the Republican delegates to the convention behind his leadership (partly through making concessions to conservatives on such questions as legislative apportionment) and played a deciding role in formulation of the new constitution.

In the winter of 1962, Romney, after several days of prayerful contemplation (he is a devout Mormon), agreed to seek the governorship on the Republican ticket. Swainson, who had proven even less successful than Williams at dealing with the legislature, was slated by the Democrats for another term. The campaign that followed was dominated by Romney's enthusiastic conception of himself as healer of the political fission that had divided Michigan. Concentrating on intangibles such as leadership and unity rather than on a specific program, avoiding close identification with other

Republican candidates, the former auto manufacturer in the end carried the day, it seemed, by the sheer force of his evangelical personality. (Labor-liberal leaders were particularly disconcerted by a Romney tactic of challenging union or Democratic speakers in union halls or at factory gates.) Even so, the Republican candidate was elected governor by the relatively modest majority of 78,000 out of 2,760,000 votes cast, and Democrats captured most other statewide offices.

In the first days of the new administration—faced with the task of gaining approval for "New Con," as it was now called—Romney appeared to regard himself as a kind of tribune of the people (somewhat in the manner of President of the Fifth Republic of France Charles de Gaulle). In his office in Lansing, the governor held weekly grievance sessions, open to all comers. Any citizen of Michigan might have five minutes to present his problem. At the end of the stipulated time, a small bell rang, and the next complainant was ushered into place.

A privately commissioned poll, taken a few weeks before the scheduled referendum on New Con, showed the constitution favored by 50 per cent of the voters, 10 per cent opposed, and the rest undecided. Between the time the poll was taken and April 1, 1963, the date of the referendum, a skillfully led coalition made up of such disparate elements as the UAW and the conservative Justices of the Peace Association (whose offices were to be abolished under New Con) converted virtually all of the undecideds to the opposition. At 3 A.M. election night, Romney and his associates were convinced that the constitution had been rejected. However, as late returns trickled in and one large error was revealed in the early tabulations, defeat was turned into victory—by a margin of 11,000 out of 1,609,000 votes cast. Meeting the press the following morning, Romney called the vote "a citizens' victory." He declared: "I'm not concerned about the impact of the vote of any one individual. I am deeply concernd about its impact on the state—my concern is with Michigan."

With the election of Kennedy, Mennen Williams had departed for Washington where he was to serve as undersecretary of state for African affairs. The following winter, Staebler stepped down as Democratic state chairman. (But not out of politics—he was elected Michigan's congressman-at-large in 1962.) At the 1961 Democratic state convention, he delivered a short lecture on the role, as he saw it, of his party: "We are the 'inquiring party.' We want to change things . . . We generally describe ourselves as liberals—a term sometimes labeled empty in newspaper editorials. It's not empty for Democrats. We mean by a liberal a person with an open mind, with a greater freedom from prejudice, from frozen ideas, and a willingness to consider the merits of the case, to listen to facts, to respond to problems."

During the twelve years that Williams, Staebler, and the leaders of the UAW sought to set the course for Michigan, things certainly had changed. The state had greatly increased its role in such fields as education, public assistance, and medical care. The cost had been considerable. In the early sixties, per capita taxes were higher than in most comparable industrial states; two-thirds of the state's tax bill was still paid through levies on consumer goods. Diversified industry, which would free the state from dependence on a car economy, had failed to appear. (In 1962, a boom in automobile manufacturing reduced the unemployment rate in Detroit below the national average—a factor which may have contributed to Romney's victory. The fall before, however, newsdealers on Cadillac Square had done a brisk trade in lists of California job opportunities.)

Whatever the price, more than a decade of innovation in state government in Michigan produced a variety of services not only greater in quantity but also in many cases superior in quality to those offered by other states. Many Michiganders continue to question the means by which the reforms of the Williams era were achieved. Few dispute the ultimate good effect of most of these increased services. By 1963, Michigan gave every appearance of having survived a leap forward into the politics and economics of the welfare state—and of having, in the process, achieved a revival of citizen participation in the mechanics and morals of government.

3

ARIZONA
THE STATE PRIMEVAL

By the desk of Senator Barry M. Goldwater, in the Old Senate Office Building in Washington, D.C., hangs an oil painting of an isolated trading post in the mountains of northern Arizona. "I would like to be up there right now," the senator told a recent visitor, "away from these damn federal bureaucrats."

Actually, as Senator Goldwater well knew, Arizona, 75 per cent owned by the federal government, is one of the last places in the nation to escape the effects of federal influence. Nevertheless, the romantic and lonely scene presented by the painting does in a way symbolize and explain the philosophy of untrammeled individualism for which the conservative senator and, to some degree, the state which he represents have come to stand.

Having achieved statehood only fifty years ago, Arizona remains, in the middle of the 1960's, at a fairly primitive level of political and social development. The presence of huge areas of open land, almost untouched, suggest both isolation and opportunity. The awesome magnificence of the Grand Canyon, in the state's northern portion, is reminder of the great works that nature, uncontrolled, may produce. To this evidence of space and force have been added the booming prosperity of Phoenix, the state's principal city, which tripled its population between 1950 and 1960. (A walk around Scottsdale, a plush Phoenix suburb, reveals, however, that many of the ranchtype houses are surrounded by barriers, high ones, indicating perhaps that the spirit, "Don't fence me in," has given way to the sentiment, "Private, keep out.") Here, if anywhere in the Western world in the middle of the twentieth century, the individual may still feel confidence in his ability to "do for himself," as Senator Goldwater likes to say.

Arizona's origins as a state were anything but conservative. The rough mountain and desert country, much of which was acquired from Mexico through conquest and purchase in 1848 and 1853 (the remainder had been part of the Louisiana Purchase), little increased its population from the time the territorial government was established in 1863 to the beginning of the twentieth century. The area's original inhabitants—Apache, Navajo, Hopi, Papapago, Pima, Maricopa, and Yuma Indians—maintained themselves in attitudes of unyielding and sometimes fiercely violent defiance to the white man and his ways. Mexicans, who had been drifting into the area against unremitting opposition from the Apaches since Marcos de Niza, the first Spanish missionary, arrived in 1539 (sixty-eight years before the first English settlement in Virginia, eighty-one years before Plymouth Rock), constituted about 50 per cent of the population. Following the Civil War, Mormons began migrating from Utah in small but significant numbers, founding their own religious communities. The Army, which manned the frontier forts as long as the Indian wars continued; the railroads, built mostly by Irish laborers; and the sprawling, open-pit copper mines drew into the territory a rugged breed of workers and fighting men.

In 1906, Arizona rejected a proposal by Congress that it enter the union with New Mexico as one state. A constitutional convention, controlled by delegates elected by railroad and mine workers, was held amid great excitement in 1910. All of the progressive reforms popular at the time, including referendum, initiative, and recall, were included in the constitution. Congress agreed to accept Arizona as a state, but President William Howard Taft declined to sign the resolution authorizing statehood until a provision for the recall of

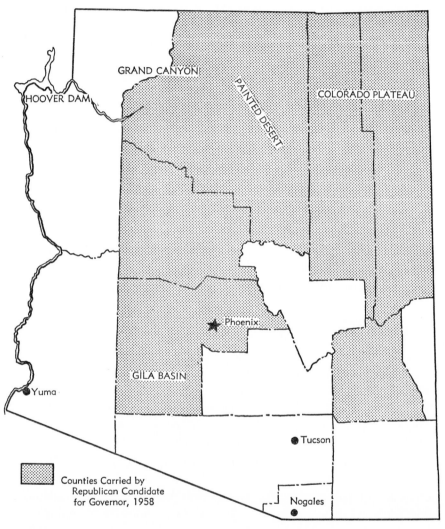

GRAND CANYON

HOOVER DAM

PAINTED DESERT

COLORADO PLATEAU

★ Phoenix

GILA BASIN

● Yuma

● Tucson

Counties Carried by
Republican Candidate
for Governor, 1958

● Nogales

ARIZONA

judges was deleted from the constitution. The objectionable passage was dropped, and on February 14, 1912, Taft put his signature to the document admitting Arizona as the forty-eighth state. Once safely in the union, the voters of Arizona swiftly amended the constitution to reinstate their power to recall judges who rendered unpopular decisions.

This radical phase did not last for very long, however. The copper mines, the railroads, and the big ranch owners who had failed to control the constitutional convention quickly established a dominance, which they have since rarely yielded, over the state legislature. In 1917, a strike sponsored by the International Workers of the World broke out in the copper mines. The state's first governor, George W. P. Hunt, promptly called out the National Guard. About one thousand workers and IWW leaders were herded into cattle cars, shipped across the state line into New Mexico, and dumped. The state had little further labor strife for many years.

Until 1950, the Democratic party was almost constantly in control of Arizona. The Republicans were able to elect a full slate of state officers in 1920 and to pick off the governorship in 1928, but otherwise the Democratic organization, built on an effective patronage machine and close collaboration with business interests, remained in power. On the national level, Arizona went Republican for president three times in the 1920's, but thereafter gave its electoral votes to the Democratic candidates. (Arizona voted for the winner in every presidential election from the time it achieved statehood until 1960.)

Despite, or perhaps because of, this long reign, the Democratic organization in 1950 was showing signs of strain. The incumbent governor, Dan E. Garvey, seeking a second term, was defeated in the Democratic primary by the state auditor, Mrs. Ana Frohmiller. During twenty-two years as state auditor, Mrs. Frohmiller had signed her name to millions of old-age and relief checks. A considerable number of the grateful recipients of these checks, it is said, had come to believe that the auditor was in some way their personal benefactress. In any case, Mrs. Frohmiller was able to win the first major party nomination for governor ever granted to a woman in Arizona. Somewhat startled, state highway officials and other stalwarts of the Democratic organization made their way to the auditor's office to promise their support in the general election. Evidently convinced that in Arizona a Democrat could not lose, and in any case a person of independent character, Mrs. Frohmiller made clear to the organization leaders that she wanted no strings attached to either her campaign or her election. In a disgruntled mood following this meeting, many of the professional politicians decided to oblige the good lady and let her win the election, if she could, by herself.

The Republican candidate for governor that year was Howard Pyle, an announcer for radio station KTAR in Phoenix, who had arrived in the state from Wyoming twenty-five years before. Pyle had been induced to make the race by the owner of a large Phoenix department store and member of the Phoenix city council (elected on a "better government" ticket): Barry M. Goldwater. Growing up in Phoenix and northern Arizona, young Goldwater had left behind him a legend of boyish escapades. (He once fired a homemade cannon over the heads of worshippers departing from the Methodist church across from his home.) He had assumed the management of the family store after his father died during his freshman year at the University of Arizona. Gradually drawn toward politics, he joined the Republican party, a proud but hopeless minority with no real hope of carrying a state election.

Encouraged by the division in the Democratic ranks, Pyle and Goldwater traveled around the state in the latter's airplane, landing on highways, in fields, anywhere that a crowd could be gathered to listen to the Republican message. Many nights they slept on the desert, under the wings of the plane. Pyle grew exhausted, became convinced that the normal Democratic majority could not be overcome. Goldwater insisted that they keep on.

Aided by the evident coolness of some Democratic leaders toward Mrs. Frohmiller's candidacy, Pyle skimmed through to election by 3,000 votes out of 195,000 cast. All other Democratic candidates, including Senator Carl Hayden, who had represented Arizona in Congress since the state was first admitted to the union, were easily re-elected.

Addressing the opening session of the 1951 legislature (unanimously Democratic in the nineteen-member Senate; sixty-one Democrats to eleven Republicans in the seventy-two-member House),

Pyle declared, "The question is, how can we afford to pay for things we would like to afford, and in many instances the things we need to afford." The legislators, making little effort to follow the turns in this line of reasoning, prepared to proceed much as before. A request by Pyle that the state school-aid formula be based on need rather than on pupil enrollment was simply ignored. (The copper companies did not object to supporting schools near their mines, but had no wish to subsidize impoverished school districts in other parts of the state.) In 1952, the legislature approved the governor's proposal that scattered executive functions be consolidated into a Department of Finance, a Department of Law, and a Department of Public Health and Welfare. Without urging from Pyle, the legislature abolished compulsory segregation in elementary schools and granted counties permission to integrate schools on a local option basis.

Republican prospects in Arizona improved markedly in 1952. Pyle was easily re-elected, running slightly ahead of Dwight Eisenhower, who carried the state for president by 44,000 votes. In a much closer contest, Goldwater was able to upset Senator Ernest W. McFarland, the majority leader of the upper house of the United States Congress and a veteran Arizona politician, by 7,000 votes. For the first time in history, Maricopa County (Phoenix) elected a Republican, John J. Rhodes, to Congress. The other Congressional seat and the legislature remained Democratic, although Republican strength rose to thirty in the state House of Representatives and four in the Senate.

Shortly after this victory, Pyle's popularity began to disintegrate. In his campaign for re-election, he had promised to take the 2 per cent sales tax from food and medicine. When, during his second term, he did not press for this change, Democrats in the legislature charged that the pledge had not been made in good faith. Meanwhile, the state courts, in response to a suit directed by state Representative L. S. Adams, Democrat, of Maricopa County, declared that Pyle's new Department of Finance was improperly drawn and unconstitutional. The legislature then repealed its authorization of the Department of Public Health and Welfare, leaving only the Department of Law standing.

Pyle opened a drive for two major objectives: change to a need formula for state school aid; and enlargement of the Senate from nineteen to twenty-eight members, with two senators for each of the fourteen counties. Both measures were opposed by the mining companies. Previously, the five largest counties had each elected two senators, while the other nine counties each elected one. The senators from the larger counties, who normally voted in support of the mining companies, thus held majority control of the Senate. Despite the opposition of the copper interests, Pyle succeeded in persuading the legislature to refer both of his proposals to a vote by the people. (The measures went through the mine-dominated Senate, so the story goes, on an evening when a key copper lobbyist had imbibed freely and was not attending to his duties.) Campaigning for affirmative votes on the two referrals in the fall, Pyle broke openly with the mine interests and criticized the legislature for turning down much of his program. "Special interest groups," he said, were "thwarting the people's will for better state government." The voters approved the enlargement of the Senate, but rejected the change in the school-aid formula.

The legislature by 1954 had had enough of Pyle. The governor's ambitious proposals in the critical fields of education, health, highways, underground water control, civil service, and finance were almost completely ignored. Speaking on the radio, still his favorite medium, Pyle called upon the voters to "take the direct and positive steps that are so plainly indicated."

The governor's troubles were measurably increased by a raid he staged in 1954 on Short Creek, a Mormon community in the northern part of the state in which the practice of polygamy survived. Intensely religious (his father was a Baptist minister), Pyle determined to break up the multiwived Mormon families by police action. At the head of a small army of highway patrolmen and deputy sheriffs (and accompanied by a flock of newspaper reporters), Pyle descended on the rural community one morning at dawn. The Mormons, who had been warned of the invasion, were assembled in the school yard, singing hymns. Children of the Mormon families were taken away to Phoenix, and superfluous wives were for a time moved from their homes. Pyle gave a dramatic description of the affair over radio.

After a few months, the children were returned to Short Creek, and polygamy was resumed about as before. The net effect of the raid was to brand Pyle as an enemy of Mormonism, even among the great majority of Mormons who had ceased since 1890 to sanction polygamy. Though constituting less than 5 per cent of the state's population, the Mormons, by reason of their cohesion and their crucial location in the low density counties, had for many years exercised great political influence.

The election of 1954 was an almost complete rout of Pyle and the Republicans. Even the *Arizona Republican* and *Phoenix Gazette,* both published by staunchly Republican Eugene Pulliam, failed to give strong support to the governor's drive for re-election. Former-Senator McFarland, running for governor on the Democratic ticket, defeated Pyle by 12,000 votes. The incumbent governor carried the two largest counties, Maricopa (Phoenix) and Pima (Tucson), by less than 500 votes each, but was steamrollered in the rest of the state. The only major Republican to survive the Democratic sweep was Congressman Rhodes, who was re-elected by 7,000 votes. (Rhodes's opponent was L. S. Adams, Pyle's old antagonist on the departmental reorganization issue. The Democratic candidate made the mistake of advertising himself a college graduate. The Republicans discovered that Adams had attended college for only a short time and revealed this fact in large newspaper advertisements run two days before the election.) Elected to Congress from the Second District was Stewart L. Udall, Democrat, member of a distinguished Mormon family from Tucson. At the time of Udall's first election to Congress, his father was a member of the Arizona Supreme Court, and two uncles were Superior Court judges. A charge by the Republicans that young Stewart was "ultra-pink" was laughed off by Arizonans who had known and respected the Udall family for generations.

Republican membership in the state House of Representatives was reduced to twenty and in the Senate to two. The House was organized by the liberals, depriving conservative Democrats and Republicans of desirable committee assignments. (The Arizona legislature, perhaps because of the normal lack of Republicans, has traditionally paid little heed to party labels or discipline. The majority faction, usually conservative in the House and always in the Senate, exercises complete control over committee assignments. Members of the minority faction are appointed either to minor committees or to none at all. Republicans have tried for years, without success, to establish a committee system similar to that in the federal Congress, where parties receive representation on committees in rough proportion to their numerical strength.) The Senate remained under conservative control, resulting in a legislative impasse throughout McFarland's first term.

Despite President Eisenhower's landslide victory in Arizona in 1956 (61 per cent), McFarland was re-elected, carrying every county, over Horace Griffin, Republican, circulation manager for the Pulliam Press. An attempt by organized labor to cut McFarland, who had refused to declare himself in favor of repeal of Arizona's right-to-work law, had no visible effect. The governor campaigned as a warm friend of the copper industry (although the mines had been supplanted by the power utilities as the most active lobbyists in the state capitol) and as champion of Arizona in the dispute with thirsty California over rights to Colorado River water. Along with McFarland, Senator Hayden and Congressmen Rhodes and Udall were re-elected.

Conservatives regained control of both houses of the legislature, and in 1957 cooperated with McFarland to kill a proposed 50 per cent increase in the sales tax. The revenue was to have been used for capital outlays for state institutions. In 1958, McFarland, who had made clear that he would run against Goldwater for the Senate rather than seek a third term as governor, submitted to the legislature a broad program for increased expenditures on welfare and education. No item in this program was enacted. Furious, McFarland called the legislature back into immediate special session. Again the governor's entire program was ignored.

Goldwater, already the recognized leader of the nationwide conservative movement, returned to the state to campaign for re-election. Paul J. Fannin, a Phoenix businessman with no previous political experience, was persuaded to run for governor on the Republican ticket. Under Goldwater's shrewd leadership, the Republicans set out to strengthen their county organizations and to mine large majorities out of Maricopa County, which by now contained 50 per cent of the state's population.

With McFarland seeking to return to the Senate, the Democratic nominee for governor was Attorney General Robert Morrison, an outspoken foe of organized gambling and the rackets. (A number of former members of the Chicago and Detroit underworlds had established residence in Arizona; some were reportedly prepared to take a financial interest in state politics.) The struggle between Senator Goldwater and Governor McFarland soon overshadowed all other state contests. The Pulliam newspapers and the *Tucson Daily Citizen* revealed that COPE, the political arm of the AFL-CIO, was pouring money and workers into the state to defeat Goldwater. Predictably, this news produced a strong reaction in the senator's favor. The Democratic campaign was further damaged by the revelation that Attorney General Morrison had as a young man been convicted in California for writing phony checks (a misdemeanor).

Both Goldwater and the shy-mannered Fannin were victorious

Figure 3. Arizona Battle Graph, 1948-62

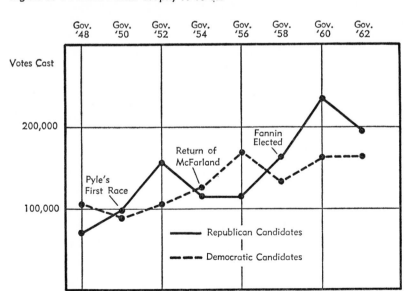

by large majorities. Goldwater increased his lead in Maricopa County from 55 per cent in 1952 to 59 per cent in 1958. All but one of the seven northern mountain counties went for Goldwater, as did Pima County (Tucson) and three of the five remaining southern desert counties. (Goldwater's only loss in the north, Gila County, had for many years been the stopper for the Democratic machine: returns from the rugged county northeast of Phoenix were traditionally held back until the rest of the state was in, at which time Gila could be counted on to return the needed majorities for approved candidates.) Fannin also carried Maricopa County and most of the mountain counties, but was shut out in Pima and the other desert counties. Paradoxically, the Democratic candidate for attorney general, Wade Church, who identified himself closely with organized labor, defeated his Republican opponent by more than 30,000 votes. Some Republicans later claimed that Church had slipped through while they were concentrating on electing Goldwater and Fannin.

As governor, Fannin was able to achieve the 50 per cent increase in the general sales tax that McFarland had successfully opposed. The added revenue was used to increase state assistance to school districts and to subsidize a plan, similar to the one that had been advocated by Pyle, to distribute school aid through the counties on a basis of need. Credit for drafting the tax law was generally given to railroad lobbyist, A. M. ("Bumps") Crawford, who died soon after. Ray Gilbert, lobbyist for the power utilities, also had a hand in drafting tax legislation during the session.

Arizona received unusual attention in the presidential campaign of 1960. Goldwater was placed in nomination for the presidency at the Republican national convention, chiefly as a symbol of conservative discontent with the party platform that had been dictated by Richard Nixon and Nelson Rockefeller. Before withdrawing his name, the Arizona senator enjoyed a tumultuous demonstration and established himself as a possible serious candidate for president in future years. McFarland, meanwhile, evidently hoping to take on Goldwater once more in 1964, had set out to deliver the Arizona delegation at the Democratic national convention to Lyndon Johnson. To the former governor's astonishment, Congressman Udall was able to snatch the delegation away from him and lead it to the banner of John Kennedy. (Udall later became secretary of the interior in the Kennedy administration.)

Nixon and Governor Fannin, seeking re-election, carried Arizona by large margins. Fannin won twelve of fourteen counties, losing only Gila and little Greenlee on the eastern border. Attorney General Church, campaigning for re-election on the declaration, "I am a labor man," lost by almost 50,000 votes to Republican Robert Pickrell. Republican strength rose to twenty-eight—still thirteen short of a majority—in the state House of Representatives and four in the Senate.

Fannin's second term was troubled by growing dissension between fast-growing Phoenix and the rest of the state. When the 1960 census showed Arizona entitled to a third congressman, a 1947 redistricting law, dividing the former Second Congressional District (the state outside Maricopa County) into an eight-county northern district and a five-county southern district, automatically went into effect. This division produced three districts widely different in population: Maricopa County, 51 per cent; southern district (Tucson and desert counties), 33 per cent; and northern district (mountain counties), 16 per cent. A division of the state into roughly equal districts could probably be achieved only by electing at least two congressmen from Phoenix.

In recent years, Phoenix has controlled the executive branch of the state government, while the outstate counties have controlled the legislature. (Tucson, the state's second largest city, was at one time inclined to form a common urban front with Phoenix. The growth of the metropolis has been so phenomenal, however, that Tucson has felt compelled to align itself to an increasing degree with the rural areas. Tucson, according to Tucsonites, is nowadays regarded by Phoenicians as "Nogales Junction"—a rest stop on the way to Nogales on the Mexican border.) In 1962, both United States senators, the governor, the secretary of state, the attorney general, the state auditor, the state treasurer, two of three members of the Corporation Commission, the three members of the Tax Commission, and four of five members of the Supreme Court were residents of Maricopa County. In the legislature, on the other hand, power remained in the hands of the less densely populated counties. Both the president of the Senate and the speaker of the House represented smaller counties. In the House, thirteen of the twenty-one committee chairmanships, including most of the important ones, were assigned to non-Maricopans. Only six of the twenty-one members on the strategically vital Rules Committee represented Maricopa County. In the Senate, one Maricopa representative had a minor committee assignment, and the other, a Republican, had none. Under the new apportionment of the House, Maricopa elects exactly half of the representatives. Party difference (the delegation is split about evenly between Democrats and Republicans) makes it unlikely, however, that the metropolitan county will be able to establish working control. In any case, Maricopa can still be outvoted twenty-six to two in the Senate.

The device of the initiative has increasingly been used by Maricopa County, which in 1962 registered 30,000 more voters than the rest of the state combined, to achieve its goals. In 1959, a Maricopa sponsored initiative turned Arizona State College at Tempe, near Phoenix, into a university, despite a contrary ruling by the state Board of Regents. In 1962, the Maricopa County Medical Association was industriously collecting signatures for an initiative to establish a medical school at Tempe, despite the fact that a professional survey, ordered by the Board of Regents, had recommended that the medical school be attached to the University of Arizona at Tucson. The smaller counties are seeking a change in the initiative requirements, which allow an issue to be presented to the public on petition of 10 per cent of registered voters (or 15 per cent for constitutional amendments), no matter where located. A small-county proposal that the initiative petition should need signatures of 10 per cent of registered voters in at least eight counties passed the Senate in 1962, but was buried in a House committee chaired by a Maricopa County member.

The rivalry between Phoenix and the rest of the state has not, as yet, been translated into partisan terms. Although the Republicans appear to be gaining more rapidly in Maricopa County (63 per cent for Fannin in 1960) than in other parts of the state, they are steadily gathering more votes in almost every county. (Even Gila County gave Fannin 46 per cent and Nixon 42 per cent in 1960.) The Democrats have difficulty exploiting outstate resistance to Phoenix, as their own liberal leadership is at odds with the conservative outstate county organizations.

Perhaps the Democrats will rally, as they did after Pyle's reign in the early fifties, and regain control of the state. Republican organizations are still practically nonexistent outside Maricopa and Pima Counties. The Democratic patronage machine, after five years under a Republican governor, still controls most state jobs. (Former-Governor Garvey, who was defeated in the Democratic primary by Mrs. Frohmiller in 1950, hung tenaciously to the job of state examiner, to which he had been appointed by Governor McFarland. The state Senate, overwhelmingly Democrat, refused in 1961 to confirm Fannin's nominee to replace Garvey. The former governor thereafter enjoyed the unusual designation "appointive State Examiner, serving without appointment.")

The Republicans, with Fannin re-elected to a third term in 1962, are, however, mounting drives to install Civil Service in the executive branch of state government and to reform the committee system in the legislature. While these changes will not be easily achieved, they seem to place the Republican party in Arizona, for the time being at least, on the side of history. As in Texas, where the Republicans also are strongest in urban areas, so-called conservatism seems to contain a considerable admixture of the good-government reform spirit that swept through earlier urbanized and industrialized states around the turn of the century. Whether reform of the rules of the game will in time lead to development of more effective working-class and minority group movements, as has occurred in other states, remains to be seen.

4

PENNSYLVANIA

BUSINESS AS USUAL

N icholas Biddle, president of the Second Bank of the United States, is reputed once to have offered a toast to "the coal and iron of Pennsylvania: may her friends ever be warmed by the first, and her enemies cooled by the second." The militant attitude expressed by this remark has always characterized the business interest of the Keystone State (so-called for an eighteenth-century cartoon which showed Pennsylvania holding the central position in the arc of the federal union). Although Biddle ultimately lost his fight to save the Bank, which had headquarters in Philadelphia, from the hostility of Andrew Jackson, the defeat did not check the increase of the state's economic power throughout the nineteenth century. Natural resources buried in the Appalachian Highlands enabled Pennsylvania to compete successfully with more advantageously located states such as New York, Massachusetts, and Illinois. Stores of iron, hard and soft coal, timber, and oil provided the basis for rapid industrial growth. In the picturesque and narrow valleys of the Delaware, the Schuylkill, the Susquehanna, the Allegheny, the Monongahela, and the Ohio, business thrived (and ruled) as nowhere else in the nation.

The governmental structure of this industrial society was maintained by a rough-and-ready political machine. In 1858, United States Senator Simon Cameron moved part of the state's Democratic organization into the newly formed Republican party. Two years later, Cameron switched the Pennsylvania delegation at the Republican national convention in Chicago to Abraham Lincoln in return for the promise of a cabinet seat. In the fall, the Keystone's twenty-seven electoral votes helped assure the election of the first Republican president. (Cameron became Lincoln's first secretary of war, a post which he managed with such blatant corruption that he had to be replaced in 1862 by Edwin M. Stanton, another Pennsylvanian.)

From that time, the Grand Old Party ruled the roost in Pennsylvania with little challenge for more than seventy years. A Democrat, Robert E. Pattison, was twice elected governor toward the end of the nineteenth century, and Theodore Roosevelt carried the state for president on the Bull Moose ticket in 1912; otherwise, the Republican reign remained unbroken until 1934. In that year, Democrats won both the governorship and a seat in the United States Senate. Pennsylvania's "Little New Deal," presided over by Governor George H. Earle, came to a swift conclusion when Republicans regained control of the state in 1938. Although it had been one of five states to give electoral majorities to Herbert Hoover in 1932, Pennsylvania thereafter voted for Franklin Roosevelt three times for president. In 1948, the state returned to the Republican presidential electoral column.

Lacking the flare of Ohioans or New Yorkers for national politics, the leaders of the Pennsylvania Republican organization pursued the interest of their state with singleminded intensity. While almost never producing a serious candidate for president (the only Pennsylvanian ever elected to the White House was James Buchanan, a Democrat, in 1856), the machine regularly used its crucial votes at Republican national conventions to assure the party's continued support for a high protective tariff, the Excalibur which the industrialists of Pittsburgh, Philadelphia, and the upstate communities regarded as indispensable to their security. After Cameron, the organization was managed by a distinguished series of state bosses: J. Donald Cameron (Simon's son, who confounded his friend,

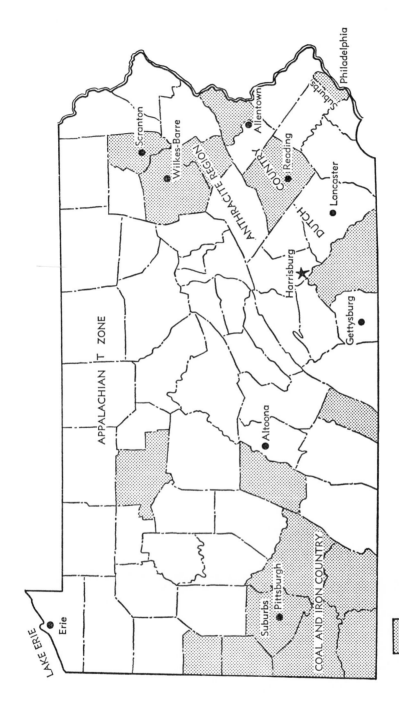

PENNSYLVANIA

Counties Carried by Democratic Candidate for Governor, 1958

Henry Adams, by favoring the "free and equal coinage of silver" in the 1890's), Matthew Stanley Quay (lean and tubercular spoilsman, defender of the American Indian, and connoisseur of Oriental art objects), and Boise Penrose (the "Old Grizzley" who, according to legend, ordered the nomination of Warren Harding for president from his deathbed in 1920). Though all were members of the United States Senate, they remained essentially state leaders, more at home at a party rally or on a hunting trip in the Alleghenies than in the polished halls of Washington. (No state capital equals that of Pennsylvania in honor done to former bosses. An heroic statue of Penrose guards the main entrance to the capitol grounds in Harrisburg, while Quay is installed beneath a recess in the rotunda.)

The hold of the machine on the state government was assured by a constitutional provision which prevented a governor from being elected to succeeding terms. Thus, from the moment of his election, the governor was in effect a lame duck. The members of the vast army of state patronage workers (by 1950 more than 35,000 jobholders, by far the nation's largest concentration of government employees completely outside the merit system) were well aware that the governor would soon be gone, while the machine and its boss would endure. Underpinning the strength of the state organization were the "courthouse gangs" operating out of most of the sixty-seven county seats. These provided additional reserves of patronage, as well as access to the rich natural resources which many counties contained. The county organizations enjoyed some autonomy; but as the courthouse jobs themselves did not pay very well, it was relatively easy for the state boss, who controlled the high-salaried positions in Harrisburg, to assure the loyalty of the county leaders.

Pennsylvania's two largest cities, Philadelphia and Pittsburgh, remained under Republican control long after most Eastern and Midwestern cities were firmly Democratic. The local organizations in these cities were managed by "contractor bosses"—men who purchased control of their city councils in order to gain lucrative contracts for construction of roads, sewers, gas lines, subways, and the other necessary adjuncts of metropolitan life. (Their activities were memorably etched by Theodore Dreiser in his novel about

Philadelphia business and politics, *The Financier*.) After the death of Senator Penrose, these city bosses, particularly the Vare brothers in Philadelphia, began to challenge the hegemony of the old state organization, based on the upstate counties. At the same time, the Mellon family of Pittsburgh, led by Andrew W. Mellon, a wealthy banker and secretary of the treasury under three Republican presidents, made its bid for control of the organization.

Unlike New York, which was settled along a single track of migration, Pennsylvania grew in concentric arcs ranging outward from Philadelphia, in the southeastern corner of the state. In the first arc are included four suburban counties, heavily populated with Philadelphia commuters and overwhelmingly Republican. The second arc, swinging from Gettysburg near the Maryland border to Easton on the Delaware River opposite New Jersey, is inhabited largely by the Pennsylvania Dutch, an industrious people who began arriving from Germany before the American Revolution. In the fertile Dutch country are some pockets of Democratic strength— York County, Berks County (Reading), Northampton County (Bethlehem and Easton)—but also two of the most populous Republican strongholds, Dauphin (Harrisburg) and Lancaster Counties.

The Dutch stopped when they reached the Blue Mountain, the front of the Appalachian Highlands, which run north from Maryland to the Susquehanna River at Harrisburg and then northeast to the Delaware. North of the Blue are the once prosperous hard-coal fields, which produce most of the nation's supply of anthracite. Populated by a mixture of Welsh, Irish, Italians, and Slavs, the five anthracite counties were long dominated by the big coal companies and the best drilled political organizations in the state. Unemployment in the coal fields in the thirties produced a slow trend toward the Democrats. West of the Blue and north of the anthracite region lies the Appalachian "T-zone," a region of forest and streams (almost half of the state's area was still forest land in 1962). Inhabited by the remnant of the nation's first great surge toward the West, the counties of this area are heavily Protestant and heavily Republican. In the southwest, beyond the Allegheny range, the T-zone phases into another series of arcs surrounding the state's second metropolis, Pittsburgh. Here, in the steel-mill towns and bituminous coal fields, the Democrats operate their own county and local machines.

As Philadelphia and Pittsburgh combined contain less than 30 per cent of the state's population, the upstate counties have usually been able to control the state government. The courthouse rings in these counties, during the civil wars that broke out within the Republican organization in the twenties, generally followed the leadership of Senator Joseph Grundy, founder and president of the Pennsylvania Manufacturers Association (PMA), who was regarded as belonging to the legitimate line of the Camerons, Quay, and Penrose. A fourth force in the struggle among the Vares, the Mellons, and PMA was the old Bull Moose faction led by Gifford Pinchot, formerly a trusted friend and lieutenant of Theodore Roosevelt and twice governor of the state. The warring groups struck temporary alliances, which had little to do with ideology (one of the most successful was between the liberal Pinchot and the arch-conservative Grundy) and enabled none to gain dominance.

As Pennsylvania was early industrialized, it also was early in developing strong industrial unions. Both the United Mine Workers and the United Steel Workers trace their origins to the company towns in the Appalachian hills. The unions, despite their economic success, had difficulty making political headway against the patronage-based county organizations. In some counties, particularly in the anthracite region, the local union leaders themselves became allies of the courthouse machines. Gradually, however, the unions began to contribute to the growth of the state Democratic party. Pittsburgh was captured by the Democrats in the early thirties, and labor claimed a large share of the credit for the election of George Earle as governor in 1934. Thomas Kennedy, vice president of the United Mine Workers, unsuccessfully sought the Democratic nomination for governor in 1938. In the late thirties, labor's own civil war, begun when the Mine Workers seceded from the American Federation of Labor, for a time diverted the attention of the union movement from Pennsylvania politics. By the end of World War II, however, organized labor was prepared to again join with the Democrats in the struggle to end the tradition of Republican rule.

Democratic hopes were given a decided lift in the late forties by the success of a reform coalition against the entrenched Republican machine in Philadelphia. Led by Richardson Dilworth, a young attorney and former Marine hero, the reformers succeeded in wresting several city offices from the Republicans in 1949. The following year, the union leaders and Democratic bosses agreed on Dilworth as their candidate for governor.

At the same time, the Republicans had resumed the internal feuds which had weakened their state organization during the twenties. Governor James H. Duff, during his four-year administration, had sponsored many progressive measures and had declined to accept the guidance of former-Senator Grundy or PMA. Unable to retain the governor's chair, he determined in 1950 to seek election to the United States Senate and to install an anti-PMA Republican as his successor. To achieve these objectives, he adopted the mantle of Bull Moose liberalism—Grundy and PMA, he said, were "high-buttoned shoes reactionaries"—and looked about for allies among the old factions. In the Philadelphia organization, just beginning to crumble under the reform assault, he gained the support of Sheriff

Figure 4. Pennsylvania Battle Graph, 1948-62

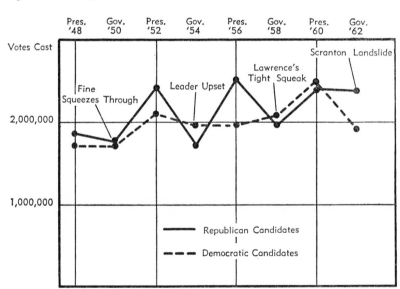

Austin Meehan, last of the contractor bosses. Upstate, he formed an alliance with a group of leaders from the suburban and anthracite counties. Known as the Blue Bell boys (for the name of the colonial inn near Philadelphia at which they sometimes dined), these leaders, while essentially conservative, had tired of PMA arrogance. As candidate for governor, Duff and the Blue Bell group selected Judge John S. Fine, political leader of Luzerne County (Wilkes-Barre), largest of the anthracite domains.

Grundy, by now almost ninety, and PMA accepted the challenge. A regular ticket, composed of Congressman John C. Kunkel, Harrisburg, for the Senate, and Jay Cooke, former Philadelphia Republican chairman and descendant of the Civil War financier, for governor, was put into the field. Following a bitterly fought primary, in which the opposing slates reported total expenditures of more than $2 million, Duff and Fine were decisively victorious.

Preceding the general election, Dilworth, though given little chance, waged an aggressive campaign in all parts of the state. On election day, he carried Philadelphia by almost 80,000 votes and sizably reduced normal Republican majorities in the suburban counties. In the anthracite region, too, he ran surprisingly well against Fine, carrying two of five counties. In the southwest, however, Democratic machines in the steel and soft-coal regions failed to produce expected majorities. (Considerable suspicion existed in Philadelphia after the election that the western Democratic leaders, who were prospering under the existing arrangement, had not been particularly anxious for a change in party control of the state government. On the other hand, the Democratic ticket may have been hurt by the fact that Dilworth's running mate, Senator Francis J. Myers, was also from Philadelphia, while Duff's home was near Pittsburgh.) In the final returns, Fine triumphed over Dilworth by 86,000 votes (compared with a Republican majority for governor of 558,000 in 1946); Duff defeated Myers by a somewhat larger margin.

The following year, the Republican machine in Philadelphia, scandal ridden and torn by internal strife, finally collapsed. Dilworth was elected district attorney, and his fellow reformer, Joseph Sill Clark, a member of one of Philadelphia's oldest and most distinguished families, became the city's first Democratic mayor in eighty-seven years. The reform coalition had not been very long in office when it began to develop internal discord of its own. To the dismay of the city's patronage-starved Democratic organization, led after 1953 by Congressman William J. Green, Mayor Clark insisted on strict enforcement of the new merit system for municipal employees. In the quarrel that broke out between Clark and the Green organization, District Attorney Dilworth, who was able to develop considerable tolerance for machine politics so long as the machine was Democratic, attempted to remain neutral.

Meanwhile, the progressive Republican faction, following its hard-won victory, had all but dissolved at the state level. Senator Duff, in Washington, proved powerless to exert authority over his recent allies. Faced with the necessity for finding funds to pay for a World War II veterans' bonus enacted during Duff's administration, Governor Fine soon made peace with the Grundyites, who still controlled the legislature. In short order, PMA was restored to its old position of influence within the state government. At Fine's request, the legislature passed a 1 per cent sales tax, the first broad-based levy in Pennsylvania's history.

As the 1952 presidential election approached, Duff became an ardent supporter of General Eisenhower for the Republican nomination. The Grundy organization favored Senator Robert Taft. (At the Republican national convention in Philadelphia four years before, Grundy had assured the nomination of Thomas Dewey by swinging the bulk of the Pennsylvania delegation to the New York governor. On the theory that he should be against whomever Grundy was for, Duff had then led a minority of the delegation to the support of Taft.) Torn between the demands of the opposing factions, Governor Fine hesitated, wavered, finally climbed aboard the Eisenhower bandwagon too late for large recognition. In November, the Republican candidate for president carried Pennsylvania by a majority of over 250,000 votes.

After a mild setback in the local row office elections in Philadelphia in 1953, many of the Democratic reformers decided that their party had little chance of winning the gubernatorial election in 1954. Dilworth declined to lead the Democratic ticket in what he judged to be another hopeless race. The city Democratic organization, which under Congressman Green's leadership was growing into one of the most formidable machines in the nation, proved less easily discouraged. Uniting with the western organization of Pittsburgh's Mayor David L. Lawrence, the Philadelphia regulars set out behind the gubernatorial candidacy of George M. Leader, thirty-seven, a chicken farmer from York County, to capture the huge patronage grab bag that waited in Harrisburg.

The Republicans nominated for governor a veteran upstate politician, Lloyd H. Wood, one of the Blue Bell boys. Wood, a rather heavy-set gentleman, gave the impression over television that he had just stepped out of a smoke-filled room. Leader, on the other hand, youthful and articulate, appeared to bristle with crusading vigor. The Democratic candidate concentrated his attack on the sales tax, which had proven unpopular with both merchants and consumers. The result was victory for Leader by almost 275,000 votes. The Democratic legions of Philadelphia and Pittsburgh prepared at last to feast at the state patronage table.

Although Leader could not have won without the huge majorities rolled up for him in the state's two largest cities, he also made large inroads into Republican strength elsewhere. He improved on Dilworth's 1950 showing in the suburban counties and carried four out of five counties in the anthracite region. The Dutch counties, in which he was regarded as a native son, gave Leader a majority of their vote; and even ten formerly unbreachable Republican strongholds in the Appalachian T-zone turned in for the Democratic candidate. In the steel region, the local Democratic machines produced the margins that had been expected of them four years before. Republican strength, unbeatable for almost a century, seemed to be dwindling to control of a few rural counties.

The immediate effect of the Democratic victory was to destroy what was left of the Republican machine in Philadelphia. Many former Republican stalwarts in the downtown wards, who had remained loyal to the GOP as long as state patronage was available, calmly switched to the opposition and thereafter delivered the same reliable majorities to Congressman Green that they formerly had made available to Sheriff Meehan and his cohorts. This development, in turn, had the effect of weakening the reform element in the Democratic party. No longer needed by the organization to carry the city, the reformers found their role in the party councils progressively diminished. Clark, who had kept the organization reeling during his four years in City Hall, stepped down as mayor in 1955 and was replaced by Dilworth. The new mayor promptly joined Green in supporting a referendum designed to modify the city's merit system for personnel. This proposal, opposed by Clark, was rejected by the voters in the spring of 1956.

Later that year, President Eisenhower's second-term candidacy swept Pennsylvania by a majority of more than 600,000. At the same time, however, former-Mayor Clark defeated Senator Duff's bid for re-election by a margin of less than 20,000 out of a total vote of 4,500,000. Heavy majorities from Philadelphia and Pittsburgh, coupled with the delayed vengeance of the Grundyites and Clark's popularity in the normally Republican suburbs, were sufficient to accomplish the surprising upset. (Luzerne County, bailiwick of former-Governor Fine, whose relations with his old ally had grown cool, went for Eisenhower by 27,000, but for Duff by only 4,000. Suburban Bucks County, Grundy's home base, gave Eisenhower a majority of 21,000, but Duff only 5,000.) Philadelphia was one of the few cities in the country in which the 1956 Democratic presidential vote did not fall drastically below the 1952 level. Congressman Green's organization, rather than the reform faction, was given credit for the showing.

The 1956 election produced Republican majorities in both houses of the state legislature. Governor Leader, already plagued by the insatiable demands of his machine supporters and the state's chronic financial difficulties, prepared to face additional woes. In 1955 the lower house of the legislature had been Democratic, but the Senate (which had not been reapportioned since 1921) remained Republican. After reaching legislative impasse on proposals for a graduated income tax and a tax on income from investments, Leader had reluctantly supported an increase of the sales tax to 3 per cent. Not surprisingly, consumers recalled Leader's campaign attacks on Fine's 1 per cent sales tax and felt themselves betrayed. Anxious to be elected to the United States Senate in 1958, the governor suddenly turned on his Democratic organization allies and sought to identify himself with reform. Several Philadelphia ward leaders were fired from their state jobs, as were the bosses of some of the western county machines. Leader indicated that Dilworth would be his choice for the 1958 gubernatorial nomination.

Congressman Green, however, had other ideas. Although working in relative harmony with Dilworth as mayor, the Philadelphia organization leaders were hesitant to entrust control of state patronage to the still occasionally hot-tempered reformer. (In 1957, Dilworth candidly commented, "The Democratic city ticket this year stinks.") Green urged his seventy-three year old Pittsburgh colleague, Mayor David L. Lawrence, to assume responsibility for maintaining organization control in Harrisburg. Though fearful that his Roman Catholic religion would hurt him in the strongly Protestant Dutch and T-zone counties, Lawrence agreed to run for governor. Rejecting pleas from some of the reformers that he make a primary fight, Dilworth accepted the decision of the bosses. Leader was given the nomination for senator.

Pondering their 1954 defeat, Republican State Chairman George Bloom and other leaders of the GOP state organization concluded that their candidate had lost because he was too closely identified with politics. No likely chicken farmers being found within their ranks, they chose as their gubernatorial candidate a pretzel maker, Arthur T. McGonigle, of Reading, whose only prior political experience had been as a fund raiser. Harold E. Stassen, former governor of Minnesota, former president of the University of Pennsylvania, and lately disarmament coordinator in the Eisenhower administration, reached for the by now fairly battered raiment of Bull Moose liberalism and entered the Republican primary against McGonigle.

Stassen's candidacy had the effect of forcing the organization leaders to give up plans for running Congressman James E. Van Zandt, a westerner, for the Senate. Onto the regular slate for senator, instead, went Congressman Hugh Scott, the only remaining Republican in the United States House of Representatives delegation from Philadelphia, whose chief visible support came from former-Sheriff Meehan and himself. Although Meehan's Philadelphia organization was by now almost wholly ineffective in general elections, the prospect that it might be put at the disposal of an insurgent in the primary was enough to bring the state leaders swiftly to terms. (According to another version of the story, Van Zandt was dropped from the ticket due to the opposition of the *Philadelphia Inquirer*.) McGonigle won the gubernatorial primary with 53 per cent of the vote to 31 per cent for Stassen and 16 per cent for William S. Livengood, a westerner and former organization stalwart. Lack of identification with politics had not seemed sufficient to rouse boundless enthusiasm for the Reading pretzel manufacturer.

Although the Republican fall campaign was conducted with visible pessimism, the result turned out to be much closer than had generally been expected. Lawrence edged through to a 76,000 vote majority over McGonigle, but Scott buried Leader beneath a margin of 113,000. Lawrence's concern over the religious issue was evidently justified—he ran behind his defeated running mate in twenty-one counties and more than 5 per cent below the Democratic showing for governor four years before in thirty-six counties, most of them in the Dutch and T-zone areas. It has been pointed out, however, that Lawrence, like Al Smith, was not merely a Catholic, but also a big-city, machine politician—a type unattractive to rural folk, regardless of religion. Actually, many persons were reportedly confused by the names into believing that Lawrence was a Yankee and McGonigle an Irish Catholic. Only heavy majorities out of Philadelphia and Pittsburgh pulled Lawrence through. Leader received the same treatment in the cities from some of the organization workers as had been accorded Duff by the Grundyites two years before. In Philadelphia, Leader ran more than 40,000 votes behind Lawrence, while in Allegheny County (Pittsburgh), he was cut by 85,000 voters who cast ballots for his running mate. Again, local loyalties may have affected the result. Scott was well known and popular in Philadelphia, while Lawrence's vote in Allegheny County was in part a tribute to his performance as mayor. Leader's own area, the Dutch country, failed to support him as it had in 1954.

As governor, Lawrence sought to establish an entente between the Democratic party and the business interest. In Pittsburgh, he had worked closely with the Mellon family and other Republican businessmen to promote the Golden Triangle (an office-building complex at the point where the Monongahela and Allegheny Rivers meet to form the Ohio) and other redevelopment projects. His efforts were not entirely unrewarded. Many businessmen who had formerly contributed only to Republicans began to give financial support to state and local Democratic organizations. Industrialists were pleased to find the governor sympathetic to the need for maintaining a good business climate—one in which the tax structure rested as lightly as possible on business. The Democratic party was to some extent relieved of its financial dependence on organized labor. Businessmen on the whole, however, particularly in and around Philadelphia, remained loyal to the Republicans, even in some cases increasing their support to the GOP. As Lawrence perhaps failed to realize, many businessmen wanted more from politics than economic privilege. The existence of a Democratic administration in Harrisburg was an affront to their view of the legitimate order of society. They wished not merely to profit, but also to govern. Many, also, were genuinely appalled by the shakedowns being conducted by Democratic politicians in Philadelphia. (By 1961, scandals reminiscent of those which Dilworth and the newspapers had exposed in the Republican regime during the late forties had begun to come to light in the Democratic city administration.)

Soundings taken throughout the state by the Philadelphia Democratic organization's professional pollster convinced Green early in 1960 that John Kennedy should be the party's candidate for president. Lawrence, mindful of the influence of the religious issue on his own election, approached the Kennedy candidacy with great caution. In the state's presidential preferential primary, which none of the Democratic candidates entered in deference to the wishes of the governor, Kennedy received 183,000 write-in votes (compared to 969,000 for Richard Nixon, whose name was on the Republican ballot). At the Los Angeles Democratic convention, Lawrence was at last carried into the Kennedy camp and permitted to make one of the seconding speeches for the future president. Green, however, received the major share of Kennedy's gratitude for delivering the Pennsylvania delegation.

In November, the 331,000 vote majority produced by the Democratic organization in Philadelphia was more than enough to overcome the 215,000 vote lead that Nixon built up in the rest of the state. Such former upstate Democratic strongholds as Berks, York, and Fulton Counties—all heavily Protestant—gave substantial majorities to the Republican candidate. On the other hand, in the anthracite and bituminous counties and in the Philadelphia suburbs —where Catholics are numerous—Kennedy ran extremely well. (Populous Delaware County, outside Philadelphia, went Republican by 52 per cent, compared to no less than 59 per cent for the last three Republican candidates for governor. The Democratic effort in the suburban counties was bolstered by tactical advice and financial assistance from Green's city organization.) In the summer preceding the 1960 election, the Democrats overcame the Republican lead in registration of the state's voters for the first time since the Civil War.

Angered by the decline of Republican fortunes, a group of businessmen, led by Philip W. Sharples, Philadelphia industrialist and chairman of the state Republican Finance Committee, began after 1960 to exert increasing authority over party strategy. "I think you should know," Sharples wrote to 1960 Republican contributors, "that there was no financial excuse for the poor political performance in sections of Greater Philadelphia or in other parts of Pennsylvania where the results were poor." The Sharples group received enthusiastic support from the state's most famous Republican, Dwight Eisenhower, who made his home in Gettysburg after leaving the White House. In Philadelphia, a group of insurgent Republicans sought to overthrow the existing organization dominated by Meehan's son, William, after the death of the former sheriff in 1961. County organizations in other parts of the state were marked for renovation. Whether because or in spite of the efforts of Sharples and his collaborators, Republicans scored broad gains in the 1961 elections. Republican Henry X. O'Brien defeated his Democratic opponent for a seat on the state Supreme Court. At the same time, Republicans replaced Democrats as mayors of Scranton, Bethlehem, York, Lancaster, Erie, and other upstate cities. The victory in Scranton was in part credited to the popularity of Congressman William W. Scranton, after whose family the city had been named, and who had the year before bucked a 15,000 majority for Kennedy in his district to win election over an incumbent Democrat by 17,000 votes.

Scenting the possibility of victory in the 1962 gubernatorial election, the Republicans immediately divided into warring factions. The Blue Bell boys allied with the Meehan organization to place Superior Court Judge Robert Woodside in the field for governor. Senator Scott, who had broken with the Meehans soon after his election, at first indicated that he would support either Congressman Scranton or Congressman Van Zandt against Woodside, an able but little-known jurist. Scranton took himself out of the race. Having assessed the relative strengths of the two alignments, Van Zandt announced that he would join the Woodside slate as a candidate for the Senate. Outraged, Scott, with the support of Eisenhower and Sharples, declared that he would himself seek the governorship. Woodside withdrew and Van Zandt became the Blue Bell candidate for governor. Scott and Van Zandt exchanged colorful descriptions of each other's political morals. With chaos approaching, Congressman Scranton agreed to become a candidate for governor if all major elements in the party would unite in his support. Chairman Bloom obtained acquiescence to this compromise from the Blue Bell faction at a meeting held in the home of Delaware County leader John McClure. Van Zandt again became a candidate for the Senate. Scott, after some hesitation, announced his approval.

The Democrats, too, indulged in some intramural party squabbling before agreeing on a choice for governor. Senator Clark, seeking re-election, indicated that he regarded Mayor Dilworth (who had been re-elected by an overwhelming majority over Harold Stassen, the seemingly always available Republican candidate for almost anything, in 1959) as his best possible running mate. Congressman Green, on the other hand, suggested that Dilworth, whose reputation had been damaged by the Philadelphia scandals, could not be elected. Dilworth stated that this time he would stay in the race, with or without the support of the Philadelphia organization. Under pressure from both President Kennedy and Governor Lawrence, Green at length withdrew his opposition, and the two old comrades of the Philadelphia reform movement became running mates on the Democratic ticket.

As matters turned out, Green proved to have been an accurate prophet. Scranton overwhelmed Dilworth, who campaigned as though seeking an award for schoolyard invective, by a majority of almost 500,000 votes. (By the end of the campaign, Dilworth had charged or implied that his opponent was anti-Semitic, anti-Negro, "effeminate," a "robber baron," an absentee landlord, and one who had "never heard shots fired in anger." "And you, sir," Scranton replied, in one face-to-face encounter, "are a desperate man.") Clark, on the other hand, was re-elected by 108,000. The Republicans carried both houses of the legislature, for the first time since 1956, by narrow majorities. The restoration of Republican rule seemed a personal victory for Scranton, whose charm and candor had created new hope in the distressed anthracite and bituminous regions. Scranton carried all but five of sixty-seven counties—a better showing even than had been made by James Duff at the height of Republican power in 1946.

Among his final executive acts, Governor Lawrence proudly bestowed upon the incoming administration an allegedly balanced budget and a fiscal surplus for the preceding year. (The figures supporting both were promptly challenged by the Republicans.) The price for this achievement was that, in 1961, Pennsylvania was well below the national average in per capita expenditures for education, highways, public welfare, and correctional institutions. (The state was well above average, on the other hand, in expenditures for employees' salaries and supplies.)

Lawrence and the legislative leaders who shared his responsibilities were caught in a cruel dilemma, no doubt. Governing an area less attractive to industry than it once had been and already burdened by large masses of unemployed workers (more than 7 per cent of the work force in thirty-one counties in 1960), they felt compelled to hold down taxes and avoid debt so business would not desert to the South or West. Yet without revenue the state could not enlarge its support for schools, highways, and parks, as the public increasingly demanded. All state polls in the fall of 1962 showed the Lawrence administration at a low level of popularity. Partly this was due to the atmosphere of machine politics that had settled over Harrisburg, but partly also to the impression of inertia that had been created by the state government.

In 1961, former-Senator Grundy had died quietly at his home in

Bucks County. He was ninety-eight years old and left an estate valued at $18 million. Until shortly before his death, he had gone to his office at least three days every week. As the old man lay dying, the PMA held its annual convention banquet at the Bellevue Stratford Hotel in nearby Philadelphia. Moving among the diners was young William Scranton, recently elected to Congress. But first speaker of the evening was Governor Lawrence, who promised "the continuation of a good business climate for Pennsylvania." The metropolitan businessmen and upstate industrialists cheered the Democratic governor to the rafters. They felt confident, perhaps, that the economic and political structure which Joseph Grundy and his predecessors had built would not soon pass away.

5

NEBRASKA

SONS OF THE PIONEERS

Nebraska," according to its junior senator, Carl T. Curtis, Republican, "is the most conservative state in the union." Democratic Governor Frank B. Morrison recently agreed, "If by liberals you mean people who believe in a lot of big government, we don't have many of them in Nebraska."

It was not always so. The Cornhusker State, located near the geographic center of North America, was during the late years of the nineteenth century and the early years of the twentieth a hotbed of liberalism and even radicalism in the United States. Settled largely by veterans of the Union Army and farmers hurrying west to take advantage of homestead legislation passed by the Republican Congress in 1862, the state was at first tied by strong emotional and economic bonds to the party of "free men and free soil." The state capital was named Lincoln, after the first Republican president, and in 1872, five years after achieving statehood, Nebraska gave 70 per cent of its popular vote for president to the Republican candidate, former–Union General Ulysses S. Grant. Immediately thereafter, however, farm problems aggravated by the great grasshopper invasion of 1874 began to draw agricultural Nebraska away from the increasingly conservative Republicans. Abjuring alliance with the Democrats, still widely identified with the rebellious South and Eastern big-city machines, Nebraskans turned to a new third party, the Populists, who promised to place the railroad, milling, and telegraph industries under strict government control. In alliance with some dissident members of the two major parties, the Populists were able to dominate state government from 1892 to 1900. The climax (and also the beginning of the end) for Populism was achieved at the Democratic national convention of 1896, when William Jennings Bryan, a Nebraskan, stampeded one of the two major parties into support of a watered-down version of the radical program conceived in the lonely reaches of the Great Plains. Bryan's famous "cross of gold" speech, dripping with rural bravado and implied anti-Semitism, rallied agrarian enthusiasm to an almost hysterical pitch, while at the same time assuring the eventual eclipse of what now could be no more than a regional movement. As Democratic candidate for president, Bryan that November lost every state east of the Mississippi and north of the Mason-Dixon line to his Republican opponent, William McKinley.

Bryan's crusade left its mark on both major parties in Nebraska. The Democrats were raised to the status of a serious contender for statewide power. The Republicans, at the same time, were prepared for the liberal leadership of George W. Norris, who during his thirty years in the United States Senate became a national spokesman for many progressive causes, most notably the Tennessee Valley Authority. During the 1930's, under Norris' inspiraton, Nebraska established two advanced institutions that have not yet been duplicated by any other state: a nonpartisan, unicameral legislature and a state-owned public power system. Both have had critics, but neither, in the middle sixties, appears in danger of being abolished.

To house the unicameral legislature, the state raised a majestic skyscraper, complete with gold door knobs, beautiful tile mosaics, and a bronze Sower, poised 437 feet above the level of the surrounding plains. Although costing $10 million and constructed in the middle of the Depression, the capitol was paid for when completed. (The building has been a subject for continuing pride and controversy. In 1954, Kenneth Evett, assistant professor of fine arts at

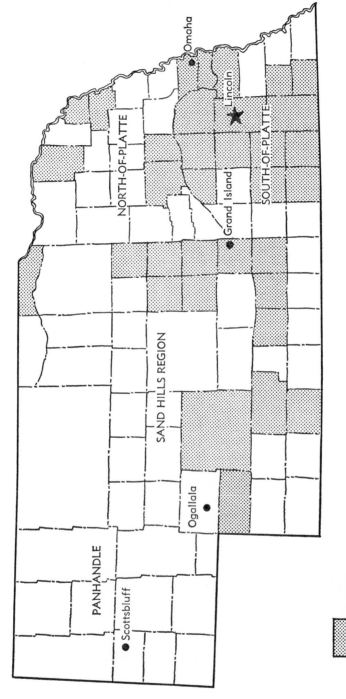

PANHANDLE

SAND HILLS REGION

NORTH-OF-PLATTE

SOUTH-OF-PLATTE

Omaha

Lincoln

Grand Island

Ogallala

Scottsbluff

Counties Carried by Democratic Candidate for Governor, 1960

NEBRASKA

Cornell University, was commissioned to paint three murals, depicting various phases of Nebraska life, for the rotunda. In one of these murals, the artist included the likeness of a bull, painted in the form of a square. Opposition to the general "modernistic" style of the paintings concentrated on the square bull. The issue was debated across the state, eventually causing an eruption of oratory in the legislature. When requested to appropriate additional funds for more paintings, the legislature concluded: "The public should be allowed to live with the first group for some time, before going farther.")

Running beneath this experimental tradition was a conservative strain that was, during the 1940's, to reassert its dominance. Many of the progressive measures were justified at the time of their adoption on the ground that they would save money (which in fact, they did—the unicameral legislature alone substantially reduced the cost of state government). It has been observed that Nebraskans are descendants of pioneers who stopped—that is, who fell out along the trail, foregoing the promised lands of California or Oregon to make do on the initially unpromising soil of the Platte River basin. The people who survived on this land, outlasting the grasshoppers and transforming what had been called the "Great American Desert" into a thriving producer of grain, grew strong, independent, and essentially cautious. In 1875, they adopted a constitution, still in effect, which narrowly limits the possible forms of taxation and forbids bonded indebtedness. (During the 1930's, the state was proudly advertised to businesses considering migration as a "white spot"—no income tax, no sales tax, no bonded debt—a distinction which it still may validly claim.) Though in economic hard times they might approve some changes in the *form* of government and though they might occasionally indulge (as in the state capitol) a lurking desire for attention from inhabitants of wealthier and more sophisticated states, they and their descendants could be relied upon to dig their heels in hard against any innovation that might threaten their pocketbooks or their personal freedom.

Contributing to the underlying conservatism of the state has been a regional rivalry which has induced a reliance on local rather than state government. (In 1960, the state collected only 37 per cent of the combined total of state and local taxes, a proportion lower than that of any other state except New Jersey.) Originally, this rivalry sprang from the mutual animosity felt between those who lived north and south of the Platte River, which curves snakelike across the state from west to east. The south-of-Platte residents, who arrived first, believed that they had been betrayed by the territorial governor who agreed to have the capital located at Omaha (north-of-Platte). With the coming of statehood, the capital was moved south-of-Platte to Lincoln (so named at the insistence of north-of-Platters, who remembered the Civil War president primarily as the man who placed the new Union Pacific railroad on their side of the river), but, as it turned out, the seat of territorial government had by that time assumed an insurmountable economic lead. This dispute is preserved in the practice, followed by both major parties, of alloting one United States Senate seat to a south-of-Platter, while reserving the other for a statesman who hails from north-of-Platte (in practice, usually, Omaha).

In recent years, a more fundamental rivalry has developed between the state's only two sizable cities, Omaha and Lincoln, on the one side and on the other the predominantly rural outstate (in fifty-four of Nebraska's ninety-two counties, 40 per cent or more of the people lived on farms in 1960). Though the state's two metropolitan counties contain 35 per cent of the population, they elect only 30 per cent of the legislators. The outstate farmers, fearful of the economic power already concentrated in the cities, are determined that they shall have no more. Complicating this division is a conviction widely held among residents of the western half of the state, the cattle-grazing Sand Hill and Panhandle regions, that they are not fairly treated by the more populous eastern counties. The Panhandle, a full day's drive by car from either Omaha or Lincoln, has developed a particularly strong sense of isolation. As a result, a kind of three-way impasse exists in the legislature, with representatives from the western and city areas taking turns to join the eastern rural majority to make certain that few bills primarily benefiting the other go through.

Nebraska's fundamental conservatism was reasserted in the 1940's by a pair of Republican United States senators, Kenneth Wherry and Hugh A. Butler. Wherry, Republican leader of the Senate and principal spear bearer for General Douglas MacArthur during the controversy surrounding the recall of the former Far Eastern commander in 1951, achieved a measure of national celebrity. It was Butler, however, who built and operated one of the most efficient political organizations the state had ever known. Under Butler's leadership, Republicans piled up seven straight gubernatorial victories by majorities that only once fell below 60 per cent. In 1952, Dwight Eisenhower carried the state for president by a majority only one percentage point below Ulysses Grant's all-time record. By the time Butler died in 1954, Nebraska was approaching one-party status, with Democrats as rare and powerless as Republicans in Virginia.

Desultory opposition to Butler's dominance had been carried on by a series of mildly liberal governors, two of whom sought unsuccessfully to defeat him in Republican primaries for his Senate seat. One of these, Dwight A. Griswold, who also had distinguished himself as chief of the United States mission to Greece in the postwar years, finally did arrive in the Senate, taking Wherry's place after the latter's death in 1952. Unfortunately, Griswold himself died in 1954, three months before Butler. Candidates in the Republican primary to succeed to his seat were two outstaters, Governor Robert B. Crosby, a moderate, and Congressman Carl Curtis, a tight-lipped conservative in the Butler tradition.

Crosby's single term in the governor's mansion had been enlivened by a state Supreme Court decision ordering general equalization of property assessments. As residents of one of the few states that continue to draw a large share of their revenue from the tax on real estate (most states now leave this resource to local government), Nebraskans are particularly sensitive to the assessment problem. Over the years, disparities had inevitably worked their way into the system, and the court held that substantial variations existed in the rates at which property was assessed in different counties. A special session of the legislature was necessary to deal with the uproar arising over the equalization. The governor put into effect what he called "Operation Honesty," a program to encourage citizens to give truthful reports to the assessors. At the end of his term, Crosby declared, "Looking back, I am actually glad it happened. It gave a substance to my governorship that I would not have foregone."

Resentment over the new assessment had, however, measurably reduced his popularity. In the primary, Curtis, as heir to the Butler machine, was nominated for the Senate.

In the 1954 general election, the Republican ticket, composed of Curtis and Roman A. Hruska for the two Senate vacancies and Victor E. Anderson for governor, rolled to easy victory. Only five counties, all rural, returned Democratic majorities for governor. Two of these exceptions, Butler and Saline, contain large colonies of Czechoslovakian foreign stock, predominantly Roman Catholic in religion. The other three, Greeley, Howard, and Sherman, grouped together in the center of the state, also have relatively high proportions of Roman Catholics. It should be noted, however, that of the state's ten counties with populations 30 per cent or more Catholic, seven voted Republican. (Nebraska, despite its central location, was the final destination for a considerable number of immigrants in the twentieth century. Its population includes almost as large a proportion of foreign stock as that of Pennsylvania and larger than that of Ohio.)

During two relatively uneventful terms, Governor Anderson imposed a regime of strict austerity, which he felt was appropriate to the state's wavering farm economy. A thorn in the governor's side during both his terms was state Senator Terry Carpenter, from the western Panhandle, who in 1956 won nationwide fame by attempting to nominate "Joe Smith" in opposition to Richard Nixon for vice president at the Republican national convention. Carpenter, a former Democratic congressman who had turned Republican during the New Deal period, picked away at what he felt to be the inadequacies of the Anderson program. By 1958, despite rising gross agricultural income, the increasing cost of conducting farm operations—the so-called cost-price squeeze—had produced widespread discontent in the state. Nevertheless, Anderson in his third-term announcement exulted, somewhat in the manner of a tribal rainmaker: "I feel quite sure that every Nebraskan is very grateful for the return of normal weather and the rains we have received. They have been a great blessing to all of us. The resulting good crops this year will be of economic benefit, but should not lead us blindly into mounting costs and higher taxes."

Evidently uncheered by this prospect, Nebraskans the following fall voted the Democrats into state offices for the first time in twenty years. Anderson lost by a little more than 1,000 votes (out of 421,000 cast) to Ralph G. Brooks, a small-town school administrator. Omaha and Lincoln went Democratic, as did twenty-five outstate counties. South-of-Platte, where Brooks resided, twenty-nine out of thirty-four counties showed a 10 per cent gain in the Democratic vote over 1954; while in the Panhandle, where Terry Carpenter had campaigned for the Democratic candidate, four out of eleven counties showed gains of 15 per cent or better. Most of the cattle-grazing Sand Hills region and the hog-feeding counties along the Elkhorn River in the northeast remained heavily Republican.

The Democrats, having been so long in the shade, created an air of novelty in the state capital. (It was discovered that an Omaha bartender, enjoying the advantage of a Scandinavian name, had been elected state treasurer, with responsibility for millions of dollars in public funds.) For some years National Committeeman Bernard Boyle, an Omaha attorney, had been assumed to be the real leader of the state Democratic party. A rival faction, the so-called New Life group, was headed by Frank B. Morrison, a gigantic orator and lawyer with outstate roots, who had perennially sought office on the Democratic ticket. Governor Brooks had been aligned with the Boyle group, but immediately set out, through an arduous schedule of speechmaking and personal appearances, to establish an identity of his own. This attempt seemed on its way to success, but the governor, at the age of sixty-one, proved physically unable to sustain it.

In April, 1959, Senator Carpenter rose in the legislature to announce that he had been reliably informed that Brooks had several days before been hospitalized with a stroke. The governor's office confirmed the story a few minutes later. Carpenter and others criticized the extent to which the governor's administrative assistant, Robert Conrad, a Boyle man, had assumed the powers of chief executive. Brooks eventually returned to his desk, but Conrad continued to carry on many of the duties of governor. The legislature turned to such normal pursuits as arguing over where federal interstate highway funds should be spent (the final formula: 23 per cent for Omaha and Lincoln, 77 per cent for rural areas), and debating the governor's complaint that the floors of the new $200,000 executive mansion trembled when he walked upon them.

In 1960, Frank Morrison charged that Boyle was using his political position to influence state agencies on behalf of his clients and defeated Conrad in the Democratic primary for governor. A few weeks later, Brooks, who had been nominated to run against Curtis for the Senate, suffered a fatal heart attack. The State Central Committee, dominated by Boyle, put Conrad back on the ballot, this time as candidate for the Senate.

The Republicans had not interpreted their 1958 defeat as a repudiation of conservatism. Party leadership passed to Senators Curtis and Hruska (the latter, in the general view, having the personality, while the former had the organization). Support for basic conservative tenets was reasserted: a balanced budget; reduction of foreign aid; no more federal aid programs, particularly no aid for schools; and no more welfare programs of any kind.

While Morrison was defeating Conrad, a bitterly fought Republican

Figure 5. Nebraska Battle Graph, 1948-62

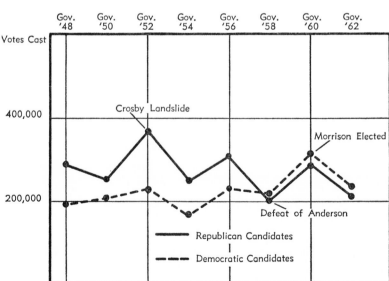

gubernatorial primary was being won by John Cooper, a business-man from a small town in the southeast corner of the state. The climax to the general election campaign that followed was reached when Cooper and Morrison debated in the auditorium of a Lincoln bank. The Democratic candidate brought his aged mother to the stage and dared Cooper to repeat in her presence charges question-ing her son's honesty. Although Nixon carried Nebraska for presi-dent by 62 per cent (his best showing in the nation), and Curtis easily defeated Robert Conrad, Morrison was elected governor by almost 25,000 votes. Omaha and Lincoln again went Democratic for governor.

The importance of the hometown-boy appeal—particularly if a candidate could claim more than one hometown—in Nebraska was indicated by the fact that Morrison made his largest gains over the 1958 Democratic showing in Lancaster County (Lincoln), where he lived, and outstate Frontier and Red Willow Counties, in both of which he had once practiced law. Lancaster County, second largest in the state, gave 62 per cent of its vote to Nixon, but only 33 per cent to the Republican candidate for governor. The Panhandle, with Terry Carpenter back in the Republican fold, went solidly GOP. Carpenter's own county, Scotts Bluff, showed a 13 per cent increase in the Republican vote over 1958. The Republican candidate's home county, on the other hand, gave him almost exactly the same pro-portion of the vote his predecessor had received two years before.

The new governor immediately announced that during his admin-istration no party official would be permitted to represent a client for pay before a state agency and suggested that both the state attorney general and bar association look into National Committee-man Boyle's past activities in this field. (Neither found grounds for action.) Later he blocked appointment of Conrad by the Kennedy administration as United States attorney for Nebraska.

Morrison's most important activity, however, was to step up the bipartisan campaign to attract new industry to the state. Nebraska, with a population of 1,411,330 in 1960 (less than that of Detroit or of Queens County, New York), had gained only about thirty thou-sand people in the last thirty years. Between 1950 and 1960, sixty-nine of the state's ninety-three counties actually lost population. These losses were due almost entirely to the decline in job opportunities on farms caused by the revolutionary mechanization of American agriculture. Unlike many of their counterparts in industry and mining, farm laborers appear to move on when work is no longer available. In 1960, Nebraska had only two counties in which unemployment was over 5 per cent and none over 7 per cent. On the other hand, twenty-four counties had lost more than 15 per cent of their population during the census decade. (In comparison, unemployment in Michigan's Upper Peninsula was much heavier, but only one county out of fifteen had lost as much as 15 per cent of its population.) Perhaps because the decline in farm jobs began before corresponding reductions in other fields or perhaps for other reasons, the jobless farmer has been much more mobile than most of the unemployed. Nebraska lacks small industry, of the kind that has held up the economies of agricultural regions like Central Ohio and Pennsylvania's Dutch country, to absorb the former farm workers. Flight from the farm, as a result, has frequently meant flight from the state. Seeking to solve this problem, the state at the beginning of the 1960's launched an economic development program under which local communities were encouraged to grant financial advantages to new industrial concerns.

Morrison, like most former governors, had his problems with the unicameral legislature. Theoretically nonpartisan, the forty-three member legislature had in 1961 about a three-to-one Republican majority. Although there is almost no sentiment for a return to bicameralism, the absence of partisan designation has, some observers feel, tended to break down legislative cohesion. There are neither majority nor minority floor leaders, and the speaker, who presides in the absence of the lieutenant governor, is usually chosen on the basis of general popularity. In a few cases—as when the Republican legislators forced a recount of the close 1958 gubernatorial election —party lines are discernible, but as a rule each senator follows his personal guiding star. Morrison and five former governors, interviewed in 1961 by the "depth reporting" class of the University of Nebraska school of journalism, all agreed that lack of party discipline in the legislature makes it difficult for a governor, himself elected under a party label, to promote his program. "There is no formal leadership," one former governor commented. "It's just like a Mexican army: all generals." The legislators themselves, many of whom attract supporters across party lines, were overwhelmingly in favor of continuing the present system.

Morrison's difficulties with the legislature, most of them minor, might easily have been greater had the Republican majority felt compelled to pursue a partisan policy. On the other hand, in a partisan election a popular Democratic governor would presumably carry a larger proportion of Democrats into the legislature. A Republican governor, in any case, would be likely to exert more influence over fellow party members whose re-elections to some extent depended on the success of his program. Most Nebraskans seem unimpressed by these considerations. Various campaigns in the last decade to return legislative elections to a partisan basis have failed for lack of popular support.

In 1962, Republicans made a determined effort behind the candidacy of Fred Seaton, secretary of the interior in the Eisenhower administration, to recapture the governorship. Seaton promised better schools, better highways, higher pensions for retired teachers. But many Nebraskans seemed to suspect that the former secretary had been too long in Washington to understand their problems. Governor Morrison turned on the homely charm and was re-elected by a majority of 24,000.

Above the main entrance to the state capitol in Lincoln is chiseled the inscription, "The Salvation of the State is Watchfulness in the Citizen." Nebraskans have, indeed, been a watchful people. In the middle 1960's, there is some evidence of a growing realization on the Great Plains that other qualities—imagination, generosity, daring —may be at least equally necessary to the state's salvation. Nor would such qualities be new to Nebraska. The capitol itself, rising above the flatlands like a beacon toward heaven, is sign enough of the creative impulses working within the hearts of the rough and practical men who manage the state's destiny. Having defeated grasshoppers, drought, and economic depression, Nebraskans are turning their attention to the effects of the permanent revolution in agriculture. Their two greatest resources, the land and their own resiliency, remain fresh and strong. And the great work of establishing humanity on the central plains of North America (mission enough for any people) has only begun.

6

NEW YORK

THE COLLABORATIVE STATE

When Americans say that their country has transcended the class war, they sometimes have in mind the complex political and economic system that has evolved in the state of New York. Apparently, it is true that the New York business community has long since ceased to strive for the company-town situation, which still exists at least as an aspiration in many industrial states, and that labor and minority groups have moderated the remorseless opposition to vested interest that forms their single-minded program in some parts of the nation. What exists in place of this simple dualism is a subtle, kaleidoscopic arrangement of interests—labor, finance, industry, agriculture, rackets; Negroes, Jews, ethnic groups, religious denominations, veterans groups, fraternal organizations—each concluding temporary accommodations with as many as possible of the others, each pursuing its own objectives without much regard for the traditional ideologies of national political parties.

This politics of accommodation has resulted not so much in a welfare state (though New York leads the nation in many of the services offered to its citizens) as a collaborative state—one in which all major interests seek more through negotiation than through aggression to achieve the goals that each separately desires. During the 1950's, this system was subjected to severe strain. In a single decade, women for the first time became more numerous than men on the voter registration books, achieving a majority of 170,000 by 1960; the five suburban counties surrounding New York City increased population at rates ranging from 29 to 141 per cent, while population in the city itself actually declined; rural population dropped in upstate counties; economic gains by the growing middle class enabled 20 per cent of the state's families to enjoy incomes over $10,000 a year by 1960; the proportion of the population over sixty-five increased 34 per cent, as compared to a total population growth of 13 per cent; and the proportion under eighteen increased 44 per cent—more than three times the general rate. In view of this record of dynamic change, it is the over-all stability rather than the occasional eccentricity that gives most cause for wonder in the politics of New York in the 1950's.

No man had a greater share in developing New York's collaborative political system than a former Michigan choirboy named Thomas E. Dewey. Only forty-eight years old in 1950 when he was elected to a third successive four-year term as governor, Dewey already had behind him a controversial and distinguished public career. He had first gained fame twenty years before as a racket-busting assistant United States attorney in the Southern District of New York. With the support of Governor Herbert Lehman, latest in a series of notable Democratic chief executives of the Empire State, he was appointed special rackets prosecutor for New York County (physically identical with the borough of Manhattan, which for more than a century has been the financial, entertainment, and underworld capital of the United States). In 1937, he was elected district attorney of New York County on the Republican and American Labor party tickets (the latter an amalgam of liberal and left-wing groups, called into being by President Franklin Roosevelt to enable New York liberals to support the New Deal without voting the line of the notoriously corrupt city Democratic machine). The following year, he ran a game but unsuccessful race as Republican candidate for governor against Lehman.

After losing the Republican presidential nomination to Wendell

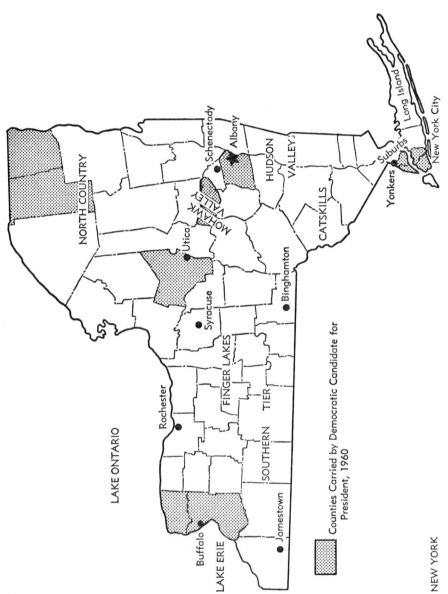

LAKE ONTARIO

NORTH COUNTRY

Schenectady

Albany

HUDSON

VALLEY

MOHAWK VALLEY

CATSKILLS

Utica

Binghamton

Suburbs

Yonkers

New York City

Long Island

Syracuse

FINGER LAKES

Rochester

SOUTHERN TIER

Jamestown

Buffalo

LAKE ERIE

Counties Carried by Democratic Candidate for President, 1960

NEW YORK

Willkie in 1940 (the galleries at Philadelphia's Convention Hall had been carefully packed with Dewey rooters, many of whom, losing their hearts to the burly Hoosier, contributed to the "We Want Willkie" roar that eventually stampeded the convention), he returned to the state political wars. He was easily elected governor in 1942, when the Democrats and the American Labor party (by then slipping under Communist control) put up separate candidates.

The state party that Dewey was thereby called upon to lead was at that moment coming out of a long era of stagnation. After the galvanic period at the beginning of the twentieth century, when Theodore Roosevelt and Charles Evans Hughes had made the New York Republican party one of the most dynamic political instruments in American history, the party had fallen under the iron grip of upstate utility and industrial interests. Beginning with Al Smith and extending through Franklin Roosevelt and Lehman, the Democrats had consistently carried the governorship (though not the notoriously malapportioned state legislature) as the champions of the public interest against this reactionary business element. Republican prospects were improved somewhat in the 1930's when State Chairman W. Kingsland Macy, Victorian mannered boss of Suffolk County on the eastern end of Long Island, broke the party control of the upstate interests. Macy also precipitated the legislative investigation of political corruption in New York City, which eventually led to the election of Fiorello LaGuardia, a former Republican congressman, as mayor.

By the time of Dewey's victory in 1942, technicians like Macy and J. Russel Sprague, leader in Nassau County, also on Long Island, had perfected reliable Republican organizations in the suburban belt surrounding New York City; while legislative leaders like Assembly Speaker Oswald D. Heck, Schenectady, had succeeded in developing a more progressive party program. Dewey utilized the machinery thus provided with virtuoso ability. Never a politician of the back-slapping, blintz-eating variety, he led his party to three successive state triumphs on the basis of effective government and ruthlessly efficient political control. During his tenure, men of tested professional capacity were recruited for service with the state government, while political appointments were awarded only to those who had survived rigorously thorough background investigations. His two frustratingly unsuccessful attempts at the presidency, as Republican candidate in 1944 and 1948, seemed only to harden his Machiavellian conviction that fear of punishment was more effective than hope of reward in maintaining political discipline. Loved by few, he was widely respected by both politicians and ordinary citizens for his integrity and administrative skill. By 1950, the presidency apparently forever beyond his grasp, Dewey was prepared to return to private life. He was dissuaded by a threat of rebellion within his own party and the spectre of a revitalized New York City Democratic organization, capable of gaining control of the model state government he had spent eight years constructing.

Tammany Hall (the popular name for the city Democratic machine, although Tammany was never more than the title of the Manhattan borough organization and supposedly passed out of existence altogether when Mayor Robert Wagner moved the organization headquarters to more virtuous surroundings following his primary victory in 1961) had for many years been a starved and anemic tiger. Long past were the days when John F. Curry, last of the great sachems, had submitted weekly lists of promotions and transfers, carrying the force of law, to city department heads during the administration of James F. Walker, the celebrated Night Mayor of Broadway. Frequently at odds with Roosevelt and soundly thrashed by LaGuardia, Tammany had emerged from the New Deal period in a condition of advanced senescence.

In the late forties, with LaGuardia dead and the liberals divided, a coalition of the Democratic organizations of the five boroughs (Manhattan, Brooklyn, the Bronx, Queens, and Richmond) found itself, almost by default, back in control of the city government. In 1949, the new machine, under the nominal leadership of Mayor William O'Dwyer, executed a coup reminiscent of the great days when New York's Democratic politicians combined the skills of Metternich and Cesare Borgia. Fearful of his chances for re-election that year, O'Dwyer was anxious to have former-Governor Lehman at the top of the party ticket to assure overwhelming Democratic majorities in the Jewish districts of the city. Lehman, who inspired an emotion close to worship among his co-religionists in New York, had been defeated for the United States Senate, his only political loss, in the Republican landslide of 1946. He was understood to be willing to take another shot at the federal legislative body.

Unfortunately, no United States senator would normally have been elected from New York in 1949. To overcome this embarrassment, it was decided that the state's senior senator, Robert F. Wagner, then in poor health at the end of a long and productive career, should be persuaded to resign one year before the end of his regular term. The somewhat delicate task of putting over this proposal was assigned to the senator's aspiring son, Robert Ferdinand Wagner, Jr., who had served as commissioner of buildings and chairman of the City Planning Commission in the O'Dwyer administration. The stratagem worked perfectly. O'Dwyer was safely re-elected, Lehman won the vacant Senate seat (over John Foster Dulles, who had received the temporary appointment from Governor Dewey), and young Bob Wagner, for his part in the transaction, was rewarded with the presidency of the borough of Manhattan.

A relatively inconspicuous but significant role in the 1949 success was played by the new leader of Tammany Hall, Carmine G. DeSapio. Elected the first Italian leader of the Hall, after an arduous struggle upward through the prevailingly Irish hierarchy of the Democratic city organization, DeSapio set out to associate the name Tammany with good works and lofty views on world affairs. Under the tutelage of a professional publicist, much addicted to purple prose, he suddenly began turning up on television panel shows and before college seminars. At the same time, he made plans to reassert Tammany's old hegemony over the other four borough organizations.

Heartened by their 1949 achievement, the Democratic high command, by now dominated by DeSapio and Edward J. Flynn, leader of the Bronx, set out the following year to bring off an even more complicated maneuver. This time the governorship was the objective. In order to swell the Democratic vote in New York City, it was decided that a mayoralty race was needed. Accordingly, President Harry Truman was persuaded to appoint O'Dwyer as ambassador to Mexico, thereby creating a vacancy for which Supreme Court Judge Ferdinand Pecora was named as Democratic candidate.

Congressman Walter Lynch, a Flynn lieutenant from the Bronx, was designated to run for governor, and Lehman went back on the ticket, seeking a full term in the Senate. The ethnic balance of the slate was impressive, carrying appeals to the large Italian, Irish, and Jewish blocs. The Liberal party, an anti-Communist off-shoot of the old ALP, endorsed the three Democratic candidates. DeSapio and Flynn were widely congratulated on the smoothness with which their scheme had been put into operation. Nobody paid much attention when City Council President Vincent Impellitteri, who would automatically serve as mayor from the time of O'Dwyer's resignation until the election, protested that he, not Pecora, should have been placed at the head of the city ticket. Even Impellitteri's charge that DeSapio had offered to toss him a judgeship if he gave up his independent candidacy for mayor created little stir.

Dewey, meanwhile, was confronted with rebellion within the Republican party. W. Kingsland Macy, pushed somewhat into the wings after his work of reconstruction in the thirties, was anxious to run against Lehman for the Senate in 1950. To achieve this end, he teamed with Frank E. Gannett, a conservative upstate newspaper

Figure 6. New York Battle Graph, 1948-62

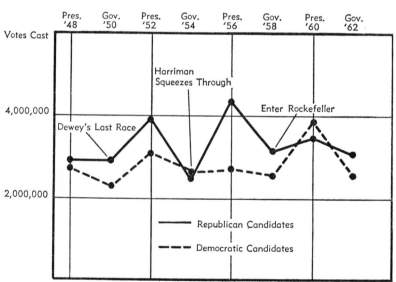

publisher, to support Lieutenant Governor Joe R. ("Holy Joe") Hanley, a former Chatauqua speaker, for the governorship. The well-financed campaign for Hanley developed so rapidly that Dewey soon discovered that the only way to head it off was by once again becoming a candidate himself. Persuaded that Hanley, aged and half-blind, could not repulse the Democratic assault in November, Dewey agreed to seek a third term. As consolation prize, Hanley was nominated for the Senate seat, which had been Macy's original objective. While he had been a candidate for governor, Hanley, who was heavily in debt, had received substantial advances from Macy and Gannett to pay off his creditors. After he had accepted the nomination for senator, the lieutenant governor made the error of writing a letter to Macy in which he explained that he had been promised that a way would be found to pay all his debts, whether or not he defeated Lehman. Early in the general election campaign, a copy of this letter found its way into the hands of the Democratic State Committee, which understandably gave it wide publicity.

Neither the balanced ticket nor the Hanley letter, however, were to be of much value to the Democrats that year. Dewey waded into the opposition with a gusto that he had sorely lacked in his campaign for the presidency two years before. Some speeches that Congress-man Lynch had made indicating sympathy with the Franco regime in Spain proved seriously embarrassing to his liberal supporters. Democratic resistance in the state legislature to construction of the New York Thruway, planned to provide a quick route from New York City to Buffalo, did not enhance the party's standing with the state's three million automobile owners. In November, Dewey was victorious by more than 500,000 votes, while Senator Lehman was at the same time re-elected by a majority of more than 250,000. An incidental victim of the election was Kingsland Macy, who was so heavily cut by fellow Republicans, evidently indignant over release of the Hanley letter, that he lost his normally safe Congressional seat from eastern Long Island. Most astonishing of all, however, was the success of the independent candidacy of Vincent Impellitteri in the New York City mayoralty contest. "Impy," as he was lovingly dubbed by the *New York Daily News,* easily defeated the selections of the two major parties, both also Italians.

The master plan of the Democratic chieftains not only had failed to capture the governorship, but also had actually cost them control of the city administration. Undeterred by these signs of voter antagonism, the Democrats in 1951 selected Joseph T. Sharkey, an old party warhorse from Brooklyn, to run for president of City Council. The Liberal party, with renewed awareness of its strategic power, put forward Rudolph Halley, fresh from his television triumphs as counsel to Senator Estes Kefauver's crime committee, and was rewarded with its first independent citywide victory. The role of the party organizations in New York City had been proven feeble, a lesson which was to remain unlearned by many political leaders until ten years later.

Again in 1952, the Liberal party was able to demonstrate its key importance. Although never able to poll as much as 6 per cent of the total state vote and practically nonexistent outside of New York City and a few suburban counties, the Liberal party was sufficiently strong virtually to assure defeat to any Democratic state candidate who did not receive its endorsement. (Some regular Democrats, notably Congressman Charles A. Buckley of the Bronx, argued, on the other hand, that the spectacle of a Liberal tail wagging the Democratic party lost more votes than it gained.) Organized in 1944 by a number of anti-Communist intellectuals and union leaders previously aligned with the American Labor party, the Liberals received generous financial support from David Dubinsky's wealthy International Ladies' Garment Workers Union. Although formal leadership of the party was frequently reserved for some well-known intellectual, like Dr. George S. Counts or Judge Paul R. Hays, both professors at Columbia University while they were Liberal state chairmen, the main burden of strategy formation was carried by Alex Rose, president of the United Hat, Cap, and Millinery Workers Union and a close associate of Dubinsky. (The third member of the old liberal union triumvirate in the ALP, Sydney Hillman, president of the Amalgamated Clothing Workers, was on the outs with Dubinsky when the Liberal party was organized and chose to return to the Democrats rather than affiliate with the new group.)

The Liberals endorsed every Democratic candidate for president and governor from 1946 to 1960 and all but one of the Democratic candidates for the United States Senate. Neither Averell Harriman in 1954 nor John F. Kennedy in 1960 would have carried New York State without the votes they received on the Liberal party line. For lesser offices, the Liberals were more selective, sometimes running independent candidates and sometimes allying with the Republicans. In 1946, for example, their endorsement enabled Jacob K. Javits, a Republican, to oust a Tammany stalwart as United States congressman from Manhattan's Washington Heights district.

The single instance in which the Liberals failed to support the Democratic candidate for senator occurred in 1952. The Democratic organization, unmoved by Sharkey's defeat in 1951, that year nominated another Brooklyn party regular, John Cashmore, to oppose Republican Senator Irving M. Ives for re-election. Several years before, Senator Ives had won the gratitude of the I.L.G.W.U. by securing a special provision in the Taft-Hartley Act to permit secondary picketing in the garment industry in situations where nominal manufacturers had subcontracted their work to outside producers. Presumably as a sign of Dubinsky's recognition of this service, the Liberals, instead of endorsing Cashmore, put forward their own candidate for the Senate, thereby assuring an easy victory for Ives.

The Republican party was further strengthened in 1952 by the election of Dwight Eisenhower as president of the United States. Governor Dewey was one of Eisenhower's earliest and most effective supporters. At the Republican national convention, he had crushed a threatened bolt by a portion of the New York delegation to the banner of Senator Taft with an icy reminder that, whatever happened in Chicago, he would be governor of New York for two more years. (Mrs. Taft, once an ardent campaigner but by then confined to a wheelchair by the effects of a stroke, was asked by a reporter, as the convention neared its climax, if it would hurt the senator much to lose. "It would hurt Dewey more if he won," she replied. Dewey, as it turned out, had no cause to suffer.)

The fall election, in which Eisenhower carried New York State by more than 800,000 votes, had the incidental result of lending support to an argument long associated with the Taft wing of the party: that Republicans were losing elections because their sympathizers did not feel motivated to come to the polls. Nearly one million more votes were cast in New York in 1952 than in 1948. (The increase from 1952 to 1960 was only 165,000.) At polling place after polling place during the registration period, a substantial number of voters answered, "1932," when asked when they had cast their last ballots.

The role of New York in the new Eisenhower administration was, initially at least, immense. John Foster Dulles as secretary of state and Herbert Brownell, Dewey's old campaign manager, as attorney general, were but the two most prestigious appointments awarded to the Empire State. As well as securing posts for New Yorkers in the national administration, Dewey gave influential advice on such decisions as the selection of California's Governor Earl Warren, his 1948 running mate, as chief justice of the Supreme Court.

As 1954 approached, Dewey made it clear that under no circumstances would he again run for governor. The state party was by now completely under his power. Macy had been treated as an outsider by Republican leaders after the Hanley episode of 1950. J. Russel Sprague, the Old Smoothie, as he was known in the party, had worked closely with Dewey on the state level, while maintaining tight control over his Nassau County bailiwick. Toward the end of Dewey's third term, a state investigation of harness racing revealed that Sprague had made enormous profits from small investments in some of the trotting tracks that were attracting huge crowds of bettors in the suburban areas. Feeling that these disclosures implied, at least to the public, that the urbane Nassau boss was trading on political influence, Dewey immediately forced his old ally to resign as New York's Republican national committeeman. Sprague hung on for a time as leader in Nassau, but his statewide influence was greatly reduced. Other party leaders, such as New York County Chairman Thomas J. Curran and L. Judson Morhouse, who became state chairman in 1954, were loyal Dewey agents.

In the General Assembly, Speaker Heck, despite his upstate background, was a vigorous supporter of the progressive Dewey program. State Senator Walter J. Mahoney, teetotaling son of a Buffalo fireman, was beginning to emerge as leader of the Republican conservatives. He had organized a revolt in the Senate against a tax increase proposed by the state administration. Although he eventually acceded to most of the governor's requests, his resolute behavior made a favorable impression on Dewey, who later came to his rescue when he was in danger of being passed over for a Senate promotion.

As his successor, Dewey selected Senator Ives, who was assumed to command a large following among New York City liberals, by reason of his identification with the Ives-Quinn Law, the first law passed by any state banning racial discrimination in employment. A balanced ticket consisting of an Italian, an Irishman, and, for attorney general, Jacob Javits, was selected to run with Ives. The outlook for continued Republican rule appeared fairly good.

Following a series of almost unrelieved defeats, the Democratic organization in New York City had at last won a victory in 1953. As mayor, Vincent Impellitteri had proven too much for even the fun-loving citizens of New York. The approaching mayoralty election, DeSapio realized, was a golden opportunity for Tammany to regain control of the city government. The borough organizations in Brooklyn, Queens, and Richmond, operating on the mistaken belief that Impy retained great public popularity, decided to back the incumbent mayor for re-election. Casting about for an opposition candidate, DeSapio accepted the suggestion of Ed Flynn, then a dying man, that the Bronx and Manhattan organizations unite in support of young Bob Wagner, who had toiled conscientiously in the party vineyards. The primary result was a smashing victory for Wagner. DeSapio moved in quickly on the three defeated borough organizations, installing new leaders amenable to his influence. In the Bronx, Flynn, who died before the primary, was succeeded by Congressman Buckley, generally an ally of DeSapio but continuing to exert power in his own right. Despite the defection of the Liberals, who ran Rudolph Halley, Wagner was elected mayor in November.

By 1954, DeSapio was able to play a dominant role in selecting the Democratic state ticket. Franklin Roosevelt, Jr., who had been elected to Congress several years before against a Tammany candidate in the first months of DeSapio's reign, campaigned for months in an effort to persuade delegates to the state convention to give him the Democratic nomination for governor. (New York is one of the few remaining states in which nominations for state offices are made by party conventions rather than in primaries.) Upstate he appeared to rouse some enthusiasm, but DeSapio, on grounds of young Franklin's reputation as a playboy and the alleged antipathy to the Roosevelt name among Roman Catholics, declined to be impressed. After consulting with Alex Rose of the Liberals, the Tammany boss decided to swing the gubernatorial nomination to Averell Harriman, one of the richest men in America, former secretary of commerce, and former ambassador to both Russia and Great Britain. On urging from Senator Lehman, young Roosevelt agreed to go on the ticket for attorney general. The other two spots, controller and lieutenant governor, were awarded to the customary Jew and Italian.

In the campaign that followed, the big names of the national Democratic party, including former-President Truman, Mrs. Eleanor Roosevelt, and Senator Lehman, stumped with uncommon enthusiasm for Harriman, already regarded as a possible presidential candidate for 1956. Senator Ives's reputed appeal to liberal city dwellers failed to develop. Despite his eight years in Washington, the state's senior senator turned out to be virtually unknown in New York City. Although Harriman was also finding difficulty drawing crowds, except when he appeared with his renowned sponsors, a *New York Daily News* poll conducted three weeks before the election gave the Democratic ticket a 300,000 vote lead.

In a desperate effort to stave off defeat, Republican strategists persuaded Ives to resurrect old criticisms of Harriman's business ethics and to seize upon a statement by one of Mayor Wagner's assistants advocating a change in the formula for state contributions to local school costs. Under the existing system, state aid was allotted on the basis of each community's ability to meet its own needs; the Wagner aide proposed that the state pay all school districts equally according to student enrollment. The attack on Harriman's character received little attention, but the school cost issue at last stimulated the until then languid interest of upstate residents in the campaign. Under the ability-to-pay concept, upstate communities had a considerably larger share of their school costs financed by the state than did New York City, with its enormously valuable taxable real estate. Republican statisticians calculated to the penny what the aid-per-student system (which Harriman vainly disavowed) would cost in state assistance to each upstate community. The Democratic lead began to dwindle and quite possibly would have completely disappeared had not a providential snowstorm on election day held down the upstate vote. As it was, Harriman won by a hairbreadth margin of a little more than 10,000 votes out of a total of more than 5,000,000 cast. The entire Democratic ticket was victorious, with the exception of Franklin Roosevelt, Jr., who, justifying DeSapio's low opinion of his vote-getting appeal, was defeated by Jacob Javits.

The 1954 election provided a good picture of basic political alignments in the state. Though elected governor, Harriman carried only five of the state's sixty-two counties, four in New York City plus the upstate Democratic stronghold of Albany. New York City cast 41 per cent of the total vote (a decline from 49 per cent in 1950). The three densely populated, relatively low-income boroughs of Brooklyn, Manhattan, and the Bronx all went Democratic by majorities of about 70 per cent. The rapidly filling up borough of Queens, soon to be second in population only to Brooklyn but still retaining a somewhat suburban flavor and including a relatively high proportion of homeowners, went Democratic by about 55 per cent; while little Richmond (Staten Island), also displaying many suburban characteristics, gave a bare majority to the Republican candidate. The five suburban counties surrounding the city—Suffolk, Nassau, Westchester, Rockland, and Putnam—cast more than 15 per cent of the total state vote (an increase from 11 per cent in 1950). All were heavily Republican, (60 to 68 per cent), though less so (except Suffolk) than in 1950 and much less so than in 1946.

The remainder of the state, with the lone exception of Albany County, long ruled by the well-drilled Democratic machine of Daniel P. ("Uncle Dan") O'Connell, turned in Republican majorities, ranging from 53 per cent in Erie County (Buffalo) to 80 per cent in little Yates County in the Finger Lakes region. Of the fifty-two upstate counties, thirty gave Irving Ives 65 per cent or more of their votes. Among residents of Manhattan and its adjacent boroughs, upstaters are often spoken of as "apple-knockers" or "hayseeders." This impression of a rural, provincial backwater existing north of Tarrytown is very far from being correct. In only four counties, in 1960, did as much as 20 per cent of the population live on farms. Up the Hudson Valley and west along the route of the old Erie Canal lies a track of middle-sized cities, containing cosmopolitan populations and work forces heavily devoted to manufacturing. This belt shows a much higher degree of Republicanism than is normally expected of industrial regions in the United States. Monroe County (Rochester), with a population of more than one-half million, 33 per cent foreign stock, 42 per cent of the work force employed in manufacturing, and 40 per cent Roman Catholic, has consistently returned Republican majorities. The same is true of Onondaga County (Syracuse), with similar statistics. Even Erie County (32 per cent foreign stock, 36 per cent manufacturing, 56 per cent Catholic), where the Democrats generally have controlled the city administration in Buffalo, went Republican in every statewide election from 1950 to 1958. In part this apparent anomaly is simply a reflection of a nationwide tendency of middle-sized industrial counties, like Kent (Grand Rapids) in Michigan and Stark (Canton) in Ohio, where home ownership is high and many companies are locally owned, to be Republican. Partly it is due to the Democratic party's dependence on New York City, which encourages all upstaters to make common cause, on issues like the school-aid controversy, with the Republicans. And partly it is due to the fact that in counties like Monroe and Onondaga the Republican organizations have over the years provided reasonably honest and effective local government.

A second belt of smaller cities, stretching from Binghamton to Jamestown along the Pennsylvania border, forms the Southern Tier. This area, one of the few in the state in which Protestants outnumber Catholics, was in 1954 overwhelmingly Republican, seven of its eleven counties going for Ives by better than 70 per cent. The other regions of the state—the Catskill country just north of New York City (containing Sullivan County, the only upstate county in the United States with a Jewish population over 10 per cent); the Finger Lakes region between the Syracuse-Rochester belt and the Southern Tier; and the North Country, the great Adirondack triangle between Lake Champlain and the St. Lawrence River—come closer to fulfilling the stereotype commonly held on Manhattan Island. More

sparsely populated than some parts of the Great Plains, these areas
are devoted mainly to agriculture, lumbering, and the tourist trade.
All in 1954 were Republican, although the North Country, suffering
from chronic unemployment and containing numerous Roman Catholics (59 per cent in both Clinton and Franklin Counties), was less
so than most other parts of upstate.

Despite the narrowness of his gubernatorial victory, Harriman set
out immediately in pursuit of the presidency. ("Somewhat," a reporter remarked at the time, "like a dignified old gentleman who
suddenly begins to chase chorus girls.") In New York politics, he
gave a free hand to DeSapio, whom he appointed secretary of state.
The Tammany chieftain took full advantage of this opportunity to
place his supporters in control of upstate Democratic county organizations. Somewhat to the governor's embarrassment, DeSapio also
became a principal promoter of the Harriman-for-president drive.
Although anxious to avoid the Tammany label, Harriman could
find no way to do so without risking offense to his by now formidable
ally. By the time the Democratic delegates assembled in Chicago in
1956, Adlai Stevenson's nomination for a second attempt at the
presidency was assured. The New York delegation was conspicuous
mainly for its manner of dress: many members copied DeSapio's dark
suits and tinted eye glasses (the latter a necessity to the Tammany
leader, who had suffered for many years from a painful optic afflic-
tion).

As candidate for the seat from which Senator Lehman was retiring, the Democrats chose Mayor Wagner. Attorney General Javits,
with the support of Dewey and J. Russel Sprague, set out to secure
the Republican nomination. Upstate leaders, who distrusted Javits'
liberalism, were at first cool. An attempt was made, while the Republican national convention was meeting in San Francisco, to suggest that the former Manhattan congressman had once flirted with
Communism. This slander had the unplanned effect of guaranteeing
his selection. Javits' backers were able to argue that he was being
maligned because he was Jewish. Fearing the charge of anti-Semitism
(Jews in 1957 composed 18 per cent of the state's population), the
Republican state committee agreed, with no great show of enthusiasm,
to make him its candidate. In November, President Eisenhower and

Javits swept the state, although the Senatorial candidate ran more than a million votes behind Eisenhower's record-breaking majority. Almost 105,000 voters who expressed a choice for president cast no vote in the senatorial contest.

The following year, the Liberals, little attracted by the scandal-ridden Wagner administration but not anxious to repeat their independent campaign of four years before, evinced interest in forming a coalition in the city with the Republicans if the latter should put forward Javits for mayor. Though his seat in the Senate was not yet warm, Javits himself seemed to look with favor upon this idea. However, Republican City Chairman Tom Curran was not inclined to coax the new senator away from Washington. Instead the Republicans nominated Robert K. Christenberry, a one-armed Marine veteran of World War I. Resignedly, the Liberals endorsed Wagner, and the mayor was victorious by almost a million votes.

Off to a fast start at re-electing Governor Harriman in 1958, the Democrats foundered in mid-summer on the problem of selecting a candidate to run for the Senate seat being given up by Irving Ives. Liberal Democrats, including Senator Lehman, were anxious that a declared liberal should be chosen for this post. Governor Harriman agreed that a liberal should be selected, but at the same time wished to have an Irish-Catholic as his running mate. DeSapio had settled on Frank S. Hogan, district attorney of New York County, whose ideological preferences were unknown. Mayor Wagner declined to become a compromise candidate, partly because DeSapio had several months before coolly explained over television that, in effect, the mayor could have the nomination only if he acknowledged the Tammany leader's supremacy in the party. Deserting his old sponsor, Wagner formed a united front at the Buffalo convention with Harriman, Lehman, Mrs. Roosevelt, and State Chairman Michael H. Prendergast, of Rockland County. DeSapio's only major ally outside the New York City organization was Peter J. Crotty, leader in Erie County. It was enough. At one point, in a hotel room conference, Harriman threatened to carry his fight to the convention floor. In the end, however, the governor bowed to the dictation of his secretary of state. Hogan was nominated by acclamation.

DeSapio's victory had been impressive, but also costly. He had provided the Republicans with proof that the Democratic party was "bossed." Worst of all, he had not only defeated Senator Lehman, but ignored him as well. The elderly but still vigorous idol of New York State liberals returned to Manhattan, determined that DeSapio's power should be destroyed. Allying with Mrs. Roosevelt, he assumed leadership of the struggling Democratic reform clubs in Manhattan, which up until then had been waging uphill fights against the Tammany organizations in their districts.

The Republicans also engaged in some early summer blood-letting. By the time their convention met at Saratoga, however, the gubernatorial nomination had been sewn up for Nelson Rockefeller, whose family fortune exceeded even that of Governor Harriman and who had carried out important national and international assignments in the administrations of Presidents Roosevelt, Truman, and Eisenhower. State Chairman Judson Morhouse, relying on polls that showed Rockefeller the only Republican with a chance at victory in November, had steered the prize to the personable millionaire in preference to Senator Mahoney and former–National Chairman Leonard W. Hall, both of whom had been longer in the party trenches. For the Senate, the Republicans nominated Congressman Kenneth B. Keating of Rochester, whose reluctance to make the race (it still looked like a Democratic year) was overcome by a telephone request, arranged by Dewey, from Vice President Nixon.

In the fall canvass, Rockefeller proved as warm in personality as his opponent was chilly. Though not the first candidate to engage in walking tours through crowded city districts, he imparted a personal style and verve to this form of campaigning. Striding along the avenues of Manhattan's Lower East Side, he grasped the hands of strangers (many of whom were clearly flattered to meet *the* Rockefeller) and got himself photographed eating blintzes and bagels in delicatessens. Keating, too, campaigned effectively in New York City as well as upstate. Harriman and Hogan labored under the stigma of "bossism." The result was a landslide victory for the Republicans in a year when the GOP was going down to overwhelming defeat in most parts of the nation. The New York Democrats, who had been 20 per cent ahead of their rivals in polls taken early in the year, must feel, said Senator-elect Keating, "like the kindergartner who failed finger painting." In four of New York City's five boroughs (Queens being the exception), Rockefeller ran 10 per cent ahead of Ives's showing in 1954. In some upstate counties his gains were smaller—he, in fact, fell behind Ives's performance on Long Island, in the North Country, and in the Syracuse-Rochester belt. In populous Erie County (Buffalo), he ran 10 per cent better than Ives.

The election gave evidence of an enormous floating vote, particularly in and around New York City and Buffalo, which paid little heed to the rules and expectations that had been worked out for New York politics. Quite clearly, many of the people who voted for Rockefeller (or, for that matter, against him) were not subject to the partisan loyalties or professional discipline of traditional politics. Moreover, these uncommitted voters, amounting to a crucial 10 per cent of the electorate, were not satisfied with a role of passive neutrality. Though little interested in standard political rewards (government jobs, contracts, economic advantage), the uncommitted in New York were becoming increasingly participants in the political process.

As governor, Rockefeller stunned many of his independent supporters, as well as professional Republican politicians, by calling immediately for an increase in personal income taxes. For weeks, a bloc of upstate Republican legislators held out against this proposal. Hoping to attract some Democratic legislators from New York City, which would benefit from the tax rise through increased state aid, Rockefeller at first resisted the advice of Republican strategists to place responsibility for the increase on the fiscal practices of his predecessor. When it became clear, however, that the minority party preferred to attack the tax measure as a "soak-the-poor" program, the governor at last opened fire on "the loose fiscal policies" of the Harriman administration. Eventually enough upstate legislators were won over to enact a somewhat modified tax plan. A withholding provision in the new law, as well as the higher rates, cost the governor dearly in personal popularity.

Rockefeller made little secret of his interest in eventually succeeding to the leadership of a national administration. Although he was able to exert considerable influence over the formulation of the

Republican platform in 1960, his ambition for the presidential nomination that year was thwarted by the long-standing commitment of most party leaders to the candidacy of Richard Nixon. At the Republican national convention, however, his jaunty manner—somewhat akin to that of an extroverted camp director—seemed to shelter plans for the future.

Hoping to recoup after his 1958 debacle, DeSapio in 1960 set out to form an alliance with the Democratic organizations in Pennsylvania and Illinois that would control the national convention and select the party's candidate for president. This scheme collapsed when Buffalo's Peter Crotty and Congressman Buckley early declared their support for John Kennedy for the presidential nomination. A mass break by the New York delegates to the Kennedy banner followed. State Chairman Prendergast, by now a DeSapio supporter, unwisely attempted to punish Senator Lehman for his leadership of the reform movement in New York City by denying the elder statesman a place in the state delegation to the national convention. The resulting outcry was so great that Prendergast was forced to make way for the former senator by giving up his own seat in the delegation.

In the fall of 1960, the floating vote that had helped to elect Rockefeller swung heavily to John F. Kennedy, giving him a statewide majority of almost 400,000. Religion played some part in this victory (five of the six upstate counties over 40 per cent Catholic switched from Eisenhower in 1956 to Kennedy in 1960); so did economic conditions (the industrial Mohawk Valley, between Albany and Utica, a site of chronic unemployment, produced five of the ten counties in the state in which Democratic strength increased 10 per cent over 1958). Something more, however, was involved. In the Southern Tier and on Long Island, where employment was high and Catholics (except in Nassau County) were relatively few, Kennedy made heavy gains over Democratic showings in both 1956 and 1958.

Again, in the New York City Democratic mayoralty primary of 1961, the independent vote was clearly responsible for giving Mayor Wagner, supported by Senator Lehman and the reform clubs, victory over a candidate endorsed by DeSapio, State Chairman Prendergast, and the five borough organizations. (DeSapio's fall was complete: he was ousted as leader of New York County and was even turned out of the party leadership of his own lower-Manhattan district.) In the general election, Wagner, while easily defeating his Republican opponent, state Attorney General Louis J. Lefkowitz, yielded 15 per cent of the total vote to City Controller Lawrence E. Gerosa, an independent Democratic candidate, who had little basis for appeal beyond his Italian name and a vague reputation for economy. At the same time, Democrats were successfully storming Republican citadels in Nassau County and Rochester, while being firmly repulsed in Syracuse and losing ground earlier gained in Suffolk County. In Buffalo, the Crotty organization lost the Democratic primary; then, by running an independent candidate for mayor, permitted the Republicans to win control of the city government.

In 1962, the Democratic party all but abandoned the effort to field a ticket for state offices. All efforts to persuade Mayor Wagner to risk his newly gained prestige in a race for governor against Rockefeller failed. Only two months before election day, the nomination was glumly bestowed upon United States Attorney Robert Morgenthau, son of Franklin Roosevelt's most famous secretary of the treasury, who shuffled through the short campaign as though trapped into performing an onerous and embarrassing ritual.

Against this dispirited opposition, Rockefeller's victory margin of just over half-a-million votes seemed comparatively slight. (Senator Javits was at the same time piling up a majority of more than one million over attorney James B. Donovan, later celebrated as negotiator of the ransom for survivors of the abortive 1961 invasion of Cuba.) In the early months of his second administration, Rockefeller was plagued by a revolt against higher taxes in the legislature and an ugly outcropping of scandal involving high Republican figures. At the end of the legislative session, the governor departed on a honeymoon to Venezuela with his second wife, the former Mrs. Margaretta Fitler ("Happy") Murphy, like himself recently divorced. The distance from Albany to the White House appeared to have grown measurably longer.

New York's politics of accommodation, developed by Alex Rose and Senator Lehman as well as by Governors Dewey and Rocke-

feller, is faced, in the middle sixties, with the necessity of absorbing
the energies of the new bloc of independent voters. Members of this
group—the new surburbanites, the unattached youths, the conscientious club women, the anxious old folks—cannot be found on the
same side of all political issues. For instance, the enthusiasm of
women's groups and the pressure of growing population for new
schools conflict with the home-owner's concern over real-estate tax
rates. Likewise, the suburbanite's voracious appetite for land may
deprive other members of the middle class of parks and open country
in which to enjoy newly acquired leisure. Most of these diverse
classes do, however, share in common a lack of attachment to the
traditional goals of political factions and parties. The economic
struggles, the ethnic antagonisms which shaped the party loyalties of
prior generations seem to many of them largely irrelevant. Finding
little in the current party rivalry to claim their interest, they have
voted as often as not for a friendly smile, a sincere tone of voice, a
flattering appeal to reason. But they do vote. If they are uncommitted, they are not disinterested. Their hearts and their minds are
stirred by concerns that they are persuaded can find solution in
politics.

The Empire State's collaborative form of government has produced
a well-balanced tax structure, a range of effective state services, a
variety of means for combating the poisons of bigotry and discrimina-
ton. The enthusiasms and problems motivating the members of the
floating bloc are, however, to some extent different in kind from the
economic and ethnic aspirations that the collaborative state has gone
far toward fulfilling. They are, for the most part, interwoven with the
changing nature of society itself. Whether they will be taken over
by some of the existing factions in the old firmament of accommodation, whether they will lead to the formation of new factions, or
whether some essentially different kind of political design will have
to be found for their expression, cannot yet be foretold.

7

TEXAS

THE DISAPPEARING MIDDLE

The conservatism of Texas is related to the conservatism of Virginia or Pennsylvania in much the same way that a skyrocket is related to a hearth fire. Texas conservatives tend to be flamboyant, streamlined, enthusiastic, and, above all, youthful. The most vocal and conspicuous supporters of John G. Tower, elected in 1961 at the age of thirty-five as the state's first Republican United States senator since Reconstruction, were amateurs in their twenties and early thirties. Tower's election, as well as Dwight Eisenhower's two victories in Texas, were made possible by substantial majorities polled in the state's five major cities, Houston, Dallas, San Antonio, Fort Worth, and El Paso, which since World War II have included ever-growing proportions of young people in their populations. In 1963, the largest and most active political organization on the campus of the University of Texas, once a Democratic preserve, was the Young Republicans Club.

The status quo, against which the conservatives later revolted, in Texas at mid-century was a strange amalgam of New Deal liberalism and wheeler-dealer politics. Its powerful symbol was Sam Rayburn, speaker of the United States House of Representatives since

1940 (except for a two-year lapse during the Republican Eightieth Congress); and its acknowledged field marshal was already Lyndon B. Johnson, elected to the United States Senate in 1948. The formula followed by Rayburn, Johnson, and their associates coupled moderate liberalism and strict loyalty to the Democratic party at the national level with firm support for such Texas-bred economic giants as the hugely profitable oil and gas industries. The liberal portion of their philosophy derived from the impoverished condition of much of rural Texas, hard hit by the Depression and struggling through continued hard times. (Even in 1960, average annual income was less than $3,000 in 58 of 254 counties.) Their alliance with the oil,

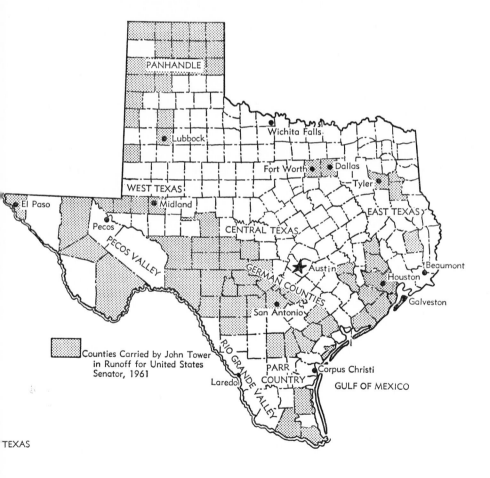

TEXAS

gas, cattle, and insurance tycoons, besides securing financial support for their political operations, expressed their own delight in the bigness, the raw power, the freewheeling ways which Texas millionaires were at that time making synonymous with the name of the Lone Star State all over the world.

Protection of local economic interests is not an unusual role for American liberals. Nobody is surprised when Midwestern progressives defend the dairy industry against incursions by the manufacturers of oleomargarine, or when East and West coast liberals approve price-fixing agreements in the shipping business. In most states, the ties that Rayburn and Johnson maintained with local businessmen would not have seriously affected their over-all liberalism. In Texas, however, the very power, the very self-conscious visibility of the great millionaires tended to turn their collaborators into cronies and their cronies into accomplices. The only way not to be identified with the big operators was deliberately to oppose them. This Lyndon Johnson and his political associates did not do.

An important fact, and potential weakness, about the reigning Democratic party leadership in 1950 was its geographic identification with East Texas—the land between the Louisiana border and a line drawn north from Austin, the state capital, through Dallas to the border of Oklahoma. Since General Sam Houston helped overthrow Mexican rule in 1836 and ten years later led Texas into the United States, this region had exerted political dominance over the entire state. After successful conclusion of the war with Mexico, there was a rush into East Texas from nearby Southern states. In ethnic background and social system, the region has ever since remained closely tied to the Old South. (A monument to the Confederate war dead on the capitol grounds at Austin reminds succeeding generations of Texans: "DIED for State Rights Guaranteed Under the Constitution. The people of the South, animated by the spirit of 1776, to preserve their rights, withdrew from the federal compact in 1861. The North resorted to coercion. The South, against overwhelming numbers and resources, fought until exhausted.")

In 1960, fifty-four of the state's counties contained populations more than 20 per cent Negro; all were located east of the Austin-Dallas line. (Negroes in Texas, unlike those in many other parts of the South, qualify and vote in about the same proportion as whites. In many rural counties, the Negro vote is heavily influenced by politically powerful whites. Negroes in the cities, on the other hand, constitute an independent force, generally following the liberal Democratic line. During the fifties, Negroes were elected to the Houston school board and the Galveston city council. The proportion of Negroes in the Texas population declined from 20 per cent in 1900 to just over 12 per cent in 1960.)

Although the state's two largest cities, Houston and Dallas, are located on the fringes of East Texas, the region's tone and political leadership have come until very recently from the rural counties and small towns. Once devoted almost entirely to raising cotton, East Texas farms, many of them small and relatively uneconomical, have in recent years been converted in growing numbers to livestock or commercial tree production. East Texas has had its share of oil tycoons. The general economy of the region has remained depressed, however—more than half of the state's low-income counties in 1960 were located in East Texas, which contained only about one-fifth of the state's area.

East Texans prominent in the state government in 1951 included Governor Allan Shivers, who had succeeded from the lieutenant governorship when Governor Beauford Jester suffered a fatal heart attack in 1949; Lieutenant Governor Ben Ramsey; and Attorney General Price Daniel. All three hailed from towns only a few miles west of the Louisiana border. (Speaker Rayburn from Bonham and Senator Johnson from Johnson City resided on the periphery of the East Texas region.) All were aware of forces at work in the large cities and other sections of the state that threatened to challenge East Texas hegemony during the coming decade.

Of the three, Ben Ramsey, San Augustine, was probably the most typical representative of the old school of East Texas politicians. Elected lieutenant governor in 1950 against twelve competitors, several of them well known, he had set about constructing a political apparatus that during the next decade was to give him influence in Austin equal to that of the governor. Through prudent use of his duties to appoint members to state Senate committees and to determine the order in which bills reached the Senate floor, Ramsey was able to assume a dominant role in legislation during his six consecutive terms as lieutenant governor. Though he used his power largely for the negative purpose of preventing bills he did not like from reaching the floor, he on occasion promoted the enactment of tax legislation and other measures. More than once he was to have his way over the opposition of a governor.

Allan Shivers and Price Daniel, both, like Senator Johnson, members of a newer breed, were more inclined than Ramsey to look beyond the confines of East Texas and even beyond the entire Lone Star State to the pinnacles of national power. Other than aspiration for high places, the two men had little in common. Shivers, tall, photogenically handsome, the very picture of a Texan, restlessly looked about at the beginning of the decade for an issue or event on which he might ride into national prominence. He had observed with keen interest the showing made six years before by the Texas Regulars, a group of conservative Democrats, dissident from Franklin Roosevelt's New Deal, who had polled more than one-tenth of the state's total vote in the 1944 presidential election. Though still a loyal party man, he was sensitive to the philosophic similarities between conservative Texas Democrats and Northern Republicans. Price Daniel, shrewd, cautious, was more strongly imbued with the "brass-collar Democrat" tradition, which was particularly strong in East Texas. (According to an old Texas saying, a brass-collar Democrat "would vote for a yellow dog, rather than a Republican.") Equally ambitious, he was less ready than Shivers to desert the party that had ruled Texas for more than a century.

Factors of unrest at work in Texas politics in 1950 were both ideological and geographic. To the left of the controlling Rayburn-Johnson faction in the Democratic party was a small but active group of liberals led by former-Congressman Maury Maverick, Sr., of San Antonio. (The site of the heroic defense of the Alamo in the struggle for independence with Mexico, San Antonio was not part of the social or political system of East Texas. Heavily populated by Catholics and persons of Mexican descent, it was a natural source for opposition to the Protestant, Anglo-Saxon "magnolia boys" of the northeastern counties.) This group in 1952 supported Ralph W. Yarborough, Austin, for governor against Shivers and sent a loyalist delegation, pledged to support the Democratic national ticket in November, to the Democratic national convention in Chicago. An uninstructed delegation, led by Governor Shivers, was eventually seated at the convention. Undiscouraged, the liberals returned home to await developments.

To the right of the dominant Democratic faction was a large and rambunctious group of conservatives, determined that Texas' electoral vote should not once more be awarded to a presidential candidate carrying the banner of the New Deal. At the core of this group were the old Texas Regulars and the Dixiecrats, who had bolted the Democratic party in 1948 to support Strom Thurmond of South Carolina for president. Their strength had been augmented by the bitterness surrounding the senatorial primary of 1948, in which the Democratic State Executive Committee declared Lyndon Johnson the victor over Coke Stevenson, a conservative former governor, by a margin of eighty-seven votes. Stevenson had been the apparent winner until returns were received three days after the election from Jim Wells County, one of the counties in the extreme southeastern corner of the state allegedly controlled by George Parr, the celebrated Duke of Duval. Parr's counties, largely populated by Mexican-Americans, had for many years displayed a tendency to cast overwhelming percentages of their vote for candidates favored by their leader. (Starr, Jim Hogg, and Duval Counties, all in Parr's supposed sphere of influence, had the distinction of producing the highest percentages in the state for the Democratic candidates for president in 1952, 1956, and 1960. The Republican vote in Starr County in 1960 was reduced to 6 per cent. Percentages in some Democratic primaries were equally remarkable. It is noteworthy, however, that the Parr counties sometimes supported *different* candidates in the primaries.) Parr laconically commented that Coke Stevenson had not protested in the past when he had been the beneficiary of heavy majorities produced by the counties of the southern tip. An appeal of the election result to the United States Supreme Court was turned down on the ground that federal courts could not "consider or take part in state election contests." The conviction persisted among conservatives, however, that Stevenson had been counted out.

The Republican party had not been a serious contender for power in Texas since the Civil War. The so-called German counties, a tier of rural counties between San Antonio and Austin populated largely by German-Americans, clinging to their Teutonic language and customs, could be counted upon to poll, presumably as an expression of their sense of difference, a considerable Republican vote in presidential elections. Some Northern Republicans who had moved into Dallas, Houston, and the Lower Rio Grande Valley continued their loyalty to the GOP. Otherwise, the party had been quiescent since Herbert Hoover carried the state for president against Al Smith in 1928. A tiny guard of patronage hopefuls, loyal to whomever led the national Republican organization, controlled the party machinery.

This comfortable arrangement was upset in 1952 when supporters of Dwight Eisenhower, led by Houston oilman Jack Porter, a former Democrat, invaded Republican precinct meetings in an effort to overthrow the old-line party functionaries who were committed to the presidential candidacy of Senator Robert Taft. The Taft faction managed to keep control of most of the precinct meetings and sent its own delegation to the national convention in Chicago. The Eisen-

Figure 7. Texas Battle Graph, 1948-62

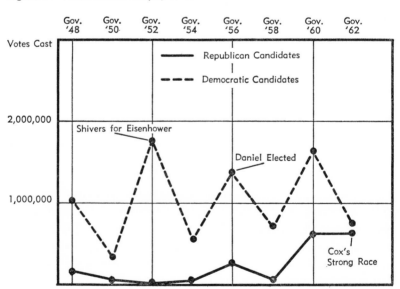

hower publicity machine, however, picked up the issue and success-fully persuaded both the convention and millions of national tele-vision viewers that the rank and file of Republican voters in Texas were being unfairly denied a voice by political timeservers. In a tumultuous postmidnight session, the convention voted to replace the Taft delegation with an Eisenhower delegation, and the stage was set for General Eisenhower's eventual nomination. Whichever delegation most accurately represented Republican sentiment in Texas, the drive staged by the Eisenhower supporters clearly had a revitalizing effect on the party in the state.

Beset by liberals, conservatives, and Republicans, the East Texas Democrats by 1952 were faced with rising sectional discontent from the other four-fifths of the state. On the plains of Central and West Texas, spreading from Fort Worth to the booming oil towns of Midland and Odessa ("the land of the high sky," according to local radio announcers), demand was being expressed for a greater share in state government. Though fanatically proud of their identification as Texans, the cowboys and wildcatters of the semiarid central plains felt few ties to the traditions and contemporary problems of the Old South. To the north, in the Panhandle region, a flourishing agricul-tural economy had attracted many former Kansans who talked from time to time of forming a completely independent state. (Under the 1845 annexation agreement, five states could be carved from the one domain if ever the citizens of Texas should so desire.) In the area beyond the Pecos River, an almost completely detached society, based on El Paso, had developed. For years, most candidates for statewide office had not even bothered to campaign in the El Paso region. Unlike residents of the Panhandle, the far westerners were anxious to be regarded as real Texans. During the 1950's, politicians discovered that a journey to El Paso was likely to produce a large vote of gratitude from the western counties. The growing population of the region made the trip a justifiable labor.

In the vast, arid triangle south of San Antonio, the local chieftains, like George Parr, had for many years carried on mutually profitable exchanges with the East Texas politicians. (Parr's own power derived from the benevolent regime his family had exercised over local Mexican-Americans for two generations.) Though relatively small in population, the Mexican-American counties played an important role in state politics due to the ability of the chieftains to deliver overwhelming majorities for their favorites. The controlled vote in the southern counties was estimated at between 30,000 and 50,000—more than enough, if the chieftains stuck together, to determine the result of many primaries. Moreover, the Mexican-Americans, having doubled in number between 1930 and 1950, were the fastest growing element in the state's populations. Whether the oldtime chieftains would be able to maintain their tight political organizations seemed doubtful. Increasingly, new leaders, like Henry B. Gonzalez of San Antonio, were persuading the Mexican-Americans to join with organized labor and the Negroes in a common liberal front.

The most spectacular changes in the state were, however, occurring in the larger cities—particularly Houston, Dallas, and Fort Worth. While most Eastern and Midwestern cities had begun to decline in population, these metropolitan centers were at the beginning of a decade of growth in which each was to increase its numbers by about one-half. Population growth was to be accompanied by the appearance of countless glass-walled skyscrapers (built in part, one suspects, just for the hell of it), and acre upon acre of individually owned family dwellings. There were to be (as yet) few slums, few of the huge apartment buildings or rowhouse developments common to older cities. Suburbs mushroomed as rapidly as in the East or California (the population of Irving, near Dallas, grew from less than 3,000 in 1950 to more than 45,000 in 1960), but huge areas of open space still remained within easy striking distance of the city centers. The young, predominantly, came to these cities, eager for new opportunities, ready to have their brass collars broken, identifying with a philosophy of individual enterprise not unlike that preached in the North by spokesmen for the Republican party.

Into this atmosphere the Eisenhower campaign of 1952 swept like a summer cyclone. The popular World War II general, himself a native of Texas, succeeded in triggering emotions of revolt which had been building for years. After Adlai Stevenson, the Democratic candidate for president, announced, in answer to a question from Governor Shivers, that he would not sign a bill affirming the state's jurisdiction over oil-bearing tidelands reaching three leagues into the

Gulf of Mexico, many major Democrats repudiated their party's national ticket. (Texas had a special claim to the tidelands, later approved by Congress at the request of President Eisenhower, based on the original agreement by which the state had joined the union.) Shivers campaigned actively for Eisenhower, as did Price Daniel (himself a candidate for the United States Senate), National Committeeman Wright Morrow, and Democratic State Chairman Wallace Savage. The Republicans reciprocated by running no candidates against Shivers or Daniel. Remaining loyal to the national Democratic ticket were Speaker Rayburn, Senator Johnson, and Ralph Yarborough, who had lost the gubernatorial primary to Shivers by about a two-to-one majority.

The result was victory for Eisenhower by more than 130,000 votes. Of the state's twenty-seven counties with populations over 50,000, only ten registered majorities for Stevenson. San Antonio and El Paso, as well as Houston, Dallas, and Fort Worth, went Republican by sizable margins. One of the German counties, Gillespie, voting 92 per cent for Eisenhower, had the honor of being the banner county in both state and nation for the victorious candidate. The Panhandle, Central Texas, the Far West, and the Gulf Coast all supported Eisenhower. Only the old brass-collar counties of East Texas and the Mexican-American counties south of San Antonio remained loyal to the Democratic standard.

The liberal Democratic faction, which had been left with the task of conducting most of the Stevenson campaign, set out immediately following the election to capture control of the party in the state. In 1953, the Democratic Organizing Committee was set up by the liberals for the purpose of prying away party leadership, not only from Shivers and Daniel, but also from Rayburn and Johnson, who had been loyal to the national ticket. With liberal support, Ralph Yarborough again challenged Shivers in the Democratic primary for governor in 1954. Both sides made enormous expenditures during the campaign. A well-informed participant later estimated that expenditures of at least $1.5 million were made for each of the two major candidates and that additional sums were spent without the candidates' direct knowledge. Shivers was bank-rolled by the big oil companies and other business interests, while Yarborough obtained contributions from some oil men who identified with the liberal faction and from labor unions, including some unions with few members in Texas. For the first time, television was widely used in a state campaign. Shivers charged that his opponent was the candidate of the CIO and George Parr. Yarborough replied that the governor was anti-labor and pro-Republican. Neither candidate obtained a majority in the first primary. In the runoff, Shivers was victorious by about 90,000 votes. The closeness of the result somewhat damaged the prestige of the aspiring governor.

The Republican party fell back into its normal somnolence in the general election. The only indication of life in the GOP occurred in Dallas, where Bruce Alger, a conservative Republican, defeated Wallace Savage, former Democratic state chairman, for Congress. Reportedly, some liberals voted for Alger rather than Savage, who had supported Eisenhower in 1952, on the theory that it would be easy to knock off Alger with a liberal Democrat in 1956.

The 1954 Supreme Court decision declaring racial segregation in schools unconstitutional caused minor political repercussions in Texas. Shivers announced that he would not permit forced integration of schools, but added that he did not believe schools should be closed to preserve segregation. Yarborough, who received considerable Negro support in his many campaigns, placed himself on record in favor of segregated schools. Within three years, one-fifth of the state's approximately seven hundred biracial school districts had desegregated by board action. The East Texas districts, containing more than 90 per cent of the state's Negroes, remained segregated, however. In 1957, fewer than 2 per cent of the state's Negro pupils attended classes with whites. A number of laws designed to preserve or at least prolong segregation were passed by the state legislature under East Texas leadership. In 1960, the first crack appeared in East Texas resistance when Houston began grade-a-year integration under federal court order. The most drastic of the anti-integration laws, which ordered that state aid be withheld from schools integrated without majority approval of the district's voters, was held to be unconstitutional in an opinion by the state attorney general.

In 1956, Shivers and Johnson, who the year before had become majority leader of the Senate (after serving as leader of the minority during the Republican Eighty-third Congress), staged a battle royal for control of the Democratic party machinery. Early in the year, Shivers implied that Johnson had drifted into alliance with liberal groups on the national level. Speaker Rayburn, who had been trying to heal the party differences, supported Johnson's decision to strike back. A coalition was formed with Democrats of Texas (the former Democratic Organizing Committee), and the Johnson group was able to take over the state convention. For their part in the triumph, the liberals were permitted to name one of their most vigorous leaders, Mrs. R. D. ("Frankie") Randolph, wife of a Houston banker, as national committeewoman. A delegation prepared to support the Democratic candidate for president was sent to the national convention in Chicago.

Shivers decided not to seek a fourth term, and Price Daniel, who had found Washington little to his liking, returned to the state to run for governor. He was opposed by Yarborough, again supported by the liberals, and W. Lee ("Pass-the-biscuits-Pappy") O'Daniel, a former governor and outspoken segregationist. In the first primary, Daniel was more than 150,000 votes ahead of Yarborough, his closest rival, but failed to receive a majority. In the runoff, some East Texas counties, which had originally supported O'Daniel, shifted surprisingly to Yarborough. Daniel's lead in Bexar County (San Antonio) fell from 28,000 in the first primary to 11,000 in the runoff; in Harris County (Houston) from 38,000 to 13,000. Only heavy majorities from Dallas and the controlled southeastern counties of George Parr and his fellow chieftains pulled Daniel through to a margin of 4,000 votes out of almost 1,500,000 cast.

Battered by the liberals in the primary, the moderate Democratic leadership was drubbed by the state's conservatives in the general. After receiving assurances from Adlai Stevenson that a new Democratic administration would make no attempt to upset the tidelands ownership law signed by President Eisenhower, Price Daniel joined Johnson, Rayburn, and Yarborough in supporting the national Democratic ticket. Shivers, once more breaking with the national Democratic party, backed Eisenhower for re-election. Democrats for Eisenhower, led by two faithful Shivers lieutenants, became active throughout the state. The combination of Shivers' political leadership and Eisenhower's continued popularity proved more than enough to overcome the concerted Democratic effort for Stevenson. The Republican margin in the state increased two percentage points over 1952. Once again, the five major cities were carried by Eisenhower. There was, however, some change in the regional lineup. In the Panhandle, twelve farm counties that had gone for Eisenhower in 1952 returned to the Democratic fold. In East Texas, on the other hand, fifteen brass-collar counties that had favored Stevenson in 1952 this time followed Shivers' leadership to support the Republicans. The largest Republican gains over 1952 were scored in Houston and the surrounding Gulf Coast. In Dallas, Eisenhower won by a slightly improved margin, and Bruce Alger disappointed liberal Democratic hopes by being re-elected to Congress by eight times the plurality he had received in 1954.

What is to be made of the oscillation from liberalism to conservatism in the few short months that separated the runoff primary from the general election in 1956? Price Daniel and other moderates, who had suffered from both shifts, must have pondered the same question. For one thing, of course, the issues in the state and national elections could legitimately be viewed as different. (William Bryant, the Republican candidate for governor against Daniel, received only 15 per cent of the vote.) Nevertheless, most Yarborough voters in August probably voted for Stevenson in November. All but two of the Panhandle counties carried by Stevenson had voted for Yarborough in the runoff. In East Texas, 39 of 69 counties withstood the trend toward Eisenhower; all but three had voted for Yarborough. In the entire state, only 47 out of 150 Yarborough counties voted for Eisenhower, while the Republican candidate for president carried 86 out of 104 Daniel counties. Evidently, the Eisenhower majority was produced by many Daniel voters added to a large number of persons who had not voted in the Democratic primary. The total vote in the second Democratic primary in 1956 was 550,000 less than was cast in the general election and 450,000 less than had been cast in the much less hotly contested Democratic primary of 1952. Clearly, many conservative Texans were ceasing to regard themselves as active participants in the Democratic party. The outlook for the future was that the liberals would continue to gain strength within the Democratic party, while the Republicans, benefiting from conservative disaffection from the Democrats, would gradually achieve the roll of genuine competitor for power in the state.

In 1957, Ralph Yarborough at last won a statewide election. In a three-way race for the remainder of Price Daniel's term in the Senate, the untiring liberal, who had, in the words of one reporter, been "a fulltime candidate" since 1952, received 38 per cent of the vote (only a plurality being required for victory) to 30 per cent for former-Congressman Martin Dies, conservative Democrat, and 22 per cent for Thad Hutcheson, Republican. (Minor candidates divided the remaining 10 per cent.) It had been a long and arduous struggle for the Austin attorney. He had traveled during five years to virtually every hamlet in the state, surviving several forced landings of the small chartered planes that were all his campaign treasuries could afford. Regardless of their political views, many Texans had come to admire his spunk. The following year, Yarborough won a clear majority in the Democratic primary for a full Senate term over William A. Blakley, a Dallas oil millionaire, who had the united support of Governor Daniel, Senator Johnson, and Allan Shivers. In the general election, he easily defeated Roy Whittenburg, Republican.

Daniel was easily renominated and re-elected governor in 1958. His closest opponent in the primary was state Senator Henry Gonzalez, San Antonio, who had conducted a lonely filibuster against the pro-segregation laws that passed the legislature in 1957. Gonzalez received 245,000 votes compared to 800,000 for Daniel, who had supported the segregation laws, and 240,000 for Pappy O'Daniel, the extreme segregationist. Liberal candidates for two vacancies on the state Supreme Court ran strong races before bowing to their conservative opponents, one an incumbent, in the runoff.

Johnson, Rayburn, and Daniel, meanwhile, had decided to end their alliance with the liberal Democrats of Texas (DOT) that had helped them overthrow Shivers in 1956. At the 1958 state Democratic convention, held in San Antonio in September, the moderates, led by Governor Daniel, were in firm control. All went smoothly until the Daniel forces, in an excess of arrogance, declined to accept two nominees to the sixty-two member State Executive Committee on the ground that the two individuals were affiliated with DOT. A wild fracas broke out in the hall, and a record vote on the issue was prevented by hasty adjournment of the convention. About a thousand liberals marched from the hall, in which the lights and air-conditioning had been turned off, to a nearby hotel where a rump convention was reconvened. Senator Johnson and Speaker Rayburn dispatched pained telegrams from Washington, deploring the means by which the two DOT members had been denied seats on the Executive Committee.

During 1959, the full strength of the Democratic party in Texas was mobilized to support Lyndon Johnson's drive for the presidency. The legislature dutifully moved the primary dates from late July and August to early May and June, so Johnson could attend the national convention already renominated for the Senate. Another new law, designed to strengthen party discipline, barred persons voting in the primary of one party from participating in the precinct, county, or state conventions of the other. (The unintended effect of this legislation was to lead more conservatives to leave the Democratic party and become avowed Republicans.) Finally, the election laws were changed to permit one person to run concurrently for two different offices—provided one was the office of president or vice president. Some liberals, notably Frankie Randolph, objected to the buildup that Johnson was receiving in his native state. For her pains, Mrs. Randolph was relieved of her seat on the National Committee in 1960.

After the campaign of Texas' favorite son had sputtered to its predictable fate at the Democratic convention at Los Angeles, the party machinery was turned to the work of carrying the state for the national Democratic ticket, of which Johnson had agreed to become the junior member. This task proved much more difficult than had at first been imagined. Allan Shivers came bounding out of political retirement to lead the Nixon-Lodge canvass in Texas. John Tower, a young professor of government at Midwestern University in Wichita Falls, campaigned aggressively as Republican candidate for the Senate against Johnson, making effective fun of the latter's dual appearance on the ballot. Protestants, heavily represented in Central Texas and the Panhandle, seemed to display more interest in the Roman

Catholic at the top of the Democratic ticket than in the Texan in the secondary spot.

As the returns began coming in on election night—and it seemed for a time that the national result might depend on Texas—Senator Johnson's headquarters in Austin suffered through some anxious moments. Early results showed Richard Nixon running strong in the cities and the Panhandle. Quite clearly, Republican strength in the state was not, as some had supposed, dependent on the personal popularity of President Eisenhower. Ultimately, the Kennedy-Johnson ticket carried Texas by 46,000 votes. Nixon's vote, however, exceeded either of Eisenhower's winning totals (1,121,000 for Nixon in 1960 to 1,080,000 and 1,102,000 for Eisenhower in, respectively, 1956 and 1952). Moreover, at least 100,000 ballots, double the Democratic majority, were thrown out by local election boards on grounds that they had been mutilated. This mutilation resulted largely from a peculiarity in Texas election law which provides, where paper ballots are used, for scratching of unwanted candidates rather than marking the name of the candidate who is desired. Many voters scratched only the name of the major party candidate to whom they were opposed, ignoring the several minor party candidates for president. In many precincts, such ballots were credited to the major party candidate who remained unscratched. In precincts where the law was strictly observed, rejected ballots ran to more than 20 per cent of the total cast. Republican protests that victory in the state had been stolen from them by local election boards, controlled by the Democrats, were ignored by the courts.

In the final returns, Nixon carried Dallas, Fort Worth, and Houston, but lost San Antonio and El Paso. The Republican candidate made sizable gains over Eisenhower's 1956 showing in the Panhandle and held his own in the German counties and in the wealthy oil-producing counties around Midland. East Texas, however, returned emphatically to its Democratic loyalties, Kennedy carrying all but ten of sixty-nine counties. The Democratic ticket also did sizably better than in 1956 in the Gulf Coast region, the Mexican counties in the south, and the land beyond the Pecos in the west, all areas heavily populated by Roman Catholics.

Republican spirits were dramatically revived in 1961, when

Tower, who had won 46 per cent of the vote in his race against Johnson, was elected by majority vote to fill out the new vice president's term in the Senate. Running against William Blakley, who had been temporarily appointed to the seat by Governor Daniel, Tower was able to carry the five major cities and to hold Nixon's gains in the Panhandle. Reportedly, many liberals, disliking Blakley's conservatism, voted for Tower in hopes of replacing him with a liberal Democrat the next time around. (Bruce Alger, beneficiary of a similar theory, was by now beginning his fourth term in the House of Representatives.)

The rising cost of state government in 1961 caught up with Texas, which for years had utilized a severance tax on the oil producers to ease its financial problems. Faced with the need for additional revenue, liberals proposed either a personal income tax or a severance tax on natural gas. Business groups, with the powerful support of Ben Ramsey, still in the lieutenant governor's chair, persuaded the legislature instead to enact a 2 per cent general sales tax, Texas' first. Governor Daniel at first opposed the sales tax, but finally, under heavy pressure from public school teachers (who were to receive an $810 annual raise from tax receipts), permitted it to become law.

Seeking an unprecedented fourth term as governor in 1962, Price Daniel was ignominiously eliminated in the first round of the Democratic primary. Leader in the first primary and winner in the runoff was John B. Connally, Fort Worth, Senator Johnson's former administrative assistant and first secretary of the navy in the Kennedy administration. Connally was supported by Johnson and, as well, by Allan Shivers, who considered that he had a score to even with Daniel. A full slate of liberal candidates, led by Don Yarborough (unrelated to Ralph) of Houston for governor, advanced to the runoff primary, where all were defeated by their conservative opponents. Only Yarborough ran a close race, carrying Houston, El Paso, and most of East Texas, and coming within 26,000 votes of Connally's total. The Republicans meanwhile nominated for governor Jack Cox, a former Democrat and Shivers' protégé, who had given Daniel a close race in the Democratic gubernatorial primary of 1960. Shivers, whose political career seemed by no means over, benignly supported

Connally in the general election, while remaining on good terms with Cox.

It was a year of some embarrassment for the liberal Democrats in Texas. The AFL-CIO, a growing power in state politics, endorsed Woodrow Bean, El Paso, for congressman-at-large, only to discover shortly before the first primary that Bean had not filed a federal income tax return since 1951. The candidate blandly explained that he did not approve of the income tax law, a sentiment which squared poorly with the liberal advocacy of a state income tax. Hastily withdrawing its endorsement, the union group was unable to recall thousands of marked sample ballots that had been distributed among Mexican-Americans. Bean was high man in the first primary, but was defeated with the rest of the liberal slate in the runoff. Between the first and second primaries, national headlines were devoted to the tangled speculations and swindles of Billie Sol Estes, a grain dealer from Pecos, who had contributed heavily to the campaigns of many Texas Democrats, mostly liberals. Senator Yarborough disclosed that his weekly television report to the people of Texas was in part financed by Estes, and federal Assistant Secretary of Labor Jerry Holleman, former president of the Texas AFL-CIO and a leader of DOT, resigned his position after admitting that he accepted $1,000 for personal expenses from the mysterious manipulator of government subsidized grain surpluses. In view of these more or less extraneous difficulties, the liberal showing in the 1962 primaries was not at all bad.

Connally's triumph over Cox in November gave one more round of victory to the old wheeler-dealer moderates of the Lyndon Johnson school. But their years, if not their days, seem numbered. The death of Sam Rayburn in the fall of 1961 lost them a solid rock of leadership, capable of drawing together many of the diverse elements in the Democratic party. Vice President Johnson, scarred by many a factional feud, appears to have lost some of the close identification with Texas that he maintained while majority leader of the Senate.*

---

* The effect on Texas politics of Johnson's succession to the presidency, following the tragic assassination of President Kennedy in Dallas on November 22, 1963, can not at this writing be foretold.

At the moment, the main drive and enthusiasm in state politics is coming from the conservatives, particularly the Republicans. The very word "conservative" has acquired a totemic value. Candidates in both parties in 1962 identified themselves on billboards and in newspaper advertisements as "conservative" or "true conservative," while even candidates endorsed by liberal groups found it necessary to announce their veneration for "conservative" principles of economy and efficiency. Cox, the Republican candidate for governor, received more than 45 per cent of the vote cast in the general election. Seven Republicans, the most since Reconstruction days, were elected to the 174 member legislature. The liberals, however, are increasingly active and have considerable prospect, by slipping through between moderate Democrats and Republicans, of coming to power within the next few years. A coalition of Negroes, Mexican-Americans, and organized labor is gradually forming and is already a formidable force in its own right.

The Republicans, despite their youthful vigor, seem not yet to have developed the political skills needed to overcome the resistance provided by 254 county courthouse based organizations. In 1962, practically every elected state and local official in Texas was a Democrat. Together, these officeholders form an army dedicated to the preservation of one-party control. But they are, to some extent, a discredited army, tied to the errors and prejudices of the past, representative of the days before the shining towers of commerce rose above Dallas, Houston, and Fort Worth, before the acres of ranchtype houses began to sprawl around the great cities. The Republican party, in Texas, has hitched its wagon to the future; and, in Texas, the future seems likely to arrive with unusual speed.

8

OHIO
SWING STATE

The Ohio Republican organization, a national force comparable in influence to Wall Street, organized labor, or a major religious denomination, has never exercised the same easy authority over its own bailiwick that was for a long time enjoyed by its counterparts in Michigan and Pennsylvania. Perhaps for the very reason that they had to learn their early lessons under fierce Democratic fire, Ohio's Republican politicians, from James A. Garfield and William McKinley to Robert A. Taft and John W. Bricker, have frequently achieved roles of eminence and even dominance in national affairs. That the state's politically stimulating atmosphere has not similarly promoted the careers of Democrats is perhaps in part accountable to the fact that, until recently at least, party competition was maintained at the expense of discernible difference in party philosophy— the Ohio Democrat became a special type, regarded with suspicion if not aversion by many of his national party leaders.

Ohio politics has been, almost by design, devoid of heroes and heroics. As the state has never accepted the control of any one metropolitan area or any single economic interest, it has rarely fallen under the spell of any single glamorous political personality. William

McKinley—good, sober McKinley, who rose from a struggling small-town law practice to preside over the disposition of ancient empires —stood perhaps highest in its affection; but behind even McKinley, almost as an appendage to his being, was always Mark Hanna. An apparent contradiction to the unheroic spirit of Ohio politics was presented at the middle of the twentieth century by the state's deep

Counties Carried by Right-to-Work
Referendum, 1958

OHIO

commitment to the career of Senator Robert Taft; but Taft, like McKinley before him (like, for that matter, William Dean Howells, another Ohio boy), was a kind of model of the unheroic leader, a proof that sturdy common sense may also claim its share of sentiment and romance.

The key position that Ohio held in the Republican party, almost from its founding, was based first on the close division of strength between the two parties, which could throw the state either way in a presidential election, and later, after five of the eight Republicans elected president between 1868 and 1920 had been Ohio men, on the mastery that Ohio politicians had exerted for more than a generation over the great and puzzling machinery—almost, in the view of one observer, like the hierarchy of a monastic order—of the national Republican party. Control of a national administration, particularly in the days of vast federal patronage, usually meant more in the Republican than in the Democratic party, for the reason that in eleven Southern states, where the Republican party after Reconstruction existed chiefly as a recipient for federal jobs, party workers were bound by unbreakable ties to a Republican president in office. As a result of Ohio's long hold on the White House, Republican leaders in the South during the nineteenth century developed the habit of accepting guidance from the masters of the party organization in the Buckeye State. This habit was forged into a solid obligation by Mark Hanna and from 1900 to 1952 Southern delegations regularly followed the lead of Ohio at the quadrennial Republican national conventions. This arrangement led in due course to the brief reign of the unsavory "Ohio gang" that surrounded the unfortunate Warren G. Harding in the 1920's; but by the forties it had produced the solid, conservative leadership of Robert Taft, son of the late president, William Howard Taft. Although he had become a kind of national symbol for Republicanism, Taft was in 1948 for the third time denied his party's nomination for president by the powerful combination of financiers and moderate liberals who controlled the Republican organizations in the East.

Among the reasons that Eastern Republican leaders insisted "Taft can't win" in 1948 was the controversial Taft-Hartley Labor Relations Act (called the "Slave Labor" Act by union leaders), which had been passed in 1947 as a curb on the growing power of national unions. When Taft's Senate term expired in 1950, leaders of the union movement determined that he should be defeated, both as a demonstration of labor's power and to head off his probable presidential candidacy in 1952. To achieve this purpose, labor was presented with a somewhat weak vessel in the person of state Auditor Joseph T. ("Jumping Joe") Ferguson, who defeated seven opponents, including Toledo's Mayor Michael V. DiSalle, in the May Democratic primary for the privilege of opposing Taft. Union leaders had attempted to persuade Murray D. Lincoln, articulate president of Farm Bureau Insurance Company (now Nationwide Insurance), to make the race against Taft, but Lincoln had been unwilling to subject himself to the unpredictable melee of a Democratic primary. Since Ferguson, a master of the rugged art of the primary, was intent on running, labor set out to make the best of its given instrument.

Unions pooled their resources to prepare a 220-page "Speaker's Handbook on Robert Alphonso Taft," which purported to reveal a record of singleminded hostility to the interests of the common man; and to distribute one million copies of a comic book, portraying Taft's career in broad and possibly libellous strokes (a union dare that the senator sue was never taken up). Ordinary negotiations with management were set aside or postponed by union officers until the all-consuming goal of Taft's defeat should be accomplished. At the same time, conservatives across the nation rallied with financial contributions to assist the senator's return.

The first major break in the campaign occurred in September at a Democratic rally in Steubenville, heart of the rough-and-ready coal mining country along the West Virginia border. Ferguson opened the program with a vituperative attack on Taft. Speaking from the same platform moments later, Governor Frank Lausche, a Democrat seeking re-election to a third two-year term (he had been defeated once between his first and second terms in the mid-forties), delivered a scolding lecture on "candidates for political office who will say anything about their opponents to win." (During the summer, at the Governor's Conference at White Sulphur Springs, West Virginia, Lausche had told reporters, "I shall not allow my party interest to overcome my interest in my country.") From that moment on, it seemed clear that if labor were going to elect Ferguson, it would have to do so without much assistance from the state Democratic organization, led by Lausche's personal lieutenant, Eugene Hanhart. Though himself a former mayor of Cleveland and product of that city's Polish community, Lausche, through indefatigable handshaking at rural county fairs and frugal economic policies, had built up a considerable following among the state's conservatives. For neither the first nor the last time, the governor had declined to sacrifice his standing with this group for the sake of party regularity.

Nothing that Lausche could have done, however, would have been of much help to Ferguson. Although Aldolph Pacifico, president of the state's United Mine Workers, later charged, "The Democratic Party, from the governor on down, defeated Ferguson," the truth was that union members themselves voted in overwhelming numbers for Taft's re-election. Annoyed by the vindictive spirit with which their leaders went after Taft and unimpressed by the allegedly discriminatory features of the Taft-Hartley Act, ordinary laborers in the cities added their votes to Taft's majorities in the rural counties to give him the greatest victory of his career. In the state's eight most populous counties, all heavily industrialized and unionized, Taft's vote rose from 45 per cent in 1944, his last previous race, to almost 56 per cent in 1950. In the same election, Lausche was easily re-elected, carrying seven of the eight populous counties. (The Republican candidate, Don Ebright, had been damaged by bitterness remaining from a heated primary battle in which one of his opponents, James A. Rhodes, the astute mayor of Columbus whose career in Ohio politics was only beginning, had charged the state Republican organization with dictatorial methods.)

From this high-water mark of conservatism, Ohio's politics in the next decade was to pursue a wildly swinging course, with neither liberals nor conservatives long holding the upperhand. In the early fifties, contrary to the more common national pattern, it was the Democratic governor, Lausche, who advocated strict economy, while the Republican legislature sought to increase expenditures. The Republican legislative majority, however, divided on such issues as a proposed conveyor belt for transportation of coal and other minerals between the Ohio River and Lake Erie (favored by the rubber

and steel interests, opposed by the railroad lobby) and reapportionment of the state's Congressional districts (favored by Republican
State Chairman Ray Bliss, opposed by Ed D. Schorr, Republican
leader of Cincinnati, and Congressman-at-large George H. Bender).
The conveyor belt proposal died in the Senate Rules Committee, after
one Republican senator had publicly warned the well-financed rubber
and steel lobby "to call off the wolves;" reapportionment, however,
was accomplished for the first time since 1913.

As the 1952 presidential election approached, Ohio Republicans
began to warm to the prospect that the party's national convention
would at last accept the opportunity to "put Taft over, that four-leaf
clover, that we'll over overlook no more," as their 1948 theme song
had gone. In the meantime, they were entertained by the complete
rout of the rival party organization in the state's presidential primary.
An insurgent slate of national convention delegates, committed to
Senator Estes Kefauver, was able to defeat a Democratic organization slate, pledged to former–United States Senator Robert Bulkley
of Cleveland, in twenty-six out of thirty contests. Among those denied
places in the Ohio delegation to the national convention were the
state national committeeman, the national committeewoman, the
president of the Ohio Young Democrats, and the state director of
the CIO Political Action Committee. At the same time, State Chairman Hanhart was defeated for re-election from his own district to
the State Central Committee.

Republican amusement was short-lived. At their own national
convention in Chicago, delegations from the East and Far West,
supported by a new breed of Republican activists from the South,
once more frustrated Taft's presidential ambitions, giving the prize
instead to General Dwight Eisenhower, who only recently had discovered that he was a Republican.

The Taft name was not, however, absent from the Ohio ballot that
fall. Charles P. Taft, brother of the senator, received the Republican
nomination for governor, despite the opposition of his own Hamilton
County (Cincinnati) organization. More liberal and independent than
his brother, Charles Taft had actually broken with the Republican
party in Cincinnati and accepted leadership of a good government
coalition, the City Charter Committee, formed to support the city's

council-manager administration. The Ed Schorr organization repaid this apostasy by permitting Lausche, again the Democratic candidate, to carry Hamilton County by almost 20,000 votes which, coupled with a 175,000 majority out of his own Cuyahoga County (Cleveland), enabled the incumbent governor to improve his showing by three percentage points over 1950. Meanwhile, Eisenhower, despite predictions that many Taft followers would stay away from the polls, was carrying the state by half-a-million votes.

The following spring, Senator Taft, having already left the mark of his personality and philosophy on the new national Republican administration, died of cancer. His passing left a gap in conservative leadership in Ohio and in the nation that has not since been filled. Lausche appointed Thomas A. Burke, mayor of Cleveland, to the vacant seat in the Senate. Republicans immediately began to skirmish for the opportunity to oppose Burke for election to the last two years of Taft's unexpired term.

Congressman Bender, who had distinguished himself as a cowbell-wielding cheerleader for Taft at several national conventions, received

Figure 8. Ohio Battle Graph, 1948-62

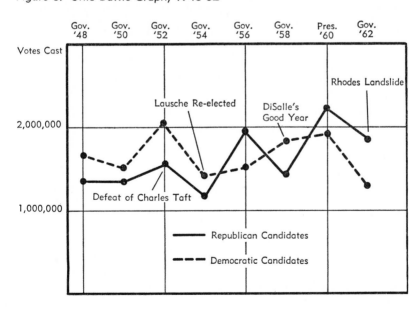

the support of the Republican State Committee. After this endorsement was made public, William Saxbe, speaker of the state House of Representatives, declared that he would oppose Bender, whom he described as a "buffoon," in the Republican primary. In the campaign that followed, Saxbe offered a number of lively characterizations of the organization leadership, including a reference to State Chairman Bliss as "a Judas goat, leading the party to slaughter." Two weeks before primary day, Robert Taft, Jr., son of the late senator, then making his own first race for the state legislature, announced that he would vote for Saxbe. Though ultimately victorious, Bender, who had full organization support, received only 57 per cent of the primary vote. Saxbe carried nineteen counties, mostly in the Miami Valley, stretching north from Cincinnati, normally the most conservative area in the state.

The general election that followed presented a good picture of basic party strengths. Neither candidate was particularly popular or well known. The majority by which Bender finally won, following a recount that cost the Democratic party $68,000, was only 2,970 votes—about one-fourth of a vote for each of the state's precincts. It was generally agreed that Burke would have overcome this narrow majority had he refrained from issuing a campaign statement supporting censure of Senator Joseph R. McCarthy of Wisconsin, then just past the peak of his spectacular career. Bender declined to comment on McCarthy or McCarthyism. The Democratic candidate received his largest vote in the triangle of heavily industrialized counties in the northeastern corner of the state, including Cuyahoga (Cleveland), Summit (Akron), Mahoning (Youngstown), and the coal-mining counties along the eastern border. Other pockets of Democratic strength existed in Toledo, rising from the state's northwestern flatlands beside Lake Erie; Dayton, in the Miami Valley; and Pike County, a sparsely populated rural district in the southern dip of the Ohio Valley. Sizable Republican majorities, on the other hand, were polled in Hamilton County (Cincinnati), most of the Miami Valley, most of the Lake Erie counties between Cleveland and Toledo, and Central Ohio, a vast rural heartland surrounding Columbus, the state capital. (The story goes that when in 1809 the legislature ordered that the capital be located at a point "no more than 40 miles from the common center of the State," the owners of the future site of Columbus, then an uninhabited wilderness along the Scioto River, won the capital designation in a card game with representatives of another community originally favored by the selection committee.) In thirty-three countries, most of them rural, the Republican candidate received at least 65 per cent of the vote.

Lausche, running against Jim Rhodes, by now state auditor and reconciled to the Republican organization he had denounced in 1950, was again re-elected, but by only half the majority he had received in 1952. His showing was at least 10 per cent better than that of the rest of the Democratic ticket in forty-nine of the state's eighty-eight counties. Deciding to give up the governorship at last, Lausche determined to run against Bender in 1956.

During his short stay in the Senate, Bender, formerly a stalwart conservative, had been transformed into a loyal Eisenhower Republican. It was to do him little good. Once again casting party regularity to the winds, Lausche nimbly announced that if elected to the Senate, he might help the Republicans organize that body in 1957, if the outcome depended on his vote. Outraged, Bender declared, "Lausche is trying to grab Ike's coattails. Those coattails are already occupied by me, and there isn't room for anyone else." But to no avail, for, once again withstanding an Eisenhower landslide, Lausche was victorious by more than 200,000 votes. (The following January, he voted with the Democrats, who without him would have had a two-vote majority, to organize the Senate.)

The Republicans did, however, succeed in recapturing the governorship for the first time in eight years. Carrying all but five counties, Attorney General C. William O'Neill easily defeated Toledo's rotund Mike DiSalle, the Democratic nominee. In thirty-three counties, including Cuyahoga (Cleveland), Summit (Akron), and Franklin (Columbus), the Republican vote for governor increased more than 10 per cent over 1954.

The Republican kingmakers, itching to get their hands back on the national party machinery, began to talk of O'Neill as possible vice presidential material for 1960. This hope was quickly blighted by a series of political blunders made by the new governor. Surrounding himself with the same men who had worked under him as attorney general, O'Neill became isolated from the county Republican leaders, who were anxiously awaiting state patronage after the long Lausche drought. Had he been able to establish himself in the role of virtuous crusader (as did Joseph Clark, under similar circumstances, in Philadelphia), the disaffection of the courthouse rings might have done him little harm. In fact, however, he succeeded, by reversing a number of his own administrative decisions, in conveying an impression of fumbling vacillation. Finally, in the highly publicized case of Dr. Samuel Sheppard, a Cleveland osteopath convicted of murdering his wife, O'Neill at first granted permission to Erle Stanley Gardner, creator of Perry Mason and conductor of a magazine feature, "The Court of Last Resort," to give Sheppard a lie-detector test; then, in the baking heat of nationwide publicity, withdrew the permission.

In January, 1958, with a new gubernatorial race about to begin, O'Neill suffered a mild heart attack. Leaping into the breach, Charles Taft announced that he would file petitions as a standby candidate for governor, in case O'Neill should be incapacitated before the primary. To O'Neill's protests of complete recovery, Taft replied that he would "not lift a finger" to advance his own candidacy, but would not withdraw from the primary on the chance that the Bliss organization might be permitted to name a candidate for governor by default. Some individuals in the state evidently raised several fingers in Taft's behalf, and when the primary ballots had been counted, the noncandidate had received 36 per cent of the vote. O'Neill, his prestige badly damaged, began to look about for some issue that would carry him through his second contest with DiSalle, who again had been nominated by the Democrats.

The business community, which had during the Lausche years striven to avoid partisan identification, was quick to provide the worried governor with an issue guaranteed to breathe new life into his campaign. That it was certain to mobilize the opposition, as well, was a risk that O'Neill perhaps felt he had to take. So-called right-to-work laws, in effect prohibiting compulsory membership in the union favored by the majority in a given plant, had been passed by eighteen states, most of them rural, beginning with Florida in 1944. Gathering the support of many businessmen and of the new conservatives then beginning to come on the political scene, right-to-work had by the middle fifties become a fighting phrase (and a profitable source of employment for some of its promoters). In 1958, the right-to-work proponents, given confidence by their success in Indiana the previous year, sought a showdown with organized labor in two major industrial states, California and Ohio.

Not all Ohio Republicans shared Governor O'Neill's sanguine view of this new issue. While more than 300,000 signatures were being obtained on petitions to put the right-to-work initiative on the November ballot, State Chairman Bliss and Senator John Bricker, up for re-election, met in July with state businessmen and industrialists at Cincinnati's Queen City Club. The two veteran politicians pleaded that the crusade be called off; but the businessmen, by now whipped up to a mood of evangelic enthusiasm, were unmoved. Bricker and Bliss returned to state headquarters in Columbus, both privately convinced that right-to-work would sink the Republican cause in November. After the state party convention, Bricker, who had been a highly popular governor in the forties and Republican candidate for vice president of the United States in 1944, told a friend, "This means the end of all of us." All, said the friend, except John Bricker. "No," Bricker insisted, "it's the end of me, too."

The senator, as it turned out, was an accurate prophet. Though running well ahead of most of the Republican ticket, he lost by more than 100,000 votes to a little-known former congressman, Stephen M. Young, of Cleveland. O'Neill went down before DiSalle (who in 1956 had said that he would "just once like to be a candidate in a Democratic year") by more than 450,000 votes, and right-to-work was rejected by an almost 1,000,000 vote margin. The initiative carried sixteen counties, most of them located in the rolling hills between the Miami and Scioto Rivers. Only two of the state's forty-two industrial counties (35 per cent or more of the work force employed in manufacturing) gave majorities to right-to-work. Democrats won control of both houses of the legislature (seventy-eight to sixty-one in the Assembly and twenty to thirteen in the Senate) for the first time in the decade. Heavy Democratic gains were scored not only in the northeastern industrial triangle, but also in the rural Ohio Valley, where fifteen out of twenty counties were suffering from serious unemployment. Riding in on the tide was Joseph T. Ferguson, the same Jumping Joe who had lost to Bob Taft eight years before, elected to a four-year term as state treasurer.

After the election, labor reported having spent $809,565 to defeat right-to-work, while committees supporting the initiative reported expenditures of $762,000 (over half of which came from bank loans secured by the Ohio Chamber of Commerce and the Ohio Manufacturers Association). Labor had demonstrated its effectiveness in a defensive situation, in contrast to its failure in 1950 when merely seeking reprisal for a law already three years old. Workers, accepting the argument of their leaders that right-to-work was a management trick, voted with rare solidarity to protect their unions. Coupled with the returns from California on the same day, the Ohio result terminated the career of right-to-work as a serious issue in American politics.

The Democratic victory had no sooner been won than Governor DiSalle fell to squabbling with a bloc of legislators from the northeastern triangle, most of them beholden to Ray T. Miller, former mayor of Cleveland. These difficulties began in a dispute over the majority leadership in the legislature and later were aggravated by a public reference by DiSalle to racket activity in one of the coal-mining counties. The dissidents at first joined with Republican legislators to block DiSalle's request for a corporate franchise tax, designed to produce $96 million in new revenue over a two-year period, but eventually were persuaded to fall back into line. Having mollified the Miller machine, DiSalle then came under fire from his union allies when he described a proposed increase in worker's death and unemployment benefits as "going too far too soon."

Despite these divisions, DiSalle was able to get most of his program through the legislature, including bills providing a 20 per cent increase in tax revenues which he argued were necessary to deal with an inherited fiscal crisis (the state had shown a $100 million deficit in 1958). Since most of the new taxes were needed to stabilize the existing state budget, DiSalle, unlike Mennen Williams in Michigan, was unable to show any great increase in services to match the enlarged tax bite. Not surprisingly, many voters held the current administration responsible for a situation that had been gathering since the end of World War II.

DiSalle got on the Kennedy bandwagon early in 1960, but only after he had been rather clearly bludgeoned out of the idea of entering the national convention as a favorite-son candidate for president himself. Even so, he had to deal with an insurgent slate, also committed to Kennedy, put into the field by the Ray Miller faction. Winning twenty-one out of twenty-nine contested places on the delegation, DiSalle was able to demonstrate his control of the party organization outside Cuyahoga County.

Leader of Ohio's delegation to the Republican national convention was State Auditor Jim Rhodes. Former-Senator Bender, who had briefly made the news in 1958 as a $250-a-day employee of James R. Hoffa "to help clean up the Teamsters Union," ran without organization support and was quietly defeated in a contest for delegate-at-large.

Most newspaper analyses prior to the 1960 election placed Ohio in the Democratic column. John Kennedy's tour of the industrial triangle was greeted with almost hysterical enthusiasm. State Democratic leaders, however, were aware from the moment of Kennedy's nomination that they were likely to lose the state. Protestantism rode into the old Western Reserve region with the pioneer wagons from New England in the early years of the nineteenth century, and it has remained strong in Ohio ever since. Later arrivals in the Ohio Valley from the South were mainly Methodists, and later still German Lutherans spread upward from Cincinnati through the Miami Valley and into Central Ohio. Roman Catholics came in considerable numbers, too, but in the sixth decade of the twentieth century, Protestants outnumbered Catholics in all but eight of the state's eighty-eight counties. (The exceptions were three counties in the industrial northeast, three rural counties, industrial Lucas County, and Hamilton County.) Unlike most industrial states, Ohio contains relatively few first or second generation Americans (15 per cent in 1960, as compared to 24 per cent in Michigan and 40 per cent in Massachusetts). Even industrial counties like Summit (Akron), Lucas (Toledo), Stark (Canton), and Montgomery (Dayton) have populations including less than 20 per cent foreign stock; in Hamilton County (Cincinnati) this figure drops to 11 per cent and in Franklin (Columbus) to 8 per cent.

Despite the Protestant roots of the majority of the state's inhabitants, religion has traditionally played little role in Ohio politics (unlike neighboring Indiana, where the Ku Klux Klan was powerful in the twenties). William McKinley was the first president to invite a Catholic clergyman to participate in his inauguration. Lausche and DiSalle, both Catholics, ran well in Protestant areas. Immediately after the conventions, some political observers doubted that Kennedy's religion would have much effect one way or the other. As the campaign progressed, however, it became evident that sentiments deeply held were being stirred. Democratic precinct workers in some rural counties sent their resignations to state headquarters. Polls taken by the Democratic organization showed that religion was the most important factor in converting 1958 DiSalle voters to Richard Nixon. On election night, Ohio was the first major barrier to break the Kennedy tide that had begun to roll in the East. The state went for Nixon by 53 per cent, as compared to 43 per cent given to the Republican candidate for governor two years before.

The rise in Republican strength was statewide and could not be attributed wholly to religion. Cuyahoga and Hamilton Counties, in which Catholics in 1957 constituted respectively 33 and 28 per cent of the population, showed Republican gains of 8 and 6 per cent. Resentment against DiSalle's tax program, the effective grass-roots campaign conducted by the Bliss organization, and the popularity of Nixon, whose father had once lived in Ohio, contributed to the Republican victory. Nevertheless, the religious factor, at least in some parts of the state, was probably decisive. In the Ohio Valley, Methodist and Evangelical country, where unemployment continued heavy, Nixon scored spectacular gains over the Republican showing in 1958—up 15 per cent in Scioto County, up 19 per cent in Lawrence County, up 17 per cent in Athens County, up 9 per cent even in always-Democratic Pike County. Interestingly, the *most* heavily Protestant area in the state, the predominantly German Lutheran northwest corner, did not produce gains for Nixon equal to those in the Ohio Valley—possibly because persons of Germanic descent were less moved by nativist emotions, possibly simply because the decline in the Republican vote in the northwest had been less pronounced in 1958. (Comparison with the 1956 results shows that Nixon received about the same percentage of the vote as Eisenhower had in the Ohio Valley, while running about 5 per cent behind Eisenhower's majorities in the Lutheran northwest.)

Beside carrying Ohio for Nixon, Republicans were able to regain control of both houses of the legislature. In the lower house, Bob Taft, Jr.—now in his fourth term—was elected majority leader. DiSalle (who did not face re-election until 1962, as a result of the lengthening of the governor's term from two to four years) immediately locked in unbreakable impasse with the new legislature. An attempt by the Republican majority to place limitations on unemployment compensation was successfully vetoed, with labor's emphatic approval, by the governor. A revenue bill, granting some exemptions from the state sales tax and eliminating a tax on resales among utilities, was also vetoed by DiSalle, but was easily repassed by overwhelming bipartisan majorities in both houses of the legislature.

In the fall of 1961, DiSalle announced that, instead of seeking re-election, he would devote himself, as a private citizen, to educating Ohioans on the perplexing problems of state government. Later, under urging from President Kennedy, he reconsidered and agreed once more to face the voters. Republicans, happily sure that the Democrats were stuck with an unpopular incumbent, fell into line behind State Auditor Rhodes, anxious for another shot at the governorship. Moving out of the wings toward center stage at a deliberate pace, Bob Taft, Jr., went onto the Republican ticket as candidate for congressman-at-large. (George Bender, who had used the congressman-at-large seat to launch himself into the Senate, had died in 1961; the following year he was posthumously accused of participating in an attempt to bribe a federal official during the Eisenhower administration.)

Still carrying the burden of his unpopular tax program, DiSalle narrowly escaped elimination in the 1962 Democratic primary and lost in the general election to Rhodes by more than half-a-million votes—the largest gubernatorial margin in the history of Ohio politics. Even reliably Democratic Cleveland turned in for the Republican candidate. The day after election, DiSalle said that he had "less respect" for Rhodes than anyone he had ever run against—a large statement—and described his victorious opponent as absolutely unqualified.

Installed at last in the governor's office, Jim Rhodes seemed to represent some condition, dimly understood, in Ohio and American politics. Like Jumping Joe Ferguson, with whom he had from 1959 to 1963 shared a corridor in the state capitol, he possessed some quality that had enabled him to surmount difficulty and defeat, returning always to the fray, ready for the next crack of the electoral whip that might land him (or Jumping Joe, or both of them) back in office. Among his first acts as chief executive, Governor Rhodes slashed the state's welfare budget and substantially reduced the state payroll.

According to a theory widely held among political scientists, close competition between the two major parties is likely to promote the increase of public services. There has not been a time in the last thirty years when Ohio politics has not been genuinely competitive. Republicans and Democrats have alternated in the governor's chair with a fair degree of regularity. Apportionment in the state Senate corresponds with reasonable equality to the distribution of population, and although a constitutional provision assuring every county at least one seat in the House of Representatives somewhat favors Republican control of that body, a determined voter upheaval such as occurred in 1958 can easily produce Democratic majorities in both houses.

The result of this almost model two-party situation has been state government that not only spends less on its services than almost any other state in the nation (forty-seventh in total general expenditures, per capita, in 1961), but also finances its operations through a tax structure resting heavily on the ordinary consumer. While the state's low rate of taxation on business and industry has no doubt contributed to the extraordinary economic growth of Ohio since World War II, it hardly permits the positive public role envisioned by liberal theorists. Neither of the state's political parties has been wholly lacking in progressive leadership. The fact remains, however, that a century of intense partisan competition, far from placing Ohio among the national leaders in expenditures for services, has enthroned thrift as the most popular and most honored of the governmental virtues.

9

MASSACHUSETTS

CAULDRON BUBBLE

The melting pot, not surprisingly, has appealed to many observers as a peculiarly apt symbol for American society. Into the crucible of the United States, the image implies, have been poured the races and nations of mankind, producing a new and distinctive species. The best qualities of all prior national types, it is suggested (assuming the observer to be a patriotic American), have blended to create the character of the new breed. If the baser aspects of the older nationalities are admitted, they are presumed to have been boiled off in the process of amalgamation. The resulting American race is a miraculous alloy, combining all of the superior characteristics that have previously been exhibited by the various divisions of humanity.

Upon examination, this symbol—as even its more rapturous proponents are likely in their calmer moments to agree—is found to be in some ways seriously misleading. The process of amalgamation has thus far been made available without substantial limitations to only a few, though no doubt the largest, of the national groups. To the extent that it has occurred, the process has usually taken the form —in language, manners, customs, and laws—of conquest by one

142

culture, the British, of all others. (Contemporary differences between British and American cultures can be explained by the experience of the New World almost without references to the effects of other national influences. The popularity in the United States of haciendas, sauerkraut, Negro jazz, spaghetti, and the like seem minor and almost pathetic exceptions to the prevalence of British ways.) In the cases where non-British cultures have made a serious impact on American society—as, for instance, the influence of the Irish on state and local politics—the action has often more closely resembled an explosion of warring elements than the peaceful bubbling of a metallic stew.

Nowhere in the United States have nations and cultures mingled in more variety and proximity than in Massachusetts. The historic port city of Boston (which dominates the state as few American cities dominate their hinterlands) has in turn provided entry into North America for hordes of Puritans and related British stocks, Irish, Portuguese, Italians, Germans, Greeks, and Russian Jews. At the same time, French Canadians and Negroes have migrated to the state after first settling in other parts of the continent. With the exception of the earliest arrivals, who received a warm welcome from the Wampanoag Indians (whom they subsequently exterminated), few of the newcomers were greeted with great cordiality by their predecessors. Each national group claimed, and sometimes later relinquished, available portions of the tough, unfertile land—Yankee descendants of the Puritans moving out from Boston Common to Cambridge, Belmont, Lexington, and Lincoln, to the far reaches of the Berkshires and to Cape Cod, all the while maintaining salients on the coast north of Boston at Newburyport, Gloucester, and Salem; French Canadians drifting down the Merrimack Valley to the mill cities of Lawrence and Lowell; Irish piling into the North, South, and West Ends of Boston, later spreading westward to Cambridge, Worcester, and Springfield; Portuguese settling around New Bedford, whose whalers had touched often at the Azores and Cape Verde Islands; Italians crowding the Irish out of North Boston and overflowing up the north shore to Winthrop and Revere; Jews concentrating first in Boston's West End, then spreading to Dorchester and Roxbury, later proceeding outward to Brookline ("the gilded ghetto") and Newton; Greeks clustering

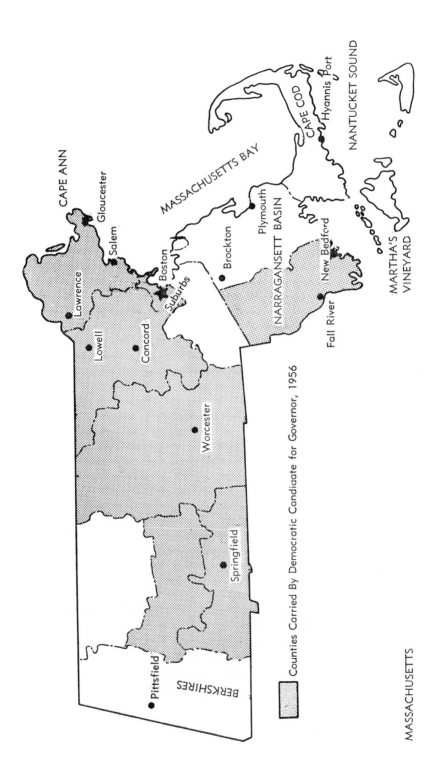

CAPE ANN

Gloucester

Salem

MASSACHUSETTS BAY

CAPE COD

Hyannis Port

NANTUCKET SOUND

Lawrence

Boston
Suburbs

Brockton

Plymouth

NARRAGANSETT BASIN

New Bedford

MARTHA'S
VINEYARD

Lowell

Concord

Fall River

Worcester

Counties Carried By Democratic Candidate for Governor, 1956

Springfield

Pittsfield

BERKSHIRES

MASSACHUSETTS

around their cathedral in Roxbury; Negroes taking over once-Irish, later Jewish neighborhoods in Dorchester and Roxbury; Puerto Ricans, the most recent arrivals, settling in Boston's South End, where a Spanish Speaking Center was established in 1957.

Succeeding each other, the nations left behind a few of their strongholds, monuments, stragglers, and places of business, so that by 1962, Boston, and to some extent Massachusetts, resembled a littered seacoast, covered with strange debris swept up from all regions of the ocean floor. Within a few paces of Charles Bulfinch's austerely beautiful statehouse on the top of Beacon Hill could be found, among other lively witnesses to the New England past: the Unitarian Service Committee, the Roman Catholic Information Center, the editorial rooms of the *Atlantic Monthly,* the Anti-Vivisection Society, the Boston Athenaeum, the Church of the New Jerusalem (Swedenborgian), the fictional residence of John Marquand's *Late George Apley,* the Parker House, Scollay Square (where the burlesque theaters and sailors' haunts were being demolished to make way for a new complex of government buildings), and the apartment residence from which the future thirty-fifth president of the United States conducted his first campaign for Congress in 1946.

Whether because of the exhausting effect of so much history or simply because of the harsh impact left by too many long New England winters, the city in which these landmarks were set produced on many visitors an initial impression of barren disorder. The government housed beneath the Bulfinch dome seemed lacking in the moral resources necessary to cope with the vast problems of the contemporary Commonwealth. The electorate appeared in many instances to be motivated by obscure hungers for retribution rather than serious desire for creative growth. The magnificent spiritual strength which, as Arnold Toynbee pointed out, enabled New England Yankees, the least likely of contenders, to triumph in the struggle for North America over the physical superiority of not only the Spanish, French, Dutch, and British Empires, but also the English-speaking inhabitants of the American South, seemed to have worn itself out at last in local quarrels and petty factions. And yet Massachusetts, beneath the vortex of inconsequential rivalries, retained some measure of its ancient pride, some remnant of its sense of historic mission. On the Cambridge side of the Charles River, almost within sight of Beacon Hill, the best minds in America were composing an empire of scholarship not inferior to those of Hellenistic Athens, Alexandria, and medieval Paris. And several hundred miles to the south, in the nation's capital, a Massachusetts man once more sat in the White House, commenting on world affairs with quotations from the New England sages while applying to space-age problems both the intellectual discipline of Harvard and the rough-and-tumble political cunning of South Boston.

The Yankees were first—not counting the Indians or improbable Vikings—in Massachusetts, and they maintained supremacy in their New England fief with a hardihood and endurance lacking among their kinsmen of New York, Pennsylvania, and much of the Middle West. While members of the Anglo-Saxon upper class in most Northern states were content to leave the management of public affairs to offspring of more recent arrivals, the Massachusetts patricians, through the instrument of the Republican party, long remained in active control of the government of their Commonwealth. Even in the 1950's, when foreign stock comprised 40 per cent of the state's population, prominent roles were played in Massachusetts politics by Governor Christian A. Herter (whose father, once speaker of the state House of Representatives, painted and donated to the Commonwealth a series of murals on historic subjects which decorate the wall of the House behind the speaker's dais), Senator Henry Cabot Lodge (whose grandfather, of the same name, blocked the entrance of the United States into the League of Nations following World War I), and Senator Leverett Saltonstall (whose grandfather, of the same name, was president of the state Senate and first mayor of Salem, and whose distant ancestor, Sir Richard Saltonstall, settled in New England in 1630, ten years after the Pilgrims had landed at Plymouth Rock).

Gradually the Irish, who had first begun to arrive in Massachusetts in large numbers following the potato famine in Ireland in the 1840's, developed an effective apparatus in the Democratic party to challenge Yankee dominance. Not until 1928, however, when the candidacy of Al Smith aroused the Irish to a wild pitch of enthusiasm, did a Democrat succeed (after the Civil War) in polling a majority of the Commonwealth's vote in a national election. (Woodrow Wilson won a plurality but less than a majority of the vote in 1912. Prior to the Civil War, Massachusetts supported an occasional Democrat, but was normally Federalist or Whig; in 1856, the Bay State gave three-fourths of its vote to John C. Fremont, the first Republican candidate for president.)

The Irish soon divided into moderates like Senator David I. Walsh, who sought to reconcile ethnic differences on a basis of equality, and irreconcilables, like the redoubtable Governor James Michael Curley (model for Edwin O'Connor's fictional hero, Frank Skeffington, in *The Last Hurrah*), who exploited and inflamed the ethnic quarrel with ferocious glee. (The comparative success of the Curley type in Massachusetts, in contrast to the more moderate Al Smith and Jim Farley in New York or the conservative Aus Meehan and John B. Kelly in Philadelphia, has been explained as the result of the unyielding opposition and scorn with which the Irish were treated by the Bay State Yankees. It may be noted, at the same time, that some Yankees, like Leverett Saltonstall, have always enjoyed a sentimental following among the Irish. When Saltonstall was opposed for the Senate in 1954 by Foster Furcolo, some of the Irish poll workers in the South End were not above advising their followers with a wink and dig in the ribs, "When you get in there, you may as well give old Salty a vote.") To the differences on policy among the Irish were quickly added fierce family rivalries, almost tribal in nature. Partly because of a sense of ethnic exclusiveness comparable to that of the Yankees, partly because their own squabbles left little room for outsiders, the Massachusetts Irish proved extremely slow in making room within Democratic party councils for representatives of the state's growing Italian, Jewish, and Negro ethnic groups. The result of all these difficulties was that Boston never developed an efficient machine of the kind found in most large Eastern and Midwestern cities, and that Republicans, though in the minority after 1928, frequently were able to squeeze through their candidates for state offices. Curley managed to lose to young Henry Cabot Lodge in a bid for the United States Senate in 1936 (thereby becoming the only important Democrat to be defeated in the year of Franklin Roosevelt's greatest triumph), and two years later, seeking to return to the governorship, lost to Saltonstall by almost 150,000 votes.

In 1948, the Democrats for the first time won a majority of the seats in the state House of Representatives and achieved a tie in the Senate. Elected as governor that year, by a majority of 390,000 over the incumbent Republican, was Paul A. Dever, member of one of Roxbury's great Democratic clans and protégé of former-Senator Walsh. A bachelor, the new governor spent most of his evenings in the Engineers' Club, near the state house on Beacon Hill, swapping yarns and gossip with political associates—many of whom eventually found their way to the state bench on his appointment. Through tolerance and wit, Dever came closer than any of his predecessors to welding the Democratic party of Massachusetts into an effective instrument of government. He pushed a hugely expanded highway program through the legislature, gained funds for new hospital construction, and even set up a commission to discover means for improving the efficiency of state government. His leader-

Figure 9. Massachusetts Battle Graph, 1948-62

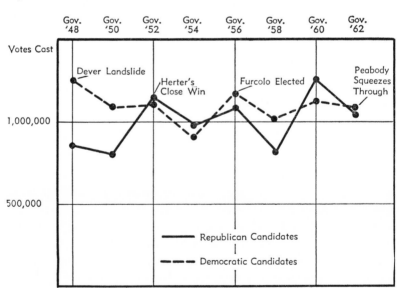

ship of the party was, however, always subject to challenge by (among many others): the eternally rambunctious Curley, then Democratic national committeeman; the powerful McCormack clan, whose most famous member, John W., was majority leader of the United States House of Representatives; and the affluent Kennedy family, related by marriage to former-Congressman John F. ("Honey Fitz") Fitzgerald.

To deal with the Republicans, who in 1950 gained a majority in the Senate, Dever saw to it that the state Department of Public Works dealt generously with requests for jobs and favors by GOP legislators. As a result, he was able to win bipartisan support for a $200 million bond issue and a $32 million increase in capital gains and personal income taxes, needed to pay for the state's new highway and welfare programs.

After engaging in a bitter gubernatorial primary in 1950, which left them almost without funds to use against Dever in the general election, the Republicans and particularly National Committeeman Sinclair Weeks (later secretary of commerce in the first Eisenhower cabinet), sought a return to the preprimary convention. This system of producing a regular slate, which had been used in the state during the thirties, would, Weeks hoped, make possible the introduction of some non-Yankee names onto the Republican ticket as well as reducing the cost of primary campaigns. Dever agreed to sign a law authorizing preprimary conventions, providing it included safeguards against the purchase of delegates which had discredited the system in the thirties. When the legislature enacted a bill without such safeguards, the governor at first returned it for reconsideration, later vetoed it.

Casting about for an opponent for Dever in 1952, the Republican high command—Senators Saltonstall and Lodge, former–Speaker of the United States House of Representatives Joseph W. Martin, Jr., and National Committeeman Weeks—stopped by the Washington office of Congressman Christian A. Herter, then completing his fifth term as representative of the Back Bay–Brookline district. Several years before, Herter had gained renown as chairman of a Congressional delegation studying postwar conditions in Europe, the report of which prepared the way for enactment of the Marshall

Plan. Offered the nomination for governor, Herter asked time to think the matter over. Retiring to his family estate at Wiggins, South Carolina, the congressman balanced Dever's still considerable popularity against the possibility that Dwight Eisenhower would head the Republican ticket as candidate for president that fall. On a winter day in 1952, state Representative Christian Herter, Jr., flew from South Carolina to Boston, carrying word that his father would accept the nomination for governor of the unofficial Republican preprimary convention that had been organized by Weeks. Through the convention method, Herter was given the regular endorsement, and the other leading contenders for the nomination, state Senator Sumner Whittier and former–State Treasurer Lawrence Curtis, were persuaded to run for, respectively, lieutenant governor and United States representative from Herter's district. At the same time, George Fingold, a former Democrat, was slated for attorney general. Dever promptly charged that Herter had the "worst public record of any man in public life in Massachusetts" and termed him "my favorite candidate for the Republican nomination for governor."

Although the Democrats held no preprimary convention, Dever, seeking re-election, began to do some slate-making of his own. When the office of state treasurer became vacant, the governor, explaining to associates that he wanted to get away from "the traditional all-green ticket," persuaded Congressman Foster Furcolo, representing the Springfield district, to resign from his federal post and accept the state office. Furcolo's presence on the Democratic ticket in November, Dever reasoned, would help the party in the Italian neighborhoods of Boston as well as in the Springfield area. The congressman agreed to make the change only after receiving a promise of the governor's support for the United States Senate in 1954 and/or the governorship in 1956.

The heated 1952 presidential campaign soon intruded its influence on Massachusetts state politics. Senator Lodge, who was up for re-election, flew to Paris to persuade General Eisenhower, then commander of NATO, to seek the Republican nomination for president. Later Lodge became Eisenhower's national campaign manager. Although most leading Republicans in Massachusetts, including Saltonstall, Weeks, and Herter, favored Eisenhower for the nomination, a vigorous minority led by Basil Brewer, publisher of the *New Bedford Standard Times,* supported Senator Robert Taft. Feeling between the two camps during the campaign that preceded the state presidential preferential primary, which Eisenhower won by better than two to one, became so intense that Brewer decided to block Lodge's return to the Senate, even at the cost of electing a Democrat.

The hostility felt by the Taft Republicans toward Lodge helped persuade yet another Massachusetts congressman, young John F. Kennedy, representing downtown Boston and Cambridge, to make a run for the Senate. Though counseled by some of his advisors that Lodge, riding high at the national level, was unbeatable, Kennedy decided that his personal timetable required that he be elevated to the Senate by 1953. While Lodge hurried around the nation rounding up convention delegates for Eisenhower, the members of the Kennedy family, including the candidate's attractive mother and sisters, were unleashed in a series of intimate teas held on behalf of the young congressman in all parts of Massachusetts.

In the Democratic presidential primary, Senator Estes Kefauver, fresh from his upset victory in neighboring New Hampshire, was high man with 30,000 write-in votes. (Eisenhower, already announced as a Republican, was second with 16,000.) Dever, however, became a leader in the movement to draft Adlai Stevenson and delivered the Bay State delegation at the convention solidly to the Illinois governor. Despite this triumph, the national convention in Chicago turned out to be a major disaster for Governor Dever. An accomplished impromptu speaker, he had been selected, on the recommendation of no less a connoisseur of fine oratory than Vice President Alben Barkley, to deliver the keynote address on the opening night of the convention. As the television cameras bore down on him in the packed auditorium, the governor first lost his voice, then droned through a prepared address of interminable length. Viewing the spectacle, many Massachusetts voters, who previously had known Dever chiefly through his "Pardon the Inconvenience, Please" signs along highways on which traffic was hampered during new construction, drew the unfair conclusion that their governor was nothing more than an old-fashioned party politician.

In the September primary, Dever, unopposed for renomination.

received only three-fifths of the total Democratic vote cast—more than 200,000 Democratic ballots were left blank for governor. Kennedy, also unopposed, ran ahead of Dever in almost every city and town. In the Republican primary, Lodge led his party ticket in most areas, but ran behind Herter in New Bedford, Basil Brewer's home territory. (Both Lodge and Herter were unopposed.)

In the general election campaign, Dever and Herter flailed each other with gusto. The governor described his Republican opponent as a "congenital enemy of the working class," while Herter called attention to "Dever's Mile of Mistakes," citing a flooded underpass, a collapsed highway tressel, and other misfortunes which had overtaken the governor's prized road-building program. Dever was somewhat embarrassed by the revelation that the legislature, before adjournment, had voted lavish pensions for its members. Herter demanded that the legislature be reconvened to correct the "sneak pension grab." The governor, pointing out that he had not personally benefited by the act, at first refused; but early in September he capitulated, calling back the legislature, which meekly repealed what the newspapers were by then calling "the 1952 goldrush." Herter continued to slash away at Dever for having signed the bill in the first place, for padding the state payroll with politicians, and for doing nothing to plug the chronic deficit in the MTA (Metropolitan Transit Authority, Boston's mass transit system). Dever replied that Herter had made "charges without proof, conviction in the public mind without evidence."

Possibly wearied by the exchange of insults, the voters in November split their tickets in all possible directions: Dwight Eisenhower, Republican, carried the state for president by 209,000; John Kennedy, Democrat, was elected to the Senate by 70,000; Christian Herter, Republican, slid through for governor by 14,000; further down the ticket Sumner Whittier, Republican, was elected lieutenant governor; Foster Furcolo, Democrat, state treasurer; and George Fingold, Republican, attorney general (the latter by a margin of 355,000).

Supported by Republican majorities in both houses of the legislature, Governor Herter achieved enactment of laws establishing several new state agencies, including a Tax Commission (ending the thirty-year reign of tax czar Henry F. Long, once secretary to Calvin Coolidge), a Department of Commerce, a Natural Resources Department, a Council for the Aging, a Youth Commissioner, and a Crime Commission. MTA was reorganized, the preprimary convention system was restored, and Dever's highway construction program was continued. (Interestingly, both Dever, a Democrat, and Herter, a Republican, were innovators during their terms as governor: the former primarily in enlarging expenditures for state services, the latter primarily in improving the apparatus of state administration.) The governor's only major defeat came on proposals that judges of the state's forty-two district courts be barred from the practice of law and for establishment of a nine-judge juvenile court circuit. The latter plan was criticized by Roman Catholic Archbishop Richard Cushing (later cardinal) as "nothing but a big pie for politicians to cut."

As the 1954 election approached, Dever, still maintaining control of the Democratic party machinery, threw his support for governor to Robert F. Murphy, a former professional football player and minority leader of the state House of Representatives. Furcolo, in accordance with his 1952 agreement with Dever, was given the Democratic nomination to oppose Saltonstall for the United States Senate. Coolness between Furcolo and Senator Kennedy, stemming from the days when both had been young congressmen in Washington, produced an incident which seriously undermined the Democratic state campaign. About to enter a New York hospital for back surgery, Kennedy agreed to appear on a radio show with Murphy and Furcolo. At the studio before the broadcast began, Furcolo urged that a strong attack be made on the record of Saltonstall, for whom Kennedy had developed a warm regard during his first eighteen months in the Senate. (Though Kennedy and Saltonstall differed in party and religion, both were Harvard men, both were born and reared within a few miles of Beacon Hill, both possessed the personal tastes and attitudes of the average member of the Boston upper class; Furcolo, of Irish and Italian ancestry, grew up in Connecticut, was educated at Yale, practiced law in western Massachusetts, and is an occasional author of humorous plays and novels.) Evidently angered by Furcolo's insistence, Kennedy not only refused to attack his colleague, but also, when the point arrived in the program at which he had promised to endorse the two candidates, simply announced his support for Murphy and "the ticket." Boston newspapers gave the incident heavy coverage, and the mutual suspicion which had existed between Furcolo and some of the Irish Democratic leaders grew stronger.

Even so, Furcolo ran a better race against Saltonstall—coming within 28,000 votes of victory—than did Murphy (down by 75,000) against Herter. The voting was as mixed as in 1952. In the Irish wards of Boston's South End, Murphy did considerably better than Furcolo. In the Italian North End and also the Jewish wards of Dorchester, on the other hand, Furcolo ran far ahead of his running mate. In western Massachusetts, Furcolo ran well, leading Murphy by 15,000 votes in Hampden County (Springfield). Both Republican candidates polled large majorities in Boston's Back Bay area, while Herter was particularly strong in the Boston suburbs and Saltonstall on Cape Cod.

During his second term, though forced to deal with a House of Representatives controlled by the Democrats, Herter was able to gain approval for a new Massachusetts Port Authority (to operate bridges, airports, and the port of Boston) and to win his fight to have district judges barred from private law practice. On his recommendation, the statute of limitations on armed robbery was extended from seven to ten years, to give the state additional time to break the Brink's robbery case. (The gang that had accomplished the Brink's job, the biggest bank robbery in the nation's history, was finally captured the following year, eight of its members receiving heavy prison sentences.) Herter's proposal that the governor's term be extended to four years was rejected by the House, where Democratic leaders feared that he would seek in 1956 to become the first four-year chief executive.

The tribal feuds within the Democratic organization, which had been temporarily stilled by Dever, broke out afresh in 1955. State Chairman John C. Carr, a Dever man, faced with a disorderly session of the Democratic State Committee, suddenly declared the meeting adjourned. A dissident faction continued in session and elected former–State Chairman William H. Burke, an ally of the

McCormack family, as Carr's successor. For a time, rival sets of party officers competed for the loyalty of the state's Democrats. The issue was brought before the state courts, which ruled that Carr had not been properly elected in the first place, and that the office of chairman had therefore been vacant at the time of Burke's election. Burke appeared to have the best legal claim to the chairmanship. Dever, however, remained as organizer of the party's annual Jefferson-Jackson Day dinner, the major source of funds for the state committee.

As the maneuvering for the 1956 presidential nomination began, Dever and Senator Kennedy sought to arrange a state delegation favorable to Adlai Stevenson. Burke and John McCormack, supported by aged but still defiant James Michael Curley, argued in favor of an uninstructed delegation. To head off the Stevenson drive, McCormack permitted his name to be put forward in the presidential preferential primary as a favorite-son candidate. Dever, respecting the power of the McCormacks, counseled that the favorite-son maneuver not be opposed. Kennedy, though aware that both he and McCormack were regarded as possible vice presidential candidates, agreed. In the April primary, despite a statewide campaign on McCormack's behalf, the House majority leader received only 26,000 votes to 19,000 for Stevenson and 47,000 blanks.

After the primary, Dever agreed to join with Kennedy in a drive to remove Burke from the chairmanship. Kennedy charged that Burke had misrepresented some remarks he had made on the wisdom of replacing Curley as national committeeman. At a May meeting of the State Committee, enlived by scuffles, name-calling, and boos, Burke was replaced by Kennedy's selection for chairman, John M. ("Pat") Lynch, former mayor of Somerville (a Boston suburb). Kennedy solemnly announced "the beginning of a new era for Massachusetts Democrats." Dever, still apprehensive over the affront to the McCormacks, urged the committee to link the party's future to the rising star of John F. Kennedy.

Herter, who was being toured around the nation as a possible replacement for Richard Nixon on the Republican ticket for vice president, decided that he would not seek a third term as governor. Lieutenant Governor Sumner Whittier was selected to bear the

Republican standard, and Furcolo, as the final installment in his 1952 agreement with Dever, became the Democratic gubernatorial candidate.

Both national party conventions proved frustrating to the Massachusetts delegations. McCormack's favorite-son candidacy for president was quickly brushed aside by the Stevenson bandwagon, and Kennedy, after nominating Stevenson, lost his hectic struggle with Estes Kefauver for the secondary place on the ticket. (According to a rumor at the convention, John McCormack helped pull the strings that led to Kefauver's victory.) At the Republican meeting, Herter not only scotched his own candidacy, but also ultimately felt obliged to make the speech which nominated Nixon for a second term. (Three years later, upon the death of John Foster Dulles, Herter became Eisenhower's second secretary of state.)

Back in Massachusetts, the Democratic factions continued their apparently ceaseless battles. At the preprimary convention, a bitter contest developed for the office of attorney general between Boston City Councillor Edward J. McCormack, Jr., nephew of the House majority leader; Joseph D. Ward, a conscientious regular party man; and Endicott ("Chub") Peabody, former Harvard football hero and member of one of New England's oldest families. Ward was endorsed by the convention, but he was subsequently defeated in the primary by McCormack. In the general election, in which Democrats swept all state offices except attorney general, McCormack was in turn defeated by incumbent Republican George Fingold, who thereby acquired a reputation as the state's best Republican vote-getter.

President Eisenhower's majority of almost 450,000 in Massachusetts failed to help the Republican state ticket. Sumner Whittier, who allegedly was regarded even by the Anglo-Saxons as a swamp Yankee (one not of the Boston upper class), lost to Furcolo by 138,000. All sections of the state supported the Democratic candidate for governor except Back Bay, a few Boston suburbs, the Berkshires, and Cape Cod. Democrats retained control of the House of Representatives, and the Republicans held a slim majority in the Senate.

Although the 1956 Democratic state platform had maintained the party's historic opposition to a sales tax, Furcolo announced soon after his inauguration that he favored this means for overcoming the state's growing deficit. (Not only was the state going about $100 million into the red every year, but also the relatively low level of state expenditures had forced the suburban communities around Boston to maintain local tax rates that were among the highest in the nation.) When Democratic state Senator John E. Powers of Boston, succeeding Dever as the party's best organizer, opened fire on the sales tax, the governor attempted to take his case to the people. The sales tax proved a poor issue on which to arouse popular enthusiasm, and Furcolo's efforts produced little more than a lasting antagonism between himself and the leaders of his party in the legislature. The Republicans, who had been moving toward enactment of a sales tax under Herter, were in no mood to assist Furcolo, and the governor's tax proposal was defeated, 223 to 8, in the House of Representatives. Having tasted blood, the legislature proceeded to scuttle most of the rest of Furcolo's program.

While permitting themselves few illusions about their chances of defeating Senator Kennedy's bid for a second term in 1958, the Republicans were hopeful on the possibility of knocking off Furcolo. At their preprimary convention in Worcester they gave their gubernatorial endorsement to Attorney General Fingold, who had become known as the state's leading crime buster. A few days later, in the middle of a hot July, Fingold collapsed in his office. After suspending his campaign for six weeks, the attorney general on the last day of August, against the advice of his doctors, appeared at a party rally in East Boston where he delivered a raking attack on the Furcolo administration. The next day he was dead, victim of a second heart attack.

With the primary only eight days away, the Republican State Committee was faced with the responsibility for selecting a new candidate for governor. Meeting in the Harvard Club of Boston, Senator Saltonstall and several other party leaders decided to give the nomination to Christian Herter, Jr., son of the former governor, who had for some time been regarded as the "white hope" of the Republican party in Massachusetts. Unfortunately, Herter's name was already on the ballot as candidate for attorney general, and the

State Committee counsel ruled that he could not legally be written in for the higher office. Support developed among some members of the nineteen-man executive committee for John A. Volpe, a newspaper publisher of Italian descent, who had been brought into the party leadership some years before by Sinclair Weeks; other committee members preferred to string along with Herter, despite the legal difficulties. The executive committee vote—ten for Volpe and nine for Herter—was so close that no recommendation was made. After two inconclusive ballots of the full committee, Herter withdrew, and the nomination was given to Charles Gibbons, last Republican speaker of the state House of Representatives.

Gibbons' campaign never got off the ground. Despite their internal troubles, the Democrats swept everything in sight in the fall election, winning clear majorities in both houses of the legislature and the Governor's Council (an antiquated holdover from colonial times, possessing veto power over many of the governor's actions) for the first time in Massachusetts history. Furcolo was re-elected by 172,000 votes, while Kennedy polled a mammoth majority of 875,000 against his opponent, Vincent J. Celeste, a little-known Boston attorney. Even young Herter lost by 85,000 to Edward McCormack, Jr., who had been named attorney general by the legislature at the time of Fingold's death.

Furcolo was even less successful with the new legislature, completely controlled by Democrats, than he had been with the last, in which the Republicans held the Senate. Not only was the sales tax again defeated by an overwhelming majority in the House, but also the governor's recommendations for an accelerated highway program, a consumers' counsel, revival of the crime commission, and a constitutional convention to modernize the state government were rejected. John Powers, now president of the Senate, and Lieutenant Governor Robert Murphy (the unsuccessful Democratic candidate for governor in 1954) led the assault on the sales tax. Powers did approve enactment of a withholding provision on the income tax, which sizably enlarged state revenues by catching thousands of citizens who had not formerly made a practice of filing annual returns.

The legislature, which each year seemed to wrangle later into the fall, was coming to be regarded as a kind of public scandal. Identification with the inertia and petty disputes on Beacon Hill contributed in 1959 to Powers' upset defeat in a race for mayor of Boston, a post which had long excited his ambition.

General displeasure with the legislature produced no popular reaction in Furcolo's favor. Graft in the Metropolitan District Commission led Attorney General McCormack to secure indictments against several state officials. Rumors of widespread corruption in the administration began to spread around the capital and to the state at large.

While most of the nation concentrated on John Kennedy's spectacular campaign for the presidency during the spring and summer of 1960, Massachusetts Democrats fell upon each other with normal bitterness and enthusiasm. Dever had died in 1958, while working on a Jefferson-Jackson Day dinner which he had planned as the kickoff for the Kennedy presidential drive; Curley the next year followed, mourned at an enormous funeral by the thousands of Boston Irish for whom his luster had never dimmed. The passing of the giants did nothing to quiet the turbulent waters of the Massachusetts Democracy. The 1960 preprimary convention in the Boston Arena produced the usual cries of treachery and threats of retribution. An amicable start was made by state Senator Powers who, "in the interest of party harmony," placed Furcolo in nomination for the United States Senate. Revolt quickly broke out among some of the delegates from Furcolo's own area, who supported young Thomas J. O'Connor, Jr., mayor of Springfield, for the Senate seat. Furcolo was given the party endorsement, but only after O'Connor had shown surprising strength. Lieutenant Governor Murphy, who had felt certain of being slated for governor, was rejected in favor of faithful Joe Ward (who had lost the primary for attorney general to McCormack in 1956). Murphy charged that he had been deprived of the gubernatorial endorsement on orders from Governor Furcolo.

The Republicans endorsed Saltonstall for re-election and John Volpe for governor. Ignoring O'Connor's entry against him in the Democratic primary, Furcolo expended large sums of money on printed literature, filmed television appearances, and the like in preparation for his campaign against Saltonstall. As primary day approached, some of the governor's advisors warned that O'Connor was gaining ground. Furcolo refused to be stirred. He later explained, "I knew that there was going to be a pretty good vote against me. But I figured that if an unknown could beat me, then Salty would be able to beat me easily." The vote against the governor was very good indeed: sufficient to provide O'Connor with a 52,000 vote majority in the primary. With the legislative session still droning on, Furcolo was a lame duck governor and a dead duck politician.

Ward edged to victory in the gubernatorial primary against Murphy and four other opponents. The resulting wounds, however, were sufficiently deep to induce many Democrats to desert to Volpe. The legislature also cooperated with the Republican candidate by remaining in session up to and past election day.

The 1960 electoral result in Massachusetts was even more confused than those of 1952 and 1956. Kennedy carried the state for president by a margin of 510,000, while Saltonstall was winning reelection by 308,000—a swing vote of no less than 409,000. Volpe also won easily, defeating Ward by 138,000. (The desertion from the Democratic candidate for governor was particularly strong in the Italian and Jewish wards of Boston. Volpe carried the North End and Roxbury wards, which were going heavily for Kennedy and had been carried in 1956 by Furcolo by, respectively, 80 and 63 per cent.) At the same time, Democrats won all other state offices and retained control of the House, Senate, and Governor's Council.

While the celebration over Kennedy's victory was still in progress, the legislature lightheartedly enacted an annual salary increase of $1,500 for each of its members, plus a $500 bonus for the extra-long 1960 session. Coupled with its large size—280 members—these raises made the Massachusetts legislature the most costly in the nation. In a generous mood, the legislature also approved salary increases totaling $7.5 million for other state employees, although all state jobholders had received across-the-board raises of $351 the previous March. On November 24, the legislature adjourned, having set a state record for longevity. A few weeks later, Furcolo, faced with a crisis in one of the major commuter railroads serving Boston, called the legislators back into special session. Sitting three days, the legislature ignored the governor's recommendations on the railroad problem, raised a few more salaries, and again adjourned. As one of his final official acts, Furcolo pronounced the special session "a dismal failure."

The example of a Massachusetts Democrat in the White House did little to inspire the next session of the legislature to more creative labors. Republican Governor Volpe was accorded the same cool treatment as Democratic Governor Furcolo. At the beginning of 1962, the legislature concerned itself with scolding one of its members who had charged on national television that collusion existed between some legislators and the state's gambling industry. The force of this chastisement was somewhat blunted by the revelation that a flourishing business in illegal off-track betting was being carried on within the state capitol itself.

The rising star of the Kennedy family, that Paul Dever used to talk about, rose still higher in Massachusetts in 1962. At the age of thirty, Edward ("Teddy") Kennedy, the president's youngest brother, announced his candidacy for the United States Senate. After winning the Democratic nomination in a bitterly fought primary against Eddie McCormack, Teddy Kennedy good humoredly polished off Henry Cabot Lodge's son, George, the Republican candidate, in the general. In a state where politics has customarily been a family affair, the Kennedy name appeared to have become a sure ticket to success. With little fanfare, Chub Peabody, a Yankee Democrat, edged to victory by a few thousand votes over Governor Volpe in the gubernatorial election. The legislature remained heavily Democratic.

In the first days of the new administration, Governor Peabody sought to purge Speaker John Thompson, a Democrat, from the leadership of the House of Representatives. Although he appeared to have the support of Teddy Kennedy, Peabody lost. The re-elected speaker thus owed little loyalty to the new governor.

At the main entrance to the old Bulfinch capitol on Beacon Hill stands a plaque honoring the service of an early governor of the Massachusetts Bay Colony, Thomas Dudley: "a Puritan gentleman, well-born, well-educated, well-rounded, self-consistent, austere, sensible, honest." Erected in 1933, the plaque seems to express the enduring respect felt by New Englanders—Irish and Italians as well as Yankees—for character of a strong and elevated, if somewhat unbending, type.

That the puritan ideal should be permitted permanently to languish in the state and city of its most perfect development seems unthinkable. There are, in fact, in the middle sixties, stirrings in favor of reform of state government, probably through a constitutional convention. Boston, after years of slumbering decay, has begun to undergo widespread physical renewal. The state economy, following a period of faltering adjustment to the flight of the textile industry, is reaping rich benefits from the technological brainpower concentrated in the two great universities in Cambridge. The work to be done remains enormous, but the spirit and determination, which once blazed the way to the establishment of a republic, are still in the New England air.*

* The death of John F. Kennedy was, of course, a national and international as well as a Massachusetts tragedy. The tradition of political gallantry (overlapping, but not identical with, puritan virtue) which was represented by the late president seems certain to be carried on by his own kinsmen and by others already on the political scene.

10

CALIFORNIA
THE NEW MEN

The journey across America ended in California. For the centuries-long trek of the Western European people, which began with the arrival of Hendrik Hudson in New York harbor in 1609, it was the last stop, the end of the trail, the completion of an adventure in human history. It was the promised land—and looked it—El Dorado, the Seven Cities of Cibola, the fulfillment of ancient dreams. It was also the end, as John Steinbeck has pointed out, to westering —to the quest that had guided men and women, of conflicting faiths and diverse origins, across a wild and beautiful continent, dedicated in common to the need and the impulse and the desire that the continent should be conquered, subdued to the enterprise of towns and the discipline of fields. At the shores of the Pacific Ocean, this quest ended. Whatever further adventures might lie ahead for humankind, the task of driving and hauling and dragging civilization across North America (Cumberland Gap, the Ohio Valley, the Great Plains, Fort Laramie, Great Salt Lake, the high Sierras) was finished.

At this place, where westering ended, sprang up a new society, belonging in part to the older American civilization, but possessing also some characteristics that appeared, at least superficially, separate and original. By 1950, this society had given birth to some odd growths: exotic pleasure palaces and wierd supernatural cults and "think tanks" and "a hundred suburbs in search of a city" (Los Angeles) and all manner of faith and nonfaith healers. (To many Northern Californians, most of these phenomena seem characteristic

Counties Carried by Republican Candidate for President, 1960

CALIFORNIA

of Southern California only. Perhaps. But it was San Francisco, not Los Angeles, that was claimed as happy hunting ground by that tribe of disengaged Bohemians of the late fifties, the beatniks.) Not the least strange of the manifestations of this new society have been the men whom it has raised to political power. Almost painfully conventional in appearance, these new leaders seem nevertheless to be products of a moral and cultural atmosphere significantly different from that of the rest of the country. Whatever their strengths or weaknesses, they and their successors are certain to play decisive roles in shaping the future history of the United States. Possessing a technology that has made it the arsenal of space-age democracy, continuing to promulgate its culture through the motion picture and television media, California, in the middle sixties, has achieved the status of most heavily populated state in the nation. Its leaders—only six of whom had advanced to federal cabinet rank before 1950—will henceforth exercise political influence of the broadest possible scope.

When the first white men, Spaniards, arrived on the golden coast of California in 1542, they found a placid Indian civilization, maintained by tribes with none of the fierceness and little of the valor of the Apache, the Iroquois, or the Sioux. The Spaniards and their Mexican successors settled down to a long and more-or-less peaceful reign, which ended in 1846 when the United States acquired California as a result of the war with Mexico.

Achieving statehood in 1850, California was "emphatically Democratic" until the Civil War. In the 1860's, the railroads arrived, establishing a dominance over state politics which they did not yield until after the turn of the century. The only important opposition to the railroad tycoons came from the short-lived Workingmen's party, led by Dennis Kearney of San Francisco, which as its major objective sought exclusion of Chinese immigrants from the United States. After passage of the Chinese Exclusion Act in 1882, the railroads resumed their harmonious sway. (Years later, in 1913, the Japanese Exclusion Act was passed over the vigorous opposition of President Woodrow Wilson and the Japanese government. In 1943, the ban against the Chinese was lifted, followed by termination of the exclusion of Japanese in 1952. The two Oriental peoples were subsequently provided with quotas for immigration based on the proportions of their national descendants in the current population. The former bans, in force for several decades, had of course fixed these proportions at extremely low levels, so no large-scale immigration of Mongolians was in prospect. By 1960, persons of Oriental descent accounted for only 8 per cent of the population of San Francisco; smaller colonies existed in the San Joaquin Valley around Stockton and Fresno, in Los Angeles, and in the Imperial Valley in the southeastern corner of the state.)

In 1910, the railroads' political control was at last successfully challenged by the Lincoln-Roosevelt League, led by Governor Hiram W. Johnson. Two years later, Johnson ran for vice president of the United States on the Progressive (Bull Moose) party ticket. Johnson remained as governor until 1917, at which time he began the first of five terms in the United States Senate. During his years in Sacramento, the state capital, he put into effect almost all of the reforms commonly associated with the Progressive Era. It was Johnson's conviction that many of the things wrong with state government could be traced to partisan politics. He therefore set up a virtually airtight merit system for state personnel that deprived the party organizations of manpower and instituted a system of cross-filing in primary elections that almost completely eliminated organization control of party candidates. City and county officials were elected without party designation. Most important, Johnson initiated a popular dislike for political parties as such—a tendency to view the party label as bearing little relation to a man's political philosophy or competence. Though originated under progressive auspices, this attitude seems over the long run to have had a conservative effect, both because it obviously favored incumbent office holders and because it gave some advantage to business and professional leaders who were likely to enjoy superior visibility in their communities.

Throughout this period, the Republican party, of which Johnson remained a nominal member, was in control of the state. The first Democratic governor in the twentieth century was elected in 1938. Democrats formed a majority in the popularly apportioned state House of Representatives from 1937 to 1941, but the state Senate, apportioned on a county representation system which strongly penalizes the more heavily populated counties, particularly Los Angeles, was not taken over by the Democrats until 1957.

From the time it was acquired by the United States, California was the destination for an ever-growing wave of migrants from other parts of the country. Population grew from less than 100,000 in 1848 to more than 10,000,000 a century later. (Between 1950 and 1960, population increased an additional 48 per cent to more than 15,000,-000.) Around the turn of the century, new arrivals came largely from the rural areas of the Middle West; the Deep South and the Northeast were also well represented. After World War I, the flow expanded from Pennsylvania, the Dakotas, and the northern Middle West, all areas which had begun to suffer economic decline. The thirties brought Okies, Arkies, and other former inhabitants of the Dust Bowl. During and after World War II, migrants came increasingly from two major sources: the cities of New York, Pennsylvania, and other Eastern and Midwestern states; and the Negro population of the South. Migration northward from Mexico also grew, so that during the fifties Spanish-speaking Americans totaled an estimated 10 per cent of the state's population. High in the Sierras, along the state's western border, Indians, placid as ever, were still significantly numerous in three sparsely populated counties.

Partly because of the change in the sources of migration and partly because of general political and economic conditions in the nation during the New Deal period, the Democrats in the thirties overtook and surpassed the Republicans in voter registration. By 1950, this advantage had been established at about 60 per cent Democrat to 40 per cent Republican, a proportion at which it was to remain more or less fixed during the coming decade.

After a few victories in the late thirties, the Democrats were unable to translate their overwhelming lead in registration into political control of the state. This was partly due to the over-all superiority of Republican leadership, partly to the nonpartisan tradition, and largely to the remarkable personality of the Republican governor from 1943 to 1953, Earl Warren.

Although he normally avoided identification with other candidates on the Republican ticket and made no effort to build up a partisan organization, Warren became so much of a California institution that his popularity undoubtedly helped to elect other members of his party. Developing a collaborative government in many ways similar to that which Thomas Dewey instituted in New York, Warren was successful in drawing much of the sting out of ethnic and economic differences which in other states contributed to the strength of the Democratic party. Normally regarded as a liberal, he remained on good terms with many conservative political and business leaders. When Hiram Johnson died in 1945, Warren appointed William F. Knowland, son of the publisher of the conservative *Oakland Tribune,* to his seat in the United States Senate.

In his first race for governor, Warren utilized the services of an adroit public relations team, Clem Whitaker and Leone Baxter. Though in later years he sometimes ran on his own, the three-term governor helped initiate the tendency to turn over the entire management of campaigns to public relations firms, performing many of the functions commonly handled by party organizations in other states. At the same time, he took some of the circus out of California politics. The carnival-like campaigns of the 1930's gave way to a more

Figure 10. California Battle Graph, 1948-62

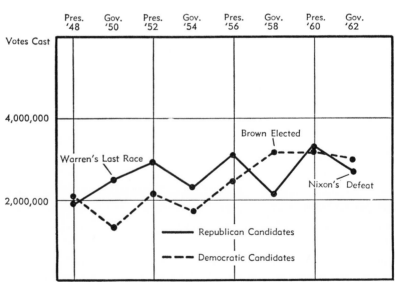

folksy approach, in which candidates seemed to strive to give the impression that they had just stepped out of an advertisement for a medium-priced automobile. The large and attractive Warren family was symbolic of the spirit of togetherness that settled over the state's politics—partisan and ideological differences were put aside by the great majority as being rather gauche and rude.

Perhaps because of his preference for a snug, uncomplicated kind of politics, Warren never looked with great favor upon the rise of an aspiring young congressman from Los Angeles, Richard M. Nixon. In 1950, only four years after first being elected to Congress, Nixon determined to run for the seat held by United States Senator Sheridan Downey, a Democrat left over from the wild and woolly days of the 1930's. Formidable obstacles stood in his way. Though Downey's health and popularity were declining, numerous Democrats were eager to take his place. In the Republican party, too, candidates, some of them veterans of the political wars, were plentiful. As assets, Nixon had a national reputation gained from his part, as a member of the House Un-American Activities Committee, in the investigation of Alger Hiss; a skillfully constructed campaign organization; and, as he liked to say, "the will to win." As was his custom, Governor Warren, running for re-election, remained aloof from all other contests.

Also seeking a new term in 1950 was Lieutenant Governor Goodwin J. Knight. After announcing that he would oppose Warren for governor, Knight, a Los Angeles attorney and former hard-rock miner, reconsidered and decided to run again for the office he had held since 1946. To his chagrin, he found himself opposed by Ray Darby, supervisor of Los Angeles County. In Knight's view, Darby had originally planned to seek the Senate seat, but had been bulldozed by Nixon into running for lieutenant governor instead.

The California Republican Assembly, a group of volunteer party workers which had been set up for slate-making purposes in place of the ineffective regular party organization, overwhelmingly supported Warren and Knight. Nixon had a much tighter squeeze. By a single vote, he won recommendation by CRA's crucial candidate's committee over former–Lieutenant Governor Frederick F. Houser.

The Democrats, meanwhile, were engaged in a brawling internecine battle of their own. Sheridan Downey, after attempting to campaign for re-election without leaving Washington, bowed to his doctor's advice and announced his retirement. The principal remaining contestants for the Senate seat were Manchester, Boddy, editor and publisher of the *Los Angeles Daily News,* and Congresswoman Helen Gahagan Douglas. Boddy opened fire on Mrs. Douglas for her "left-wing" voting record. Senator Downey, sidelined but still vocal, joined in criticizing his colleague for her votes against Truman Doctrine loans to Turkey and Greece. Douglas headquarters responded by accusing Boddy of conducting a "red smear" campaign.

Under cross-filing, the California primary had by this time been converted into a trial run for the general election. All major candidates entered in both party primaries. Warren, who had won both party nominations in 1946, was overwhelmingly renominated by the Republicans and in the Democratic primary carried twelve of fifty-eight counties, including San Francisco, against the leading Democratic candidate, James Roosevelt, son of the late president. In the Senatorial contest, Nixon and Mrs. Douglas won the nominations of their respective parties. Boddy, who proved lacking in popular support except in a few mountain counties, ran behind Nixon in the Democratic primary. Although Nixon failed to carry any counties against Mrs. Douglas in the Democratic test, his total vote in the two primaries was well ahead of the congresswoman, a sign, according to most analysts, that he would be victorious in November. Goodwin Knight defeated Darby and two Democrats to win the nomination of both parties for lieutenant governor. A contest in the Republican primary for attorney general resulted in nomination of former–Republican State Chairman Edward S. Shattuck, who had been endorsed by the CRA, over incumbent Fred Napoleon Howser, whose office had become involved in scandal. The bitterness of the struggle among Republicans for this office lent encouragement to the campaign of the Democratic nominee, Edmund G. ("Pat") Brown, district attorney of San Francisco, who had lost to Howser in 1946.

The combined effects of Johnson's laws and Warren's personality had reduced party divisions in California almost below the level of visibility. In a very general way, San Francisco and the north were Democratic, while Los Angeles and the south were Republican.

In practice, this meant no more than that attractive Democrats tended to do a bit better in the north than in the south, while the opposite was true for Republicans. Regional loyalties, however, often overcame partisan preferences: Warren, a northerner, ran ahead of James Roosevelt, a southerner, in the 1950 Democratic primary in two of four San Francisco Bay Area counties.

More than 40 per cent of the state's population was concentrated in the sprawling Los Angeles metropolitan area, including Los Angeles and Orange Counties. About 20 per cent more was piled into the San Francisco Bay Area. A third metropolitan area, San Diego, strongly Republican, accounted for an additional 7 per cent. The Bay Area had arrived at a level of steady but gradual growth by 1950. The other two metropolitan areas were at the beginning of a decade of dynamic population expansion.

Beyond the coastal mountains separating the three metropolitan areas from the rest of the state lay rich farm country, also rapidly filling up. In the fertile Sacramento and San Joaquin Valleys, running, respectively, north and south from San Francisco Bay, the canning industry and other light industries had partially taken up the unemployment slack from the increasingly mechanized farms. At the southern end of the San Joaquin Valley, around Bakersfield, petroleum production had created boom conditions comparable to those of West Texas. Though Earl Warren captured four counties in the two inland valleys in the 1950 Democratic primary, both tended to be more Democratic than the rest of the state. (In ten out of sixteen valley counties, the population was more than 20 per cent foreign stock, mostly Mexican, Italian, and German. Roman Catholics outnumbered Protestants in all but four counties—three of which were considerably more Republican than their neighbors.) South of the Tehachapi Mountains in the southeastern corner of the state were three counties, San Bernardino, Riverside, and Imperial, formerly arid desert but now crossed by rich tracts of irrigated farmland. With Roman Catholic Mexicans and members of fundamentalist Protestant sects both heavily represented in their populations, these counties were normally Republican.

Of the state's remaining thirty-two counties, only nine had populations exceeding 50,000. All nine of these medium-sized counties were strung along the coast from Los Angeles to the Bay Area and from San Francisco to the Oregon Border. The coastal counties, devoted to agriculture, timber, fishing, and the tourist trade, were usually Republican. The smaller counties, mostly in rough and mountainous country, tended toward the Democrats, perhaps as a holdover from the days when the Republicans had been identified with the railroads and the cities.

Following the 1950 primary, interest centered on the race for the Senatorial seat between Richard Nixon and Helen Gahagan Douglas. The Republican candidate, taking up the attack that Boddy and Downey had begun, charged that his opponent had a voting record similar to that of Vito Marcantonio, "who admittedly follows the Communist line in the House of Representatives." In addition to Mrs. Douglas' votes against the Truman Doctrine, he cited her opposition to an investigation of purchase of American patents by the Soviet Union and her support of the drive to abolish the House Un-American Activities Committee. Nixon's manager, Murray Chotiner, flooded the state with pink circulars—the subsequently famous pink slips—comparing the voting record of the Democratic candidate and Congressman Marcantonio.

Mrs. Douglas responded by dubbing Nixon "Tricky Dicky" and predicting that his election would result in an economic depression. Nixon, she said, had voted with Marcantonio—"who follows the Communist party line"—on foreign policy issues, whereas she had voted with the New York congressman on domestic issues only. The hatreds aroused by this exchange were to follow Nixon through the rest of his career. At the time, however, the controversy undoubtedly assured his election. Casualty lists had begun to appear from the Korean War and the charge that Mrs. Douglas had failed to oppose Communism with vigor certainly destroyed whatever chance she may have had. Several leading Democrats, including Emmet Hagerty, later San Francisco Democratic chairman, and George Creel, Woodrow Wilson's public information chief in World War I, announced their support for Nixon.

Warren, who had angered Nixon by failing to endorse any of his Republican running mates, rolled up a majority of almost 65 per cent against James Roosevelt. At the same time, Nixon, carrying all of the south, most of the Bay Area, and all but six northern counties, defeated Mrs. Douglas by a majority of almost 60 per cent. The only victorious Democrat at the state level was Pat Brown, elected attorney general over Edward Shattuck, who had conducted an inept campaign and had suffered from lack of Warren's endorsement.

Following their 1950 defeat, the California Democrats divided into bitterly warring factions. Glenn M. Anderson, a liberal, was named state chairman, but valley Democrats, some of whom had supported Warren and Nixon, joined with the Boddy faction to elect Fred Trott, a conservative, as vice chairman. State Senator Hugh M. Burns, Fresno, urged that Roosevelt resign as national committee-man and declared that the party leadership was dominated by "left-wing crackpots." Vice Chairman Trott called for selection of a "middle-of-the-road Democrat" as candidate for United States senator in 1952 "so there will be no talk of right and left wingers in the campaign."

A drive in the legislature to tighten controls on lobbyists turned up the fact that Arthur H. Samish, a free-wheeling agent for liquor and other interests, had contributed $5,000 to Brown's campaign for attorney general. Brown denied any knowledge of the contribution. The 1951 legislative session was further enlivened by controversy over apportionment of California's seven new seats in the United States Congress. The eventually approved apportionment scheme, designed to elect a maximum number of Republicans, came to be known as "watering," after Laughlin E. Waters, chairman of the assembly reapportionment committee.

The state Democratic organization was all but demolished by events of the 1952 presidential campaign. A national convention delegation, pledged to President Harry Truman, was entered by party leaders in the spring primary. When Truman withdrew his name, a frantic attempt was made to persuade Adlai Stevenson to permit the delegation to fly his standard. When this effort failed, the delegation was pledged to Attorney General Brown as a favorite son. Several of the original Truman delegation, including James Roosevelt, switched their support to Estes Kefauver, who had entered his own delegation in the primary. The result was overwhelming victory for the Kefauver delegation. Allying with the liberal faction, the Kefauver supporters were subsequently able to take over much of the party machinery.

Earl Warren, meanwhile, had been staging his own bid for the presidency. Although telling friends that it was an American tradition to nominate a returning war hero for president, he regarded himself as a "long–long shot possibility" if Eisenhower and Taft should deadlock at the convention. During the legislative session, the governor spent three days of the week in Sacramento, one on the road, and three campaigning in the Wisconsin primary. He won a few delegates in Wisconsin, but later lost to Eisenhower in Oregon. In the California primary, a conservative delegation, pledged to former-Congressman Thomas H. Werdel, was easily defeated by the Warren slate.

Shortly before the convention opened, Warren, at the Governors' Conference in Houston, signed a round-robin telegram from Republican governors urging "fair play" in settling the dispute over seating of rival Taft and Eisenhower delegations from Texas and Georgia. The telegram had the effect of tipping the scales in favor of the Eisenhower delegations, eventually resulting in a first ballot nomination for the "returning war hero." Warren realized when he signed the telegram that it would probably have a decisive influence on the nomination.

Returning from Houston to California, Warren joined the state delegation which was just leaving by special train for the convention. At Denver, Nixon, who had been in Chicago observing pre-convention maneuvers, came aboard. After talking with the governor, he toured the train, promoting Eisenhower's candidacy on the ground that there was no chance for Warren. (Before the convention, Nixon had sent a questionnaire to 20,000 California Republicans asking who their second choice would be if it became apparent that Warren could not win.) When the convention balloted for president, California's vote was cast solidly for Warren by the governor's close personal friend, Senator Knowland, chairman of the delegation. After Eisenhower's nomination was assured, Knowland, who would probably have been selected for vice president had Taft headed the ticket, sought the attention of the chair, apparently wishing to change California's vote to the winner. He was ignored, evidently on purpose, by Congressman Joseph Martin, permanent chairman of the convention. Warren was not invited to participate in the hotel room huddle which that evening chose Nixon as Republican candidate for vice president. The governor felt that Nixon owed the nomination in part to his earlier efforts to soften up the California delegation for Eisenhower. The feeling between the two men, never warm, hardened into fixed dislike.

Following the convention, Warren stumped energetically, mostly in labor districts in the East and Middle West, for the Republican ticket. The smoothly functioning Eisenhower campaign was momentarily jolted by disclosure that Nixon, while a senator, had been beneficiary of an $18,000 fund raised by California Republicans to help defray the cost of his quest for national attention. The vice presidential candidate responded, more or less successfully, with his celebrated Checkers speech (so called for his reference to the Nixon dog) on radio and television. Though the speech won him the sympathy of millions of Americans—and persuaded Eisenhower that he had not become a political liability—it placed him in a defensive position from which he never after seemed quite able to escape. (Years later, when Nixon was running for governor of California, a journalist reported frequently hearing the comment, "Why does Nixon always have something to explain?")

In November, the Eisenhower-Nixon ticket carried California by more than 56 per cent of the vote. At the same time, a referendum to abolish cross-filing was narrowly defeated, while a Republican counterproposal to place the name of each candidate's party on the primary ballot was approved. A referendum repealing tax exemptions for parochial schools was defeated by only 77,000 votes out of nearly 5,000,000 cast on the proposition. (While Roman Catholics in 1957 accounted for 22 per cent of the population of California compared to only 15 per cent enrolled Protestants and 6 per cent Jews, considerable latent Protestant sentiment reportedly existed, particularly in the two inland valleys.)

Although Adlai Stevenson fell far short of carrying the state, he did succeed in revitalizing the liberal element in the Democratic party. Early in 1953, Democratic State Chairman George Miller called a meeting to discuss, "What's Wrong with the Democratic

Party?" at Asilomar, a YWCA recreation center on the Pacific Coast between Los Angeles and San Francisco. To the surprise of Miller and Allan Cranston, idea man for the project, about 500 persons, mostly Stevensonian "eggheads," attended. Cranston presented a plan for the organization of Democratic clubs and councils which would endorse candidates and thrash out issues between meetings of the legally required party conventions.

While Cranston and Miller were completing their plans, another effort, "Dime a Day for Democrats," had been initiated in the Los Angeles area by Culbert L. Olson, governor of California in the New Deal period. The two groups met at the same time in Fresno in November, 1953, and a marriage of convenience, somewhat to Olson's annoyance, was arranged. Cranston was elected president of the combined organization, which was titled the California Democratic Council (CDC).

Democratic prospects in the state were further improved by the appointment of Governor Warren, following a hurried visit to Sacramento by United States Attorney General Herbert Brownell, as chief justice of the United States. Before his appointment, Warren had expressed the view that the Republican controlled legislature had "failed to keep pace with the needs of the State." Conservative Republicans, expecting a more responsive attitude from Goodwin Knight, who in 1950 had criticized Warren as too liberal and too friendly to labor, were stunned when the new governor became an outspoken champion of organized labor. In Washington, meanwhile, William Knowland, majority leader of the Senate since the death of Taft, was emerging as a national spokesman for conservatism.

The CDC, at the instigation of State Chairman Miller, in 1954 gave its support to Richard P. Graves, executive director of the League of California Cities, for governor. Graves switched his registration from Republican to Democrat only a few weeks before receiving the CDC endorsement. Although denounced by former-Governor Olson as "not a true Democrat," he was victorious in the Democratic primary. For the first time in years, a full slate of Democratic candidates was fielded in the general election. Party designation on the primary ballot, coupled with the efforts of the CDC, deprived many Republicans of the two-party nominations which they had formerly received. Indeed, the only two-party endorsement at the state level was that given to Attorney General Brown, who defeated Fred Napoleon Howser, seeking a comeback, in the Republican primary.

It was not, however, to be an entirely happy year for Democrats. Two of their candidates for Congress, James Roosevelt and Robert L. Condon, an incumbent, were publicly disowned by Democratic National Chairman Stephen Mitchell—the former because of his sensational divorce trial and the latter because he had been banned by the Army as a security risk from an atomic test in Nevada. Mitchell's declaration was followed by a more mildly worded disavowal from Attorney General Brown. State Chairman Miller, on the other hand, suggested that Mitchell "keep his nose out of California politics."

A struggle broke out in the Republican party for the state vice chairmanship. Under the law that alternated the party chairmanship between the north and the south, the vice chairman chosen in 1954 would normally become chairman in 1956—a presidential year. Governor Knight proposed for the post Howard Ahmanson, a millionaire savings-and-loan executive, who had contributed heavily to Knight's campaigns. Ahmanson also received the support of Senators Knowland and Thomas Kuchel (the latter, a two-term state controller, having been named by Warren to Nixon's seat when the latter became vice president). In a bold move to take control of the party, Nixon entered Ray Arbuthnot, a wealthy cattle man, as opposition candidate for the vice chairmanship. A group of congressmen, acting for Nixon, flew from Washington to California to bolster the drive for Arbuthnot. Knight issued a bitter statement attacking Murray Chotiner, also operating at the convention for the vice president. Only through a dramatic appeal by Senator Knowland from the convention floor was Ahmanson selected and party control preserved in the hands of the governor. (As matters turned out, Ahmanson had suffered a heart attack by 1956 and declined to seek the chairmanship.)

Carrying the burden of the national campaign for the Republican party in 1954, Nixon, by reviving charges that the Truman administration had been "soft on Communism," further contributed to the enthusiastic loathing with which liberals had come to regard him. Perhaps in response to the concentrated hatred of which he was the object, his own air of self-righteous belligerence began to grow. Speaking at San Mateo, near San Francisco, he ordered several henchmen to march to the front of the auditorium a heckler, whom he then lectured in stern language and tones. The "hate Nixon" phenomenon, stronger in California than anywhere else in the nation except Washington, D.C., was in part a reflex of the confused liberal conscience of the time, but in part was certainly provoked by the vice president himself. Had he been the product of an older and more settled political tradition, Nixon might have lasted out the liberals' scorn and won the respect of the nation on grounds more firm than his wife's "good Republican cloth coat." (He might also never have been elected vice president.) Instead, he tended to become what the liberals most wanted him to be—humorless, devious, sometimes misleading. The sincerity of his desire to serve his party and his country (not necessarily in that order) could hardly be questioned, but the means which he chose to render that service continued to cause disquiet to many who might otherwise have wished him well.

In the California gubernatorial election Knight, with strong support from organized labor, easily defeated Richard Graves. Losing only eight valley counties, Alameda County (Oakland), and eight small northern counties, the Republican candidate received 56 per cent of the total vote (8 per cent less than had been given Warren in 1950). Kuchel was returned to the Senate over Congressman Samuel Yorty, Los Angeles, who had attracted some notice by mailing out four million pieces of campaign literature, all under his congressional frank, at a cost to the federal government of $120,000. Congressman Condon was defeated, but Roosevelt, running in Yorty's old district, a section of Los Angeles not famous for an overly critical attitude toward human frailty, won 60 per cent of the vote.

Safely installed in the governorship, Knight began to listen sympathetically to suggestions that he might replace Nixon as Republican candidate for vice president in 1956. Harry Finks, a vice president of the AFL-CIO and close associate of the governor, predicted that labor would oppose Eisenhower nationally if Nixon were again his running mate. Other emissaries journeyed from Sacramento, exploring the possibility of a Knight candidacy.

On the Democratic side, Adlai Stevenson and Estes Kefauver, both of whom had contributed to the resurgence of liberalism in the state four years before, appealed for support for their presidential candidacies at the 1956 CDC convention in Fresno. Although no endorsement was made, 80 per cent of the delegates signed a petition favoring Stevenson. State Senator Richard Richards, Los Angeles, was endorsed for the United States Senate over Sam Yorty, who wished to try again. The former congressman treated the delegates to an address in which he charged that the convention was "rigged, stacked, packed, and wired."

Stevenson's delegation in the California presidential primary included Attorney General Brown (who had observed the 1952 convention from the gallery, after losing in the primary to Kefauver) and most of the important party leaders. Former-Governor Olson and pension promoter George McLain were among the few well-known names on the Kefauver slate. Both presidential candidates campaigned vigorously across the state. The result was overwhelming victory for Stevenson, leading shortly thereafter to Kefauver's withdrawal from the national contest.

After Stevenson was nominated at Chicago, the California delegation discovered itself to be divided among supporters of Kefauver, Hubert Humphrey, and John Kennedy for the vice presidency. As the excitement mounted in the hectic balloting, a San Francisco delegate, Ben Swig, owner of the Fairmont Hotel, urged that the delegation switch solidly to Kennedy. Although Kennedy's strength in California increased on the next ballot, Brown, at the climatic moment in the race, announced California's vote as almost three to one for Kefauver. The manner in which the attorney general arrived at this count was never made entirely clear. Kefauver, in any event, was nominated.

The Republican national convention was held in 1956 in San Francisco's Cow Palace. When the California delegation met, just before the convention opened, in the Sheraton-Palace Hotel, Governor Knight refused to withdraw his opposition to the renomination of Nixon for vice president. With the backing of Senator Knowland,

Nixon supporters rammed through a resolution binding the delegation to vote for the vice president as a unit. The Knowland-Nixon forces also won a contest with a Knight slate for party offices. Not until President Eisenhower, shortly before the balloting was to begin, announced that he favored Nixon for another term, did Knight agree to support the vice president. As chairman of the delegation, Governor Knight a few hours later cast California's unanimous vote for the man whom he had hoped to replace.

The Eisenhower-Nixon ticket again carried California in November, by a margin about 1 per cent less than that of 1952. The Democratic cause had not been greatly aided by a six planeload blitz of out-of-state senators and governors, one of whom, Governor George Leader of Pennsylvania, generously suggested that after the election Vice President Nixon might be retired to "an offshore island," evidently referring to the federal prison on Alcatraz. While losing the presidency, the Democrats gained seats in both houses of the state legislature. A tie in the state Senate was later broken when two Republicans joined the Democrats, permitting the latter party to organize the upper house for the first time in the twentieth century. Senator Burns of Fresno, who himself had bolted the Democrats to support Warren for governor in 1950, was elected president of the Senate.

In the new legislature, Governor Knight immediately encountered resistance to his efforts to settle a long-standing dispute over terms on which surplus northern water could be channeled to the thirsty south. Southern Democrats and Republicans insisted on a constitutional amendment guaranteeing the south's permanent access to northern water. Northern legislators refused to approve the amendment. A new Department of Water Resources was eventually authorized, but the legislature refused to appropriate funds to implement a projected California Water Plan so long as Knight remained governor.

Early in 1957, California politics were thrown into turmoil by Senator Knowland's announcement that he would not seek re-election to the Senate in 1958. Having never quite forgotten his closeness to the vice presidency in 1952—had Taft been elected with Knowland as vice president, Knowland would have been president in 1953—the conservative leader had evidently been impressed by the fact that in the twentieth century eight governors but only one senator had been nominated for president. (Very possibly, this calculation failed to take into consideration the increased importance of the Senate in American politics. In 1960, most important candidates for president, including the eventual winner, were senators.)

Knight hastily demanded that Knowland "stay out of the governor's race in California." The senator, who had won the nominations of both parties in 1952, gave no sign that he intended to comply with this directive. Speaking at a Sacramento Chamber of Commerce gathering, Knowland announced his support for a right-to-work law for California. A poll, commissioned a few months before by Southern California businessmen, had indicated both popularity for right-to-work and an advantage for Knowland if he should contest with Knight for the Republican nomination for governor.

Delighted by this division in the enemy camp, Democrats sensed that the governorship was at last within their reach. Efforts were made to persuade Attorney General Brown to accept the Democratic nomination. Brown, who had previously declined to seek the governorship against Warren, felt no great enthusiasm for a race against the still-popular Goodwin Knight. In August, 1957, Congressman Clair Engle, representing a safe district in the northern part of the state, agreed at a meeting of state Democratic leaders to run for Knowland's Senate seat on condition that Brown become a candidate for governor. An ultimatum was served on the attorney general, giving him until September to make up his mind. Brown took off for Coconut Island, near the Island of Oahu, to discuss matters with Edwin W. Pauley, a close personal friend and heavy contributor to former Democratic campaigns. Pauley, who had been appointed Regent of the University of California by Knight, had earlier advised Brown to run for the Senate rather than oppose the incumbent governor. Surveying the situation as it had begun to develop, the two men ultimately agreed that Brown should seek the governorship.

Making a swing around the state during the fall, Knowland began to attack "labor bosses," whom he charged were "out to liquidate" him from politics. Though still not an announced candidate, the senator clearly was planning a race for governor. His strategy was simple:

by embracing right-to-work, he would win every antilabor vote in the state; his opponents, Knight and Brown, who under cross-filing would run against him in both primaries, would divide the labor vote. The result would be certain victory over Knight in the Republican primary and a greater total vote than Brown's in the two primaries —still regarded as a long step toward final victory. Some Knowland strategists even believed that there was a serious possibility that the senator could capture both nominations. Nothing was farther from Knowland's intention than to force Knight out of the contest for governor. From the start, his campaign was based on the assumption that there would be three major candidates.

Other powerful persons in the Republican party viewed matters differently. In San Francisco for a speaking engagement in October, Vice President Nixon hinted that there would be only one Republican candidate for governor. Important party contributors, including Ahmanson and Norman Chandler, publisher of the *Los Angeles Times,* began to urge Knight to run for the Senate instead of seeking re-election. Mrs. Norman ("Buffy") Chandler added her formidable energies to the pressures building up on Knight.

The governor, nevertheless, declared himself a candidate for a new term. Ill with the flu, he departed for Arizona after promising to stay in the race "come hell, high water, pressure from friends, or threats of withholding of campaign funds." A few days later, word was leaked from the governor's desert retreat that he had agreed to give up the governorship and become a candidate for the Senate.

Vacationing in Greece, George Christopher, mayor of San Francisco, who had announced that he would run for the Senate as a Republican after being assured that Knight would not seek the seat, accused the governor of a "double-cross." Surrounded by his Greek kinsmen, who had been overjoyed by his candidacy, Christopher affirmed that he, at least, was in to the finish.

Returning from Arizona, Knight flew to Washington where he met briefly with President Eisenhower in the White House and Vice President Nixon at the Capitol. After leaving Nixon, he announced that "in the interest of party harmony and to aid the Eisenhower administration" he would run for the Senate seat to be vacated by Knowland. The switch, he said, was "by my own decision;" he denied that there had been "threat of any kind" by any Republican leaders or his financial backers. Back in California, Knowland had already announced his candidacy for governor.

Brown, who also by now was an announced candidate, assailed Knight as a "confused and wavering incumbent deserted by his own party." Knowland, he said, was a "reactionary who views the State's highest office as only a pawn in presidential power politics."

The CDC, meeting in Fresno early in 1958, unanimously endorsed Brown for governor. After accepting the endorsement, Brown, who apparently had no foresight of the general Democratic sweep in the making, left the convention without taking any part in selection of the rest of the ticket. Congressman Engle was rather narrowly endorsed for the Senate over Peter Odegard, a member of the University of Califorina faculty and an outspoken liberal. Otherwise, a highly liberal slate was chosen, including Glenn Anderson for lieutenant governor and Allan Cranston, father of CDC, for controller. Resolutions were passed condemning the right-to-work initiative and advocating trade with Red China, repeal of the Taft-Hartley Law, and ultimate repeal of the state sales tax.

In the June primary, Brown ran more than 500,000 votes ahead of Knowland in the two primaries. Knowland's chances of overcoming this lead in November were regarded as practically nonexistent. In the Republican primary for senator, Mayor Christopher, who had remained true to his word to stay in the fight, polled almost three-fourths as many votes as Knight.

Convinced that Knowland could not win, Knight set out to try to save his own political career. Billboards, sponsored by the Retail Clerks Union, appeared supporting Brown for governor and Knight for senator. Attempts by Knowland to present a façade of unity were rejected by his running mate. At no time after the primary did Knight urge Knowland's election. The split between the two became final when Mrs. Knowland, who had been energetically campaigning for her husband, sent out some two hundred letters castigating Knight and suggesting that the governor had a "spaghetti spine." Knight responded by agreeing with Brown that Knowland wished to be elected governor only so he could run for president.

The Democratic campaign was momentarily upset when the Young Democrats of California, meeting in Hollywood, passed a resolution demanding immediate withdrawal of American troops from Lebanon. (President Eisenhower had intervened to prevent civil war in the Middle Eastern nation in July.) Brown repudiated the resolution, declaring it a "mistake." The Republican candidates, intent on quarreling with each other, failed to take advantage of the opening.

Despite the opposition of Knight and other members of the Republican ticket to the right-to-work initiative, which was to be voted on in the general election, Knowland made it the center of his campaign. Brown ignored Knowland's invitation to debate the issue, but used it to solidify organized labor behind the Democratic party. The almost nonpartisan nature of California politics, carefully cultivated over the years by Earl Warren and other Republican leaders, was practically destroyed in a single summer. Democrats managed at last to achieve the working-class identification which long had eluded them.

The result was a massive Democratic victory in November. Brown received 60 per cent of the vote, carrying fifty-four out of fifty-eight counties. (The exceptions were two southern coastal counties and two mountain counties.) Knight and most other statewide Republican candidates were defeated by similar margins. Democrats achieved majorities of fourteen votes in both houses of the legislature. Right-to-work was rejected by more than two to one, although the initiative carried several normally Republican coastal and southern counties that Knowland lost.

As governor, Brown pushed through the legislature increases in personal income, business, and luxury taxes, which enabled him not only to eliminate the deficit which had beset the last Republican administration (expenditures exceeded revenue by $200 million in 1958), but also substantially to increase the state's services. A Fair Employment Practices Commission was established and an Office of Consumer Counsel was created. Hiram Johnson's cross-filing law was at last abolished. The vexing water problem was carried a long way toward solution, through Brown's success in overcoming objections of northern legislators to an almost $2 billion water distribution program. At the same time, the governor persuaded southern representatives to give up their earlier insistence on a constitutional amendment prohibiting the north from cutting off the water at some future date. A bond issue, specifying only vaguely where water projects were to be constructed, was approved.

The only major issue on which the legislature failed to follow the governor was his request for a law abolishing capital punishment. This defeat led to Brown's highly publicized anguish and vacillation over the fate of Caryl Chessman, a convicted kidnapper and attempted rapist, who died, after eight stays of execution, in the gas chamber at San Quentin prison in May, 1960.

Although he had denied any presidential ambitions before the 1958 election, Brown admitted on a national television program a few days after defeating Knowland that he would run for president if his party wanted him. During the next two years, the governor at times told friends that others no better qualified than he had aspired to the presidency. As the quadrennial conventions approached, Brown declared to reporters, "Many people want me to be more than just a favorite-son candidate."

The people to whom the governor alluded did not include John F. Kennedy, by then embarked on his remorseless quest for convention delegates. From November, 1956, until July, 1960, the Massachusetts senator made seventeen trips to California, not, as he liked to say, "to look for butterflies." Hubert Humphrey and Stuart Symington also scouted the California terrain. A CDC boomlet began for Chester Bowles. Even Adlai Stevenson, officially not a candidate, turned up in Sacramento to have pancakes with Governor Brown.

Meeting in a Carmel church sanctuary, ten state Democratic leaders put together a convention delegation, pledged to Brown as a favorite son and including supporters of all major and several minor presidential candidates. A poll of five key districts in Los Angeles County, commissioned by the Kennedy organization, showed that in a primary Kennedy would decisively defeat Brown, then in strong disfavor for his handling of the Chessman case. Kennedy placed the results of this poll on the Senate desk of Clair Engle in Washington. Frightened by the prospect of a bruising intraparty battle, Engle and Congressman John Shelley, one of Kennedy's earliest California supporters, persuaded the Massachusetts senator not to enter the California primary. Brown's slate won the primary by a margin of only two to one against a delegation pledged to pension promoter George Mc-

Lain. (McLain was in the race merely to demonstrate the size of his following. Many of his votes undoubtedly came from Democrats who had grown dissatisfied with Brown.)

National committeeman Paul Ziffren, whom Brown claimed had surreptitiously urged Kennedy to enter the primary, was removed from his party post at the governor's insistence. A week before the Los Angeles convention was to begin, Kennedy's managers claimed they had a pledge from Brown to release his delegation. Brown neither confirmed nor denied this story. At a closed caucus of the California delegation, the governor issued a statement in which he announced his support for Kennedy and told the delegates they were "free to exercise independent judgment." Brown at once denied that this statement meant what it said. It meant only, he claimed, that his delegates were free to support whom they wished once he had released them. Kennedy's California backers, despairing of the governor, put on their own campaign to capture the delegation. Lieutenant Governor Anderson rallied the liberals behind the suddenly resurrected Stevenson campaign. Senator Engle, a Symington supporter, declared himself "more confused than ever." At the first open caucus of the delegation, held in a motion picture studio, a poll showed the delegation badly divided, with Stevenson and Kennedy each holding about a third of the votes.

This division was maintained on the first and only ballot of the convention. California cast votes for five candidates, including one-half vote for Governor Brown. When Senator Engle, chairman of the delegation, read Brown's name, there was an enthusiastic chorus of boos from all parts of the hall.

Two weeks later, Richard Nixon rolled to his expected triumph at the Republican convention in Chicago. (Having declined a seat in the California delegation, William Knowland observed Nixon's nomination from the press section, where he was stationed as reporter for his father's *Oakland Tribune*.) In the campaign that followed, both candidates eagerly courted California's favor. Kennedy proposed creation of the Peace Corps in San Francisco, and Nixon promised to make President Eisenhower a roving ambassador of good will in Los Angeles.

Early returns from California on election night indicated that Kennedy had carried the state, but the Democratic lead gradually fell until Nixon was only a few thousand votes behind. Absentee ballots, counted several days later, enabled the Republican candidate to carry his native state by a bit more than 35,000 votes out of more than 6,000,000 cast. Los Angeles and the Bay Area went for Kennedy, but San Diego and the coastal counties supported Nixon. In the Sacramento and San Joaquin Valleys, where Democratic strength was usually greatest, Nixon equaled Eisenhower's showing in 1956. In the end, pride in the local boy probably was decisive in determining the outcome.

After his defeat, Nixon returned to California. For a time he practiced law in Los Angeles, earned far more money than had ever come his way in public life, and built a home in Beverly Hills. It seemed not enough. Within a year he had declared himself a candidate for governor of California in 1962.

From the start, his candidacy faced enormous obstacles. Within the Republican party, Goodwin Knight and Joseph Shell, conservative minority leader of the state Senate, were anxious to run for governor. Pat Brown, beginning to overcome the unpopularity that had surrounded him in 1960, seemed a formidable candidate for re-election. Moreover, the Democratic lead in registration had been translated into normal Democratic control of the state. Brown had begun, as Warren and Knight had not done, to build a partisan political organization (dominated, in the opinion of many, by Jesse "Big Daddy" Unruh, speaker of the Assembly and arch-foe of CDC). Although the bulk of state personnel were still protected by the merit system, appointments to the state's numerous boards and commissions were more and more filled after satisfactory answer to the question, "Is he a Democrat?" Some Democratic leaders were urging a return to a partisan system of election for city and county offices. San Diego and Orange Counties, the last urban Republican strongholds, were both sliding toward the Democrats. Basking in the light of the nonpartisan sun during the Warren era, Republicans had failed to build up the bases of strength in rural and suburban areas that their party maintained in other states. Most rural counties were Democratic, while the suburbs were unpredictable.

The state's highly emotional conservative movement, centered on Los Angeles, was a source of some strength but also of great peril to the Republican party. California conservatives were devoid of the reform spirit that helped to motivate their allies in Texas and Arizona and little attached to the rural verities associated with conservatism in Virginia and Ohio. In California, conservatism was predominantly urban and more an old than a young people's movement. (In 1960, all but two of fourteen Republican congressmen were elected from urbanized districts; eight of the state's ten rural districts were represented by Democrats. In Los Angeles County, seven districts were represented by Republicans, two of whom were declared members of the ultraconservative John Birch Society. The average proportion of the population over sixty-five in these districts was 12 per cent, compared to 7 per cent in the five districts represented by Democrats.) More than in most states, conservatism was an expression of frustration, insecurity, and irrational hostility. Such a movement threatened either permanently to divide the Republican party into quarreling factions or to drive it toward a position at which it would be attractive only to a minority of extremists.

For a time, it seemed possible that the old Nixon luck might work. Early opinion polls showed the former vice president leading over Brown. Goodwin Knight was removed from the campaign—after throwing scorching criticism on Nixon's personal integrity—by illness. Senator Shell was eliminated in the Republican primary, after winning about one-third of the vote cast. But as the day of final reckoning approached, it seemed clear that Nixon's knockout punch was as lacking as it had been in 1960. (Whether he ever truly possessed such a punch is a question that is likely to be debated by students of politics for generations. In part, undoubtedly, Nixon's career was carried forward on the tide of circumstance, and when circumstance ran the other way, his vaunted tactical powers seemed to drop from him. Nevertheless, the years had perhaps made a change in Richard Nixon. Cast as the young man in a hurry, he found it difficult to take on another role. Moreover, a decade of public criticism seemed to have inhibited the dogged, sometimes brilliant will to win that once had gained him rapturous admirers, as well as bitter foes.) According to the former vice president's own estimate, he was headed for victory until Republican chances were blighted two weeks before election by President Kennedy's firm stand in the international crisis created by the installation of Soviet missile bases in Cuba. (Nelson Rockefeller, William Scranton, and George Romney were not similarly affected in New York, Pennsylvania, and Michigan. Neither, for that matter, was Thomas Kuchel, re-elected to the Senate by close to 700,000 votes in California.) In any event, the voters of California returned Governor Brown to office by a majority of almost 300,000. On the day after election, Nixon bade farewell to politics with a rambling and largely gratuitous attack on the nation's press. (Brown, who watched the performance on television, commented, with the sympathy of a fellow technician, "Nixon will regret that as long as he lives.") But the end—the real end—had come on election night itself, when Nixon, with only a few precincts in but enough to show his tested political apparatus which way the wind was blowing, referred to California bitterly as "the boondocks" in a televised interview with one of the Eastern commentators.*

The California of Pat Brown and Richard Nixon differed sizably from that of Hiram Johnson. The Golden State of the fifties and early sixties was more heavily populated, more prosperous, more culturally sophisticated; it was also much less sure of its values and purpose. The political leaders of the new California were like brokers in a market of spectral properties. In a system that depended almost entirely on personality, their personalities were curiously blurred. If they had gained in flexibility, and even practicality, they had lost grievously in the moral firmness which might alone have brought new order to the milieu of changing attitudes in which they operated. (The resemblance between Nixon's television delivery and that of an announcer giving a toothpaste commercial was noticed by many observers, not all of them unfriendly.)

Products of the shifting society that they sought to govern, the new men failed, with few exceptions, to offer creative direction to the energies unleashed by the fantastic growth of their state's population and economy. Senator Knowland, the only leader of the period who knew clearly what he wanted, was attuned to an age permanently gone. Nixon, probably the most able of the state's leaders, was necessarily absent during much of the decade and when present seemed more concerned with political shadow boxing than with confronting problems of substance. Governors Knight and Brown contributed to

---

* Interest in Nixon as a possible presidential candidate in the winter of 1964 indicated, in Mark Twain's phrase, that the news of the former vice president's political death had been grossly exaggerated.

the enlightened tradition that kept California's state government among the most progressive and best financed in the nation; neither, however, provided political leadership likely to inspire public dedication or confidence.

The result, perhaps, was not too serious. The state's economy has continued to prosper. (Median annual family income in both Los Angeles and the Bay Area in 1960 was around $7,000; in the inland valleys and the isolated mountain counties, on the other hand, income was much less and unemployment was high.) Population has increased at an astronomic rate. State services, well above the national average, are constantly expanding. The state's vast public university system provides education comparable to that available at the great private institutions of the East. And on the beaches along the golden coast, thousands gather each day to accept the benefaction of the sun.

If visitors are sometimes troubled by the rootless, restless quality of California life, this may reflect a conservative prejudice against the state's free-and-easy ways. If political dissent is more widely supported and less responsible than elsewhere in the nation, this may be attributed to a kind of social vitality. If religious enthusiasm sometimes finds odd means of expression ("like Palestine a century before Christ," in the view of one scholar), this may result from the tapping of new spiritual depths. If Los Angeles remains the worst-planned city in America, this may be explained as a part of the dynamism of growth. Most of the strange and disturbing aspects of California culture can be regarded as evidences of underlying vigor.

The difficulty is that too little of this vigor, in the middle sixties, is being led to socially or personally constructive means of expression. The Birchites and the beatniks, the false prophets and the phony promoters, all in their different ways, are wastefully expending an incalculable amount of human creativity. Without positive leadership, the state will in all likelihood continue to scatter its remarkable energies in a manner certainly diffuse and potentially destructive. Such leadership, of a kind to harness the varied forces of mere existence to the transcendent objectives of integrated society, has not yet appeared.

PART TWO

PATTERNS OF
STATE POLITICS

11

RULES OF THE GAME

Politics, like any other organized human activity, operates according to rules, both formal and informal. The informal rules, while often important, are both flexible and vague. (The tradition that a successful politician never breaks his word, for instance, has so many notorious exceptions as hardly to be classifiable as a rule at all.) The formal rules, on the other hand, are set forth in federal and state laws. Statutes affecting state politics may conveniently be divided into four categories: (1) laws dealing with elections, including laws regulating political parties; (2) laws governing apportionment of state legislatures; (3) laws controlling the administration of state government; and (4) laws determining the method of election and duties of the state judiciary.

ELECTIONS AND POLITICAL PARTIES

In most states, general elections, in which the candidates of the major parties and any independents who may have qualified vie for elective offices, are held on the first Tuesday after the first Monday in November. (In Michigan, prior to passage of the 1963 constitution, several state officers were elected on the first Monday in April in odd-numbered years. Under New Con, the spring general elections have been eliminated.)

Primary dates, on the other hand, vary widely, both among the states and within the same state from year to year. In five of the states studied, primary elections for state offices are usually held in May or June. Virginia since 1952 has held its primaries in July, Michigan votes in August, and Arizona and Massachusetts put off the preliminary contests until September. In the tenth state, New York, candidates for state offices are nominated at party conventions. Delegates to these conventions are elected any time from July to early September, according to the date fixed by the current legislature. There has been some trend toward a spring date for the primary—sometimes, as in Texas in 1960, to strengthen the position of a local favorite in a presidential year. Nebraska moved its primary date from August to May in 1955, despite the protests of some legislators that country dwellers might have difficulty getting to the polls over roads made impassable by spring rains.

Party conventions, once employed almost universally to nominate candidates, are still sanctioned by law in several states. Only New York, among the states studied, leaves conventions with final control over major party nominations. Texas requires only those parties polling 200,000 or more votes for their candidate for governor to hold primaries the next election year. Until recently, the Republicans were able to take advantage of this law to make all their nominations by convention. In Virginia, too, the Republicans usually nominate by the convention method. In Massachusetts, conventions meet to endorse regular candidates in advance of the primaries. Candidates rejected by the convention may run in the primary. Dissident Democrats in Massachusetts have frequently taken advantage of this privilege and have sometimes been successful in overturning the convention choices. The preprimary convention was abolished in Nebraska in 1953. In that state and in Arizona, parties hold postprimary conventions for the purpose of adopting party platforms. Since 1958, Arizona Republicans, on the advice of Senator Goldwater, have prepared a "Declaration of Policy" rather than a platform. In Michigan, only the nominee for governor is chosen in the primary. Candidates for lesser administrative offices are selected at postprimary conventions. This system permits a defeated candidate for governor to go back on the ticket for another office, as Secretary of State James Hare did in 1960. In practice, the candidate for governor has usually picked his running mates. (The nominee for lieutenant governor formerly was selected in the primary, but under New Con will be chosen at the convention.) California also holds postprimary conventions, the functions of which are narrowly limited by law. The important gatherings in the Golden State are the preprimary conventions of the unofficial Republican Assembly and Democratic Council. These act as slate-making bodies in place of the regular party organizations, which are prohibited by law from so doing.

In all states studied except Michigan, a voter may participate in the primary election of only that party of which he is a registered member. Michigan permits the voter to participate in either (but only one) party primary. California's celebrated system of crossfiling, under which candidates might run in both party primaries without partisan designation, was modified to require party designation after the name of the candidate on the primary ballot in 1952 and was finally abolished in 1959. A similar cross-filing law was repealed in Texas in 1955.

Poll tax laws remain in force in Virginia and Texas. In both states, the tax rate is $1.50 per year. (Most Texas counties exact an additional fee of 25 cents.) Payment of the tax is due in Virginia no later than six months before the day of the general election and in Texas by January 31, in order for the voter to qualify for the year's primary and general elections. Poll taxes must be paid, therefore, while issues and candidates for the coming elections are frequently unknown or unclear. Persons over sixty in Texas may obtain poll tax exemptions. In Virginia, bloc payment of poll taxes by interested candidates or parties was reported to be common only in the Southwestern Highlands. Bloc payments in Texas were said to be very common for Mexican voters in the El Paso area and the Rio Grande Valley.

Rudimentary literacy in English is required for voters in Arizona, California, Massachusetts, New York, and Virginia. In New York, where by 1962 only about 120,000 Puerto Ricans of an estimated 700,000 immigrants from the United States' island possession had qualified as voters, an effort was underway to broaden the requirement to include literacy in Spanish. California Democrats, who felt that some of their potential supporters were being turned back at the polls on grounds of illiteracy, sponsored enactment of a state law in 1961 requiring that challenges be made in advance of the election. Many Arizona Indians and Latin Americans have reportedly been disfranchised for illiteracy. In Virginia, the literacy test was once used to keep Negroes from voting, but when an attempt at rigid enforcement was made in 1958, it proved to be more of an obstacle to many whites than to most Negroes. It has since been practically abandoned.

LEGISLATIVE APPORTIONMENT

The subject of apportionment of state legislatures has recently become a cause of major interest to many progressive groups. After the Supreme Court in 1962 offered the possibility of judicial remedy in cases of gross malapportionment, a sizable number of legislatures, under threat of court action nullifying the election of their members, set about enacting new apportionment laws. Although the enthusiastic predictions, in some segments of the press and elsewhere, of revolutionary changes likely to result from these developments were no doubt exaggerated, the effect of reapportionment on many state governments should certainly be considerable.

The apportionment problem takes two forms: states in which legislatures have consistently violated their own constitutions by failing to reapportion; and states which in their constitutions, following the example of the United States Senate, give representation to area, usually counties, as well as to numbers. The Tennessee case, which gave rise to the Supreme Court decision, was of the former kind.

Of the ten states studied, only Massachusetts in 1963 had representation approximately equal to population in both houses. Arizona, California, Nebraska, and Michigan provide in their constitutions for a senate in which representation is at least partly by area. In all of these states, representation by area was given majority approval in statewide referenda held since 1952. New York, Ohio, and Pennsylvania also require constitutionally that every county (except sparsely populated Hamilton County in New York) shall have at least one representative in the lower house. Although it can not seriously be argued that counties enjoy the same legal relationship to states that states hold to the federal government (constitutionally a union of semisovereign equals), there remains a widespread feeling that some form of county (or town) representation is necessary if the integrity of smaller communities is to be maintained. In this view, state citizens deserve to be represented not only as atomistic units but also as members of geographical communities. In the background of this belief, probably, lies a Jeffersonian distrust of the political sentiments generated by big cities. Whether the courts will attack constitutional representation by area as well as unconstitutional failure to reapportion remains uncertain.

A third problem of apportionment, springing from the district system of representation, has so far been given little consideration. Generally, outside the South and Southwest, the strength of the Democratic party is concentrated in a few large cities, while the following of the Republican party is more evenly distributed over whole states. Thus, overwhelming Democratic victories in the city districts produce fewer representatives, even under apportionment based entirely on population, than more closely contested Republican victories in a large number of upstate districts.

In the lower house of Michigan and the upper house of Ohio, both of which are apportioned in a manner correlating closely with the distribution of population, Republicans remained in control through most of the fifties, although Democrats usually won statewide majorities for governor. In New York, apportionment on the basis of complete one-to-one equality would still almost always produce Republican legislatures because statewide Democratic strength is based largely on huge majorities in New York City, which would elect only about 40 per cent of the state's legislators. The movement of population out of large cities and into suburbs is likely to intensify this problem for the Democrats. Unless the allegiance of suburban counties to the Republican party can be shaken, Democratic strength in legislatures may dwindle, regardless of any reapportionment by numbers.

While producing shifts of party control in relatively few legislatures, fair reapportionment would undoubtedly increase representation for groups—Negroes, Puerto Ricans, suburbanites, workers attracted by new industries—who have been involved in recent migrations, thereby affecting the internal structures of both major parties. The political power of upstate rural counties, though likely to remain substantial, will probably be sizably reduced as a result of the Supreme Court's 1962 decision.

EXECUTIVE POWERS

Another handicap to effective state government, at least as serious as legislative malapportionment, is posed by the often paralyzing division of administrative powers within the governmental structures of many states. This reckless diffusion of responsibility and authority may be traced to the traditional American distrust of strong executive power in government, springing from experience with the British Crown in pre-Revolutionary times, and to the Jacksonian belief in the long ballot, under which as many officials as possible are elected directly by the people.

The fear of executive power led to prohibitions against a governor succeeding himself, such as those still in force in Pennyslvania and Virginia; to two-year terms for the governor, as in Massachusetts, Nebraska, and Texas (and Michigan, before adoption of the 1963 constitution), which keep the chief executive a perpetual candidate for re-election; and various governors' councils, as in Massachusetts, or boards of commissioners, as in Arizona and Michigan, which exercise autonomous executive authority. The long ballot led to the direct election in many states of officers such as lieutenant governor, secretary of state, attorney general, state treasurer, and controller, all members of the executive branch with no responsibility to the state's nominal chief executive, the governor.

At best, these devices have placed actual executive authority in the hands of extralegal political organizations, as in Virginia or Pennsylvania, which endure while governors come and go. At worst, they have created a condition of chaos in the executive branch of government, as when Mennen Williams in Michigan was for four years in the early fifties surrounded by politically hostile executive officers; or when the governor and attorney general of Texas carried on a lengthy feud in the early sixties; or when the Republican lieutenant governor of Nebraska succeeded the Democratic governor after the latter's death in 1960. In a few states, like New York and California, strong governors have at their disposal machinery to put their programs into operation; but even in these, legislative majorities, which may often be hostile for reasons previously discussed, may block action by denying necessary funds.

There is some indication that many voters approve and enjoy the existence of prolonged impasse within the executive branch of government. (In Pennsylvania in 1961, a referendum that would have eliminated the prohibition against the governor succeeding himself was defeated by 85,000 votes. Both major parties had officially endorsed the proposal.) Aside from pleasure in the titillating gossip thus provided, such sentiments seem to spring from a rather severe application of the doctrine of balance of powers. For the office of controller, by its nature a watchdog post, this attitude is not unreasonable. The office of lieutenant governor, too, should probably in some way be subject to popular election, although means should be worked out, as in the national government, to assure that the chief executive and his potential replacement are at least of the same party. For all other executive offices, however, including the governor's chief administrator (secretary of state), fiscal officer (treasurer), and legal officer (attorney general), there can be little doubt than an appointive rather than an elective means of selection would better serve the cause of efficient government.

JUDICIAL SELECTION AND RESPONSIBILITIES

The third great branch of state government, the judiciary, runs the gamut in the ten states studied from intimate involvement with partisan politics to almost pure nonpartisan status.

Close to the partisan end of the scale are Pennsylvania, New York, Texas, and Virginia. In the first three states, judges are nominated and elected on party tickets, just like legislative and executive officers. In New York, where Supreme Court justices in the metropolitan area are paid more than justices of the United States Supreme Court, judgeships are highly coveted prizes, usually awarded to faithful contributors or party workers. Election to the state legislature is often viewed as the first step to a judicial career. Once on the bench, judges are almost always endorsed for re-election by both major parties.

Because Republican candidates seldom can hope to be elected to judicial posts in New York City unaided, the leadership of the Republican controlled legislature regularly exacts pledges for Democratic endorsements of some Republicans as condition for creating new judgeships for the city. Judges play powerful roles, through their right to appoint attorneys as guardians and referees in lucrative estate settlements, in both major party organizations. In Pennsylvania and Texas, judges are similarly exposed to involvement in politics.

In Virginia, judges of the Supreme Court of Appeals and all other major trial court judges are elected by the legislature. In practice, this has meant that all of the state's judges—even those serving in predominantly Republican or insurgent districts—owe their appointments to the Byrd Organization. Election contests coming before the courts have a tendency, all things being reasonably equal, to be decided in favor of the Organization. (The Organization normally puts men of high caliber on the bench, and from time to time the courts have found against Byrd Democrats where fraud has been proven. Particularly in the fiercely competitive "Fightin' Ninth," however, the Organization stalwarts are comforted by the knowledge that the courts are presided over by their political allies.) Virginia circuit judges enjoy broad appointive powers, including the rights to name county electoral boards, school trustee boards (which in turn elect county school boards), and welfare boards, and to fill any vacancies which may occur in county offices. The Republican party in Virginia has waged a long and unsuccessful battle to strip judges of their appointive powers.

Judges of higher courts in California and of all courts in Massachusetts are appointed by the governor. In the Bay State, the system of lifetime appointment has tended to insulate judges from their former political attachments. In California, too, the courts have effectively been kept out of politics. (During the Brown administration, however, judges have increasingly been appointed on a partisan basis.) Once appointed, higher court judges go on the ballot without opposition, to be either confirmed or rejected by the voters. None has ever been rejected. Judges of lesser courts are elected on a nonpartisan basis. Incumbents are rarely defeated for re-election.

Judges are also elected without partisan designation in Arizona,

Ohio, and Michigan. In Arizona and Ohio, however, candidates for judgeships are chosen in party primaries, resulting in more (in the case of Ohio) or less (in the case of Arizona) close identification of the nominees with their parties. Candidates for Michigan's Supreme Court are nominated by party conventions, producing an intensely political atmosphere on the court. During the fifties, the Michigan Supreme Court swung from a five-to-three Republican advantage to a five-to-three Democratic advantage. In 1961, six out of eight Supreme Court justices, including former-Governor Harry Kelly, had won major elective offices before coming to the court. The new majority on the court produced a series of prolabor decisions in unemployment and workman's compensation cases, which were vigorously criticized by Republican legislators and businessmen.

Only Nebraska among the ten states studied has maintained a state judiciary almost completely free of partisan influence. In 1962, Nebraskans adopted a form of the so-called Missouri Plan, which provides for selection of judges on the Supreme and District Courts by the governor from a list submitted by a nominating commission, composed of three attorneys, three citizens, and a Supreme Court justice as chairman. The appointed judge will serve for a period of three years, after which the voters will decide only if he is to remain on the bench. County Court judges in Nebraska will continue, as before, to be elected on a nonpartisan ballot.

12

CONDITIONS OF PLAY

Powerful social and economic forces create the arena in which the game of state politics must be played. Most of these are outgrowths of historic processes, often traceable to events enacted and ideas conceived far beyond the borders of the state.

Major conditioning factors which over a long period have operated on state politics may be classified as: (1) tradition itself, the tendency of political divisions to endure after rational differences have disappeared or grown slight; (2) national political alignments; (3) sectional rivalries within the states; (4) aspirations of ethnic and religious groups; and (5) pursuit of security or privilege by economic groups.

TRADITION

The Civil War, it has been said, is still the most important issue in every American election. What is meant, of course, is not that slavery and secession are subjects for campaign debate, but that many voters continue to cast ballots according to party divisions established as a result of the nineteenth-century conflict between the Southern states and the federal government.

The solid South, binding conservative Southerners to the nationally liberal Democratic party, is the most conspicuous example of the persistent influence of the war. No less a product of that conflict, however, is the "normal Republican majority" that still exists in some Northern states. As the party of rebellion the Democratic party remained abhorrent during the final third of the nineteenth century to many former soldiers who had fought for the Union cause. For many Northerners, the Republican party, originally a radical movement, became symbolic of respectability as well as of patriotism. When Nebraska farmers in the 1890's desired to overthrow the dominance of Republican bankers and railroad tycoons, most of them could not bring themselves to do so through the instrument of the Democratic party. The result was the short-lived Populist movement, which quickly lost strength when it later amalgamated with the Democrats.

The cross-currents of the Civil War also won loyal supporters for each party in areas largely controlled by the other. Residents of Virginia's Southwestern Highlands, like the inhabitants of most of the Appalachian region that stretches spinelike down the middle of the South, felt little sympathy with the Confederacy and later became staunch Republicans as an expression of their hostility toward the planter aristocracy of the Tidewater and Piedmont. Likewise, pockets of Democratic strength were established in former Copperhead strongholds of the North, such as the Ohio Valley and some of the Dutch counties of Pennsylvania.

The hostility of many of the Pennsylvania Dutch toward the Republican party is traceable to an even older tradition, that of anti-Federalism, established in the first years of the Republic. Resenting central government taxation, the Dutch made common cause with the opponents of Alexander Hamilton's Federalist party and its successors, the Whigs and the Republicans. Deriving from a similar tradition, the farmers of New York's Hudson Valley aligned themselves with the Democratic party until the goldbug campaign of 1896. They then shifted emphatically to the Republicans and have since formed a solid bulwark for the GOP. The Pennsylvania Dutch counties, carried by Nixon in 1960 and by William Scranton in 1962, may be in the process of moving toward a permanent Republican attachment.

Traditional antipathy of country dwellers toward cities has often solidified the upstate or rural vote against the party that controls the state's metropolis. This tendency has helped the Republicans in New York, Ohio, and Michigan, while it has aided the Democrats to some degree in California. Relative strength of the Democratic party in upstate Pennsylvania was, until recently, partly due to the long dominance of the Republican machine in Philadelphia. The upsurge of Republican activity in the cities of the South and Southwest during the 1950's may have helped Democrats maintain their control over most rural counties in those areas.

Persons tracing their descent from early American colonists have, outside of the South, usually identified with the Republican party. The Grand Old Party has become the beneficiary of those sentiments of belligerent patriotism and national solidarity which usually assist conservative or monarchist parties in European countries. Added to this group have been more recent immigrants of similar ethnic and religious backgrounds, as well as immigrants of other backgrounds eager to join themselves to a nationalist tradition. Partly in reaction to this nativist spirit, the bulk of immigrants from non–Anglo-Saxon and non-Protestant countries has traditionally given its votes to the Democratic party. This tendency was strongly re-enforced among immigrants concentrated in metropolitan areas like New York City and Cleveland, which, when the newcomers arrived, were Democratic islands surrounded by rural Republican seas.

The influence of pure tradition—that is, voting the way one's father did—on these alignments can easily be exaggerated. Most were originally based on social or economic differences, many of which still operate. Southern conservatives who continue to support the Democratic party are perhaps motivated as much by fear of the effects of two-party competition on the race question as by memories of the Civil War. Laborers and farmers in upstate Northern counties who consistently vote the straight Republican ticket may feel realistic concern over the threat posed by metropolitan dominance to their social and economic security. Persons of Irish, Italian, and Slavic descent who remain loyal Democrats after leaving their ethnic communities may be protesting the discrimination which they still encounter in suburban and upstate towns.

Moreover, party differences based on tradition may serve a useful function in the maintenance of party organizations. The party itself, particularly in those states in which patronage is an important factor, often becomes an object of fierce loyalty. The Irish or Jewish insurance salesman who "always votes Democratic" may simply be registering his interest in keeping his brother-in-law employed at the county courthouse.

NATIONAL ALIGNMENTS

Americans do not, as a rule, separate state and local from national politics. The party which gains majority support for its approach to national and international problems is likely to increase its share of elective offices at the state and local levels.

This was particularly true during the New Deal period, when Democrats were able to capture control of previously unbreachable Republican citadels in the governments of Pennsylvania, Michigan, California, and other states. Likewise, the gradual increase of national conservative strength, beginning in 1938 and continuing through the years of World War II, was accompanied by Republican recovery in many state and local governments. ("In Washington, where the bureaucrats live, there is still a Democrat in the White House," Earl Warren was able to say in an uncharacteristically partisan speech at the Republican national convention of 1944, "but out where the people live, the country is predominantly Republican.") President Truman's dramatic reversal of the conservative trend in 1948 occurred while Democrats were recapturing state governments in Massachusetts, Connecticut, Ohio, Michigan, and Illinois. National conservative resurgence in 1950 and 1952 was matched by return of Republican control in all of these states except Michigan and Ohio, plus Republican victories over entrenched Democrats in Arizona, Colorado, Indiana, Maryland, and five other states.

The elections of 1956 and 1960 were anomalous in this respect, as in both years the percentages won by the Democratic candidates for president were far below the average showings of Democrats running for state and local offices. This, no doubt, was in part due to an increased willingness among voters to split their tickets; chiefly, however, it resulted from the fact that in neither year did the presidential contests reflect the true relative strengths of the parties on national issues. The nation in 1956 still approved President Eisenhower's personal conduct of the central government, but had turned against the Republican party, as evidenced by Democratic control of both houses of Congress. For religious and other reasons, John Kennedy was personally unacceptable in 1960 to many voters who indicated by their votes in congressional contests that they favored the Democratic philosophy on national problems.

A striking exception to the normal connection between national politics and state and local alignments was the failure of the Republican party to grow in the South during the fifties, despite the good showings made in Southern states by Republican presidential candidates. The continued importance of the Democratic party in maintaining white supremacy in the South has no doubt blighted Republican prospects in that area. Over the long haul, continued popularity of national Republican candidates may lead to the emergence of the GOP as a competitor for state and local offices in the South. Such a development may be in progress in Texas. In Virginia, on the other hand, the Republicans have failed to enlarge substantially on the gains they made in the early fifties.

The relationship between voting for national and state offices is due in part to the fact that the parties take, in general, the same approach to state problems that they take to national problems. The Democratic state parties, even in the South, are with few exceptions more liberal—more willing to expand state services, more anxious to shift the tax burden onto business and the well-to-do, more ready to appeal for central government assistance, more committed (outside of the South) to action on civil rights—than are their Republican opposites. If voters are in a liberal mood on national issues, it is not surprising that they should at the same time favor liberal solutions to state problems. The predictable result of such a prevailing sentiment would be Democratic strength at both levels. That the Democrats did somewhat better during the fifties in state than in national elections was probably due to the existence of a sizable number of voters who preferred a liberal approach on domestic issues (the only kind that state governments deal with), but retained some reservations about the Democratic position on questions of foreign policy. Voters thus might, with no feeling of inconsistency, cast ballots at the same time for Dwight Eisenhower for president and the Democratic candidate for governor of their state. (Of the twenty-five non-Southern states electing governors in 1956, twenty-four were carried by Eisenhower, but only thirteen chose Republican governors.)

The effect of popular national leaders, like Franklin Roosevelt and Dwight Eisenhower, on state elections is often debated. On the whole, nationwide trends on issues seem to have more influence in state contests than the popularity of national leaders. Near the height of his wartime popularity, Roosevelt was unable in 1942 to turn back the conservative trend which elected Republican governors in New York, Pennsylvania, Ohio, and California. Eisenhower did even less well in his appeals for Republican victories in state contests in 1954 and 1958.

Control of state governments may, on the other hand, be of substantial assistance to a political party at the national level. Legislative majorities carry with them the power to reapportion Congressional districts every ten years—as in 1961 was demonstrated to the equal dismay of New York Democrats and California Republicans. Loyal armies of state jobholders in states where patronage is still an important factor may help a national candidate (although entrenched Democratic organizations in New York, Pennsylvania, Ohio, and Arizona made no visible dent on the Eisenhower sweep of 1956), and control of election machinery may have profound effect on the outcome of close national contests like that of 1960. Although some patronage and much prestige are available to state organizations of the party in power at the national level, many state politicians appear to regard national politics largely as a sport—played for the love of the game. Failure of a national candidate to rouse the heartfelt enthusiasm of state and local party workers—as occurred in both of Adlai Stevenson's campaigns—may easily deprive him of much of the practical support that he might otherwise receive.

SECTIONAL RIVALRIES

Sectional rivalries within the states tend to develop either between large geographic regions or between metropolitan areas and their hinterlands. Examples of the former are the struggle between Northern and Southern California and the long standing feud between north-of-Platters and south-of-Platters in Nebraska; examples of the latter are the antagonism that exists between New York City and the upstate "appleknockers" and the dread with which the spiraling population of Maricopa County is regarded by the rest of Arizona.

Friction between geographic regions may be fed by little more than traditional hostility, as appears to be the case in the Platte River feud. The conflict in California, which involves control of surplus water and apportionment of the state legislature, is more serious in nature. In some cases, geographic isolation may promote feelings of sectional separatism, as in western Nebraska, the Panhandle and El Paso regions of Texas, and the Northern Peninsula of Michigan. Areas which over a long period have exercised political power out of proportion to their economic or numerical strength, like East Texas, the Southside of Virginia, and the anthracite region of Pennsylvania, usually develop a sense of sectional cohesion. Historic political alienation, like that of Virginia's "Fightin' Ninth," may also lead to a spirit of sectional unity and pride. In some states, sectional rivalries which would seem predictable have failed to develop. Little antagonism exists between eastern and western Pennsylvania, partly because both natural regions expend their sectional energies on internal metropolitan area–hinterland feuds and partly because they are so completely separated by the Appalachian Mountain barrier that they normally simply ignore each other. Sectionalism is practically nonexistent in Ohio, apparently because potential regional divisions have been subordinated to the statewide struggle between urban and rural interests.

Sectional conflict between geographic regions may find many forms of political expression. Traditionally one United States senator is elected from each of the two main divisions of Nebraska, Pennsylvania, and California. (A similar tradition assigns one of New York's senators to the city and the other to the upstate.) Though parties in these states have at times ignored the traditional practice, it has usually been when geographic balance could be achieved in some other way. The division between Northern and Southern California is acknowledged by the state law which requires party chairmanships to be rotated every two years between northerners and southerners.

Sometimes—though rather rarely—sectionalism (as distinguished from urban-rural rivalry) may find partisan expression. Leanings in Michigan's Northern Peninsula and New York's North Country toward the Democrats during the fifties were in part the result of feelings of alienation in those regions toward the rest of their upstates, in both cases heavily Republican. More usually, sectionalism contributes to the power of a leader or group within a state's dominant party. In Southside Virginia's Fourth Congressional District, for instance, 56 per cent of the qualified voters participated in the 1961 gubernatorial primary, giving the Organization choice a majority of 72 per cent. In two insurgent districts, the Ninth and the Tenth, only 20 and 27 per cent, respectively, of the voters turned out, giving the insurgent candidate majorities of 71 and 67 per cent. The importance of Southside cohesion to the continued rule of the Organization is obvious.

Of greater significance in contemporary American politics than rivalry between large geographic regions is the struggle between highly urbanized metropolitan areas and their upstate hinterlands. Few states escape the latter quarrel. New York City, Los Angeles, Philadelphia, Detroit, Boston, Omaha, and Cleveland all feel themselves to some degree victimized by the governments, particularly the legislatures, of their respective states. The hinterlands in all of these states, plus Texas and Arizona, are at the same time frightened by the potential economic and political power of their cities. Only in Virginia, of the states studied, did relatively harmonious relations prevail between urban and rural areas. This is partly because Virginia's cities are not very large (Norfolk, the largest, had a population just over 300,000 in 1960), partly because the legislature has been fairly generous in dealing with annexation and other problems of the cities, and partly because of the homogeneity of the state's population.

Metropolitan and upstate regions commonly quarrel over apportionment of state legislatures; over the hunger of cities for annexation of surrounding territories; over disposition of state assistance for education and highway construction; and over such miscellaneous problems as subway rates in New York City, Sunday closing laws in

Philadelphia, and extension of the MTA in Boston. Large cities in most states receive a smaller share of the state government's expenditures than either their share of the state population or their contribution to its revenues. Representatives of rural areas argue that roads and schools, as a matter of fact, cost more per capita in sparsely populated regions, and that the wealth of the cities makes them better able to finance their own services. Municipal officials, faced with deteriorating public facilities and the flight of their wealthier citizens to the suburbs, are little impressed by either argument. (Median annual family income in three of New York City's five boroughs in 1960 was about $500 below the state average. The same was true of Boston and Cincinnati. For most other Eastern and Midwestern cities, median family income was close to the state average. Income in the cities, however, was far below that of the suburbs: in Detroit, median family income was $6,000, compared to $7,500 in the suburbs; in Philadelphia, $5,800, compared to $7,200 in the suburbs; in Cleveland, $5,900, compared to $8,000 in the suburbs.) In the fast-growing cities of the Southwest, where the well-to-do still as a rule maintain homes within the city limits, municipal problems are less acute. Here, too, however, the cities are demanding a larger share of the state's aid.

The traditional urban-rural conflict has been complicated during the past decade by the extremely rapid growth of suburbs. Suburban Bucks County, near Philadelphia, increased its population 113 per cent between 1950 and 1960; Suffolk County, on New York's Long Island, was up 141 per cent; Norfolk County, south of Boston, increased 30 per cent; Macomb County, near Detroit, grew 119 per cent; and Orange County, south of Los Angeles, gained 225 per cent. The new population in the suburbs came from both the cities and the hinterlands. New York City, Boston, Philadelphia, Pittsburgh, Cleveland, Cincinnati, Detroit, and San Francisco all lost population (while their metropolitan areas in every case gained), as did many upstate counties.

Normally Republican, the suburbs are in a state of political transition in the middle sixties. Democrats have made inroads in such traditional Republican strongholds as Middlesex and Norfolk Counties, Massachusetts; Nassau and Suffolk Counties, New York; Delaware and Bucks Counties, Pennsylvania; and Orange County, California. More severely underrepresented in most state legislatures than the cities, the suburbs are clamoring for attention. Suburban homeowners, seeking large public expenditures for roads and schools and at the same time anxious to prevent increases in local property taxes, turn more and more to their state governments to finance public services.

That the suburbs will ally permanently with the cities, however, seems doubtful. For one thing, fear of city taxes and corrupt city government discourages any lasting political bond with the metropolitan centers. For another, the tradition that many states are governments "of the cities, by the county, and for the suburbs" has not wholly disappeared. Republican legislators, aware that many of the large contributors to their party reside in suburbs, are likely to respond more sympathetically to suburban demands than to those of the usually Democratic cities. Finally, the prestige value of membership in the Republican party remains in many suburbs a great, though diminishing, factor. Conversion to Republicanism is for many suburbanites a sign of liberation from old ethnic and class loyalties.

The concept of the suburb has in recent years become in some ways socially and politically misleading. In most suburbs, the majority of the work force no longer commutes to the central cities. Many are employed in industries that have been established in or near suburban communities, and many others work at service occupations in the suburbs themselves. Some suburban counties, like Nassau and Suffolk (Long Island), Arlington and Fairfax (across the Potomac River from Washington, D.C.), Clermont (east of Cincinnati), and San Mateo (south of San Francisco), remain primarily residential; while others, like Middlesex (Boston), Delaware (Philadelphia), Macomb (Detroit), and Orange (Los Angeles), have become or are becoming industrialized. Usually included in the suburbs are communities like Cambridge, Massachusetts; Yonkers, New York; Pasadena, California; and Dearborn, Michigan—all populous and important cities in their own right. Not surprisingly, the Republicans, as a rule, have retained control more successfully in residential than in industrial or separate city suburbs. (Exceptions, of course, are numerous. Scandals in local government contributed during the fifties to Demo-

cratic gains in the Long Island counties, while suspicion of Philadelphia and a well-drilled county organization has kept Delaware
County Republican.)

Changes in the nature of the upstate counties also have complicated the urban-rural rivalry. The actual farm population is rapidly
declining. Even in states like Virginia, Nebraska, and Texas, where
many truly rural counties still exist, the trend in population is toward
the large and middle-sized cities. In Eastern, Great Lakes, and Far
Western states, terms like "appleknockers" (New York), "cornstalk
brigade" (Ohio), and "cow counties" (California), loosely used to
describe all nonmetropolitan areas, are very misleading. The farm
vote, as such, is becoming insignificant in many states. Of 201 counties in Massachusetts, New York, Pennsylvania, and California, only
13 in 1960 had as much as 20 per cent of their populations living
on farms. In only 13 out of 171 counties in Ohio and Michigan did
this figure pass 30 per cent. Losing inhabitants almost as fast as the
farm counties were the coal- and iron-mining regions of Pennsylvania,
Eastern Ohio, and Michigan's Upper Peninsula. Having lost the
sources of their once great economic prosperity, these regions cling
tenaciously to the powerful roles they have for many years occupied
in their states' politics.

Middle-sized cities have sometimes given rise to urban-rural divisions within the hinterland itself. In upstate New York, the industrial
towns of Amsterdam, Salamanca, and Auburn have long been Democratic enclaves in Republican counties. Similarly, Toledo, Dayton,
and Steubenville have created pockets of Democratic strength amidst
the prevailing Republicanism of rural Ohio. In Nebraska, Lincoln
has frequently made common cause with the state's urban giant,
Omaha. In some Southern states, middle-sized cities recently have
tended to go Republican in national elections, while the surrounding
country remained Democratic. In 1960, twenty-three of the thirty-
two independent cities of Virginia were carried by Richard Nixon,
while only forty-nine of ninety-eight counties gave majorities to the
Republican candidate for president.

In the conflict with the metropolis, the hinterland cities have more
often felt their interest lies with the rural areas. Such a calculation
has long helped to keep Republicans in control of most cities of

upstate New York and Michigan. The improved showing of Republicans in some upstate Pennsylvania cities in recent years may be in part due to the fall of Philadelphia to the Democrats. In Arizona, Tucson, with some reluctance, is moving in the middle sixties toward alliance with the rural counties against Phoenix. Even so large a city as San Francisco has felt obliged, in the struggles over control of surplus water and reapportionment of the legislature, to place its sectional interest before the common urbanism which it shares with the state's metropolitan colossus, Los Angeles.

It has become common to suggest that America's cities, containing an overwhelming majority of the nation's current population, are the victims of malign state governments, subject to the control of rural dominated state legislatures. This situation, it is argued, is particularly unjust since 70 per cent of the population lives in cities. (This figure on occasion has risen on gusts of oratorical fervor to even higher levels, and on one memorable evening in the United States Senate was fixed by an enthusiastic speaker at 90 per cent.) The 70 per cent figure is borrowed from the 1960 census which reported that 69.9 per cent of the current population resided in urban areas. According to the census definition, an urban area is any community with a population exceeding 2,500. In other words, 70 per cent of the American people do not live on farms or in small villages. This is not to say that they live, in the normal sense of the word, in cities.

Another statistic released by the Census Bureau revealed that 62.9 per cent of the people live in "standard metropolitan areas"—in general, counties which contain at least one city with a population over 50,000. This comes closer to approximating the true proportion of city dwellers in the population, but it still includes many completely rural areas, as well as all the suburbs and the middle-sized upstate cities which are nonmetropolitan in character.

Actually, only 27.4 per cent of the population in 1960 lived in cities with populations over 100,000. This figure probably approaches the true big-city population of the United States. An additional 21.1 per cent lived in the suburbs of metropolitan areas with a total population above 500,000. The rest of the population, 21.4 per cent, lived in middle-sized cities and towns. These figures—30 per cent rural,

27 per cent big city, 21 per cent suburb, and 22 per cent middle-sized city—probably give a rough but reasonably accurate breakdown of the kind and extent of urbanization in the United States in 1960. Clearly, no one group held anything approaching a majority—let alone 70 per cent. (Deluded confidence in the 70 per cent figure contributed to the shock experienced by metropolitan spokesmen in 1962 at the crushing defeats administered in both houses of Congress to the proposed Department of Urban Affairs. Predictably, the agents of the big cities blamed their defeat on malapportionment rather than on any weakness in their analysis.)

The size of the four blocs—and the subdivisions within the blocs—makes it necessary in most states for the leaders of all divisions to bargain and negotiate with all others. The likelihood that any one bloc will gain dominance in the forseeable future is slight. More realistic apportionment of legislatures would place some divisions, particularly the suburbs, in more favorable positions. It would not, however—except in a very few states, like Arizona—radically alter the present balance of the four major population blocs.

ETHNIC AND RELIGIOUS GROUP ASPIRATIONS

Aspirations of ethnic and religious groups have profoundly affected the nature of state politics. Although the power of these forces has sometimes been exaggerated—they have often yielded precedence to economic, sectional, or ideological factors—there can be no doubt that in many states they provide the foundations on which the political parties are constructed.

The most important instance of ethnic group influence on politics is, of course, the determined resistance offered by Southern whites to the participation by Negroes in many aspects of government and society. As V. O. Key demonstrated in *Southern Politics in State and Nation* (1950), relatively small groups of whites residing in counties heavily populated by Negroes have frequently succeeded not only in maintaining dominance over their own counties, but also in gaining complete political control of entire states. This result has been achieved through the instrument of the Democratic party. By strictly limiting participation in the Democratic primary and by foregoing division into a two-party or multiparty system, white supremacists have kept power in their hands for almost a century. Not only Negroes, but also many whites, as Key pointed out, have effectively been denied a part in government. The condition for this achievement has been undeviating one-party loyalty. Despite their conservative disdain for the liberal principles of most leading national Democrats, the white supremacists have regularly paid this price.

Counties heavily populated by Negroes (in most of which the Negro vote itself is small) have usually polled majorities for the Democratic national ticket, even when other parts of the states in which they are located have been tending Republican. In Virginia in 1960, John Kennedy carried 58 (45 per cent) out of 130 counties and independent cities; of 39 constituencies with populations between 25 and 50 per cent Negro, Kennedy carried 20 (51 per cent); of 15 constituencies more than 50 per cent Negro, the Democratic candidate carried 12 (80 per cent). Of 22 Southside constituencies more than 25 per cent Negro, all but two went for Kennedy; while of 32 constituencies in the northern Tidewater and Piedmont more than 25 per cent Negro, the Democratic candidate's share fell to 12, hinting at a sectional influence re-enforcing that of the race issue. In 1956, the Republicans made much greater inroads into the Negro populated counties for Dwight Eisenhower. Even in that year, 18 of the 29 Virginia counties and cities carried by Adlai Stevenson had populations more than 25 per cent Negro.

In state contests, the Negro populated counties are even more emphatically Democratic than in national elections. In 1953, Ted Dalton, Republican candidate for governor, carried 29 constituencies, only 2 of which were more than 25 per cent Negro. (One of the exceptions was Norfolk, where Negroes themselves vote in considerable numbers.) Negro populated counties are also bulwarks of the Byrd Organization in Democratic primaries. In the 1961 gubernatorial primary, the insurgent candidate captured 37 of a possible 131 constituencies; in the 54 constituencies more than 25 per cent Negro, he won only 6. Similarly the anti-Organization candidates for governor in 1949 carried 32 of 125 constituencies, but only 1 of 15 over 50 per cent Negro.

The significance of returns from Texas counties heavily populated by Negroes is less clear, since Negroes in the Lone Star State reportedly vote in about the same proportion as whites. However, since in rural counties Negroes reportedly often vote as instructed by politically powerful whites, returns may be taken as some indication of the voting behavior of whites in Negro populated counties. In 1960, Richard Nixon carried 82 (32 per cent) out of 254 counties in the entire state, as compared to 5 (16 per cent) out of 32 counties more than 25 per cent Negro. Moreover, Nixon's percentage of the total vote in the 6 East Texas congressional districts in which Negroes are concentrated was 43 per cent, compared to 49 per cent for the entire state. Senator John Tower, who in 1961 became the first Republican to win a state election since Reconstruction, carried only 3 of 32 counties more than 25 per cent Negro in his runoff contest with Senator William Blakley, conservative Democrat.

Even in the South, Negroes themselves, particularly in the cities, are voting in increasing numbers. In Virginia in 1961, there were about 105,000 registered Negroes—about one-tenth of the state's qualified voters. (Negroes number a bit more than one-fifth of the state's total population.) The Negro vote, although not well organized, was becoming a force to be reckoned with in Norfolk and Richmond. In general, it was cast against Organization candidates. Voting in about the same proportion as whites, Negroes in East Texas were joining with Mexican-Americans in the south and southwest to lend support to liberal candidates. Don Yarborough, liberal candidate for governor in the 1962 Democratic runoff primary, carried twenty-seven of thirty-two Texas counties more than 25 per cent Negro against his conservative opponent.

In some Northern states, the Negro vote has come to assume crucial importance. Amounting to 9 per cent of the population in New York and Michigan, 8 per cent in Pennsylvania and Ohio, and 6 per cent in California, Negroes, voting as a bloc, can swing the outcome one way or the other in close state elections. Since the New Deal period, Northern Negroes have tended to vote overwhelmingly for Democratic candidates. Dwight Eisenhower made some inroads on the Negro vote, particularly in 1956, but in 1960 the great majority of Negroes supported John Kennedy. Negro loyalty to the Democratic cause is due in part to the memory of Franklin Roosevelt, in part to the continued militancy of Northern Democrats on civil rights issues, in part to economic identification with the party of the workingman, and in part to the fact that Negroes are heavily concentrated in huge cities where Democratic organizations are strong. (In 1960, Negroes numbered 30 per cent of the population in Detroit, 29 per cent in Cleveland, 26 per cent in Philadelphia, and 14 per cent in New York City; but less than 10 per cent—usually much less—in all but thirteen of three hundred counties in Michigan, Ohio, Pennsylvania, and New York.) In many cities, the Negro vote is well organized and forms an important support to the local machine. In a 1958 Democratic primary contest in a Philadelphia district largely populated by Negroes, a machine candidate for Congress easily defeated a candidate backed by the city's reform group, the CIO Political Action Committee, and most Negro church leaders. (Both candidates were Negroes.) In the 1961 mayoralty primary in New York City, the Negro vote was cast heavily for Robert Wagner, who had reform support, against the Tammany candidate. However, J. Raymond Jones, leader of the Democratic organization in Harlem, was supporting Wagner. Mennen Williams would have lost at least two of his races for governor in Michigan without the overwhelming majorities he received from Negro districts in Detroit.

Negro leaders commonly complain that they receive too little, both in jobs and recognition, from the political organizations which often could not win without their backing. This situation, to some degree, has begun to change. The Democrats now regularly assign to a Negro the presidency of Manhattan borough. One seat each in the Congressional delegations from New York, Philadelphia, Detroit, and Chicago is regularly held by a Negro. Fair Employment Practices Commissions have been established in several states. In at least one city, Tucson, Negroes have switched their support from Democratic to Republican candidates (in 1961) as a result of failure of a Democratic administration to enact an antidiscrimination law.

General failure by Republicans to attract Negro support has led some Republican leaders, including Senator Barry Goldwater, to suggest that their party should modify its traditional strong civil rights position in an effort to win the support of Southern whites. This advice is unlikely to be followed by Republicans from urbanized states, not only because swaying even a small portion of the Negro vote may be decisive, but also because the Negro cause has won the sympathy of many minority groups, particularly Jews, who do on occasion vote for individual Republican candidates, like Senators Keating and Javits of New York and Senator Scott of Pennsylvania.

Persons of foreign stock—immigrants, and natives with at least one immigrant parent—also, with large exceptions since World War II, predominantly vote Democratic. Of the ten states studied, foreign stock in 1960 was most common in Massachusetts (40 per cent) and numbered more than 20 per cent of the populations of New York, California, Michigan, and Pennsylvania. Only in one state, Virginia, was it less than 10 per cent. Although most heavily concentrated in large cities, foreign stock is much more evenly distributed over whole states than is the Northern Negro population. In Massachusetts, foreign stock is heaviest in Boston, but accounts for more than 30 per cent of the population in all but four of the Bay State's fourteen counties. Foreign stock constitutes more than half of the population of New York City, more than 40 per cent of San Francisco, and more than 30 per cent of Detroit, Buffalo, Cleveland, and Pittsburgh. Non-metropolitan areas heavily populated by foreign stock include the Mohawk Valley of New York, the anthracite region of Pennsylvania, Ohio's northeastern triangle, Michigan's Northern Peninsula, north-eastern Nebraska, the border counties of Texas and Arizona, and the Sacramento and San Joaquin Valleys of California.

Some of these cities and regions, notably the Mohawk Valley, the anthracite region, and northeastern Nebraska, have traditions of Republican strength. Most were susceptible during the fifties to the appeals of such varied Republican candidates as Dwight Eisenhower, Nelson Rockefeller (in New York City and Buffalo), Earl Warren (in the Bay Area and the central California valleys), and Barry Goldwater (in southern Arizona). By 1960, however, all (with the exception of the corn-and-hog counties of northeastern Nebraska) were tending Democratic. Of the sixty counties in the subject states containing more than 30 per cent foreign stock, forty were carried by John Kennedy. (Of the exceptions, nine were in suburban or upstate New York, and three were in California.) In the 1960 or 1958 gubernatorial election, whichever was more recent, thirty-six of these counties had voted Democratic. (Of the twenty-four counties in the minority, fourteen were in New York.)

The composition of foreign stock population is dissimilar in different parts of the country. Italians are heavily represented in almost all metropolitan centers, as well as in central California and the Pennsylvania coal regions; Irish are still numerous in Boston and Manhattan; Poles form the largest single division of foreign stock in Detroit, Cleveland, Buffalo, and the hard-coal region of Pennsylvania; Czechs are numerous in Pittsburgh and Cleveland; Germans are heavily represented in New York City, Buffalo, Detroit, Pittsburgh, and northeastern Nebraska; Russians (many of them Jewish) are second only to Italians in New York City; Canadians are numerous in Massachusetts (largely from Quebec Province) and Michigan (from the English-speaking provinces); Finns form a major strain in Michigan's Northern Peninsula; Lithuanians are common in the anthracite region; immigrants from the United Kingdom of Great Britain and Northern Ireland are spread over the entire nation; and Mexicans supply the largest blocs in southern Texas, Arizona, and California. Beyond the foreign stock are descendants of earlier waves of migrants, no longer sizably revealed in census statistics, but still playing important roles in establishing the political characteristics of various parts of the country. These include Germans in Pennsylvania, Ohio, Michigan, and Texas; Scandinavians in Nebraska and Michigan; Portuguese in Massachusetts; Chinese and Japanese in California; and British and Irish almost everywhere.

Persons of British Protestant stock, whose ancestors presided over the birth and early development of the United States, remain in all parts of the country members of the core ethnic group. Even where not numerically strong, as in most heavily populated cities, the Yankees, or wasps (white Anglo-Saxon Protestants), as they are sometimes called, continue to wield social and economic power. If nothing else, they command the formidable resource of history. (In the chamber of the Massachusetts state House of Representatives, politicians of Irish and Italian descent carry on their work beneath a circular border of names commemorating the heroes of the early Commonwealth—without exception, Yankees.) During the twentieth century, many members of this group have felt themselves under siege, culturally as well as economically, from the more recent arrivals. For the most part, outside of the South, they have aligned themselves with the Republican party, sometimes with its most conservative elements.

A small but significant minority, like Joseph Clark of Pennsylvania and Endicott Peabody in Massachusetts, has sought to give leadership to the more liberal segment of the Democratic party. (The rosters of most chapters of Americans for Democratic Action are composed almost entirely of British and Jewish names.) Deriving from the good-government Progressives who revolted against corrupt Republican state machines around the turn of the century, these liberal defectors are found mostly in Eastern and Great Lakes states. A second, somewhat larger minority of Anglo-Saxon Northern Democrats, located mainly in the Border States and Middle West, traces its origin to the old Jacksonian equalitarianism, which, as a political force, was largely scattered by the Civil War.

With these exceptions, the Anglo-Saxons and their allies among German and Scandinavian Protestants provide the unshakable foundation of Republican strength in many states. A 1957 study of church membership showed eighty-five counties in Pennsylvania, Ohio, Michigan, and Nebraska to be more than 40 per cent Protestant. All but one of these, Northampton County (Bethlehem) in Pennsylvania, voted for Richard Nixon in 1960; all but twenty voted for the Republican candidate for governor in 1960 or 1958, whichever was more recent, although in each case the Democratic candidate had been elected. All eight counties more than 30 per cent Protestant in New York, Massachusetts, and Arizona voted for both Nixon and the 1960 or 1958 Republican candidate for governor, as did Orange County, the most Protestant county (23 per cent) in California. In the two Southern states studied, Virginia and Texas, Nixon carried twenty-five of forty-five counties more than 50 per cent Protestant. Though by now outnumbered in some states, white Protestants give the Republican party a base of irreducible support on which it can fall back during periods of general disfavor with the electorate. (The Protestant churches, as such, appear to have little direct political influence, except in holding the line on Sunday closing laws and the like. Strongly Protestant Virginia in 1956 ignored the pleas of most church leaders and denominational publications to cast negative votes on a referendum, sponsored by the Byrd Organization, to strengthen laws against the integration of public schools.)

The first great rivals of the Yankees for political power were the Irish. Arriving in the United States in large numbers from the middle to the end of the nineteenth century, the Irish took over and maintained the organizations of the Democratic party in most Northeastern states. (In Philadelphia, on the other hand, they were for a long time predominantly Republican.) Traveling west as railroad construction workers, they frequently established pockets of Democratic strength in Midwestern states as well. Little interested in theory, essentially conservative, the Irish, by controlling much of what was in effect the opposition party during most of the seventy years following the Civil War, helped prevent the development of an ideological basis for American politics. Though gaining political control of many cities and some states, Irish politicians usually had to be content to support Anglo-Saxon defectors for state and national offices. In 1928, behind the candidacy of Al Smith, they waged an epic struggle for the presidency. The result was crushing defeat for the Democratic ticket.

After 1936, the Irish began to lose interest in their century-long feud with the Yankees, partly because they were long since victorious in cities like Boston and New York, partly because they were achieving amalgamation with the older stock, and partly because they had begun to resent the growing importance of Jews, Italians, and other foreign stocks in the Democratic party. By 1956, it was commonly agreed that a majority of Irish voted for Eisenhower for president. (A *New York Times* survey of the 1956 vote showed that the one identifiably Irish district in New York City went almost 80 per cent Republican.) In 1960, a Bostonian of Irish descent was at last elected president of the United States.

As John Kennedy's campaign organization had predicted when he was seeking the nomination for vice president in 1956, his presence on the national Democratic ticket recaptured the great majority of Irish voters who had been straying into the Republican camp in recent years. Since 1928, however, times had changed. Unlike Al

Smith, Kennedy by no stretch of the imagination could be regarded as the personification of distinctively Irish aspirations. Rather, the young Boston millionaire strove in manner and intellectual style to identify himself with those very Yankee patricians whom his fore-bears had fought so hard to overthrow. The Irish themselves were for the most part pleased enough that their kinsman in the White House spoke with the tongue of Harvard and Hyannis Port. They wished no more than that they or their children might do the same.

Following Kennedy's victory the political future of "the green" seemed uncertain. Though still controlling the Democratic organizations of most Northeastern states, they were increasingly conservative, increasingly suspicious of the representatives of the "newer nations" (as James Michael Curley had called the Jews, Italians, and Slavs) who crowded them for places at the Democratic table. In the end, many of them, it seemed possible, would find themselves most comfortable in alliance with their ancient enemies, the Anglo-Saxon Protestants.

The situation of the Irish has always been deeply influenced by their bond to the Roman Catholic Church. Religion, above all else, originally set them apart from the Yankees, and lent passion to the feud between the two national groups. More recently, Catholicism, by nature conservative, has contributed to the estrangement that has developed between many of the Irish and other participants in the Democratic front. While normally refraining from direct involvement in politics in the United States, the Catholic hierarchy, particularly since World War II, has seemed to display more sympathy for Republican than for Democratic candidates. (Francis Cardinal Spellman, for example, usually found occasion to have himself photographed with Thomas Dewey during the latter's campaigns, although he never said a word publicly in Dewey's behalf.) Lay Catholics have no doubt been slower than the hierarchy in giving up Democratic ties. In 1956, however, 106 out of 126 counties more than 30 per cent Catholic in ten states studied voted for Eisenhower. Even in 1960, with a popular Catholic leading the Democratic ticket, 40 of 87 counties more than 30 per cent Catholic in 8 non-south-western states supported Richard Nixon. Of these counties, 40 (not in all cases the same 40) had voted for the last Republican candidate for governor. In Texas and Arizona, where Catholics are largely of Mexican origin, only 4 of 39 counties more than 30 per cent Catholic voted for Nixon. The gradually developing rapprochment between Protestants and Catholics on such issues as anticommunism and the permissibility of prayer in the public schools, as well as final settlement of the question of whether a Catholic could become president, will probably further weaken Catholic identification with the Democratic party.

Germans, arriving in the East and Middle West in large numbers during the nineteenth century (some, like the Pennsylvania Dutch, had been in America since colonial times), at first suffered the same frustrations as did the Irish, with the same political results. The strength of the Democratic party in Ohio was for many years based on that state's large German population, while in Pennsylvania the German counties long provided the only havens for job-seeking Democrats. Gradually, however, the common Protestantism which many Germans shared with the Yankees and the dominance of Irish Catholics in the Democratic party induced a majority of persons of Teutonic stock to affiliate with the Republicans. The effect of two world wars, in which Democratic administrations directed hostilities against the German nation, completed the process of making the German-American vote normally Republican.

Italians and Eastern Europeans, who did not begin mass migration to the United States until the end of the nineteenth century, found the organizations of both major parties already tightly controlled by their predecessors. They at first tended to join whichever party was dominant in the area where they located, thus becoming Democrats in New York City, Boston, and Cleveland, but joining the Republicans in upstate New York, the Pennsylvania coal fields, and Michigan. Over the years, these ethnic groups were drawn by economic and religious ties toward the Democrats. Resistance by the Irish to inclusion of Italians in Democratic leadership in some states slowed and later (as in Massachusetts) threatened to reverse this trend. Many persons of Italian and Eastern European stock remain Republicans and many more are for all practical purposes independent. Members of these ethnic blocs have contributed to the huge floating vote which in recent years has enlivened the politics of New York, Massachusetts, and California, among other states.

In New York, the presence of diverse ethnic strains has led to the institution of the balanced ticket—the practice of including a Protestant, an Irish Catholic, an Italian, and a Jew on party slates for state offices. (In New York City, the Protestant now normally gives way to a Negro, usually running for office in Manhattan; in Buffalo, place must be found for a Pole and, if possible, a German.) The balanced ticket has taken hold slowly in other Eastern states, where Yankee Republicans and Irish Democrats have displayed extreme reluctance at giving up absolute control of their respective parties. In Western states, where ethnic feelings are less strong and slate-making processes often chaotic, it still plays little role. Even in New York, politicians debate the value of the practice. The 1958 Republican state ticket, it is pointed out, did very well in Italian neighborhoods without including a single candidate of Italian name. Recent successes of Republican raids, staged with Italian candidates, on Democratic strongholds in Massachusetts and Rhode Island indicate, however, that the popularity of the balanced ticket is likely to increase rather than to wane.

The Jewish population, concentrated in major metropolitan centers, is numerically important in only a few states. In the ten states studied, only twelve counties, according to the 1957 survey of the National Council of Churches, contained populations more than 5 per cent Jewish. These included seven New York counties, Suffolk (Boston), Philadelphia, Cuyahoga (Cleveland), Los Angeles, and San Francisco. Only in Brooklyn (39 per cent) and the Bronx (38 per cent) were Jews the largest single denomination. Though few in numbers, Jews, through political skill and importance as fund raisers, have achieved key roles in many party organizations, particularly those of New York, Pennsylvania, and Massachusetts. No group has, since the New Deal period, remained so constant to the Democratic party. In Boston in 1956, the heavily Jewish twelfth ward produced a majority of 80 per cent for Adlai Stevenson. The vote for Stevenson in the twelfth ward was almost exactly the same as that for the rest of the Democratic ticket, while in the entire city the candidate for president ran 15 per cent behind the majority of the Democratic candidate for governor. A *New York Times* survey of voting behavior in election districts in New York City the same year showed predominantly Jewish districts going for Stevenson by almost 75 per cent, while identifiable Italian and Irish districts were voting for Eisenhower by margins ranging from 60 to as much as 80 per cent. (Negro districts supported Stevenson by majorities between 64 and 74 per cent.)

Jewish loyalty to the Democrats is based in part on the humanitarian tradition in Jewish culture and in part on irritation at economic and social slights suffered over the years from Yankee Republicans. In comparison with the Irish, Germans, Italians, and Slavs, Jews show little wish to amalgamate with Yankee culture. The temptation to convert to Republicanism as they move up the economic ladder is therefore not so great. Jewish Republicans, like Jacob Javits and George Fingold, have usually run ahead of their party tickets in Jewish districts, but have rarely carried these districts against non-Jewish Democrats. In primary elections, Jews, partly out of uneasiness over their alliance with Irish and Italian politicians in the Democratic party, have frequently supported antiorganization candidates. Reform candidates ran well in Jewish districts in the 1954 Democratic primary in Philadelphia, as did Mayor Robert Wagner in his 1961 primary battle against Tammany Hall in New York, even though the Tammany candidate was himself Jewish.

Mexican-Americans in southern Texas, Arizona, and California are irregularly Democratic. In 1960, sixteen Texas counties contained more than 20 per cent Mexican foreign stock in their populations (a figure which did not, of course, include the many third- and fourth-generation Mexican-Americans). All but two of these voted for John Kennedy. In 1956, however, nine of sixteen Mexican counties supported Dwight Eisenhower. In his successful race for the United States Senate in 1961, Republican John Tower carried six of the Mexican counties in the runoff election. Frequently voted in blocs by political chieftains like George Parr, Mexicans have sometimes given the margin of victory to conservative candidates in Texas Democratic primaries. In the 1956 runoff gubernatorial primary, liberal Ralph Yarborough carried only three of sixteen Mexican populated counties against Price Daniel; in the 1962 gubernatorial runoff, liberal Don Yarborough captured four of the same counties. Mexican-American liberals like Henry Gonzalez, who in 1962 was elected to the United States Congress from San Antonio, have, on the other hand, recently had considerable success in leading Mexicans, particularly those living in cities, to vote for liberal candidates. In the first round of the 1961 senatorial election, Gonzalez himself finished first or second in eleven of sixteen Mexican populated counties. Santa Cruz County in Arizona, more than 50 per cent Mexican foreign stock, was normally Democratic during the fifties, although it voted for Dwight Eisenhower twice and Barry Goldwater once. In 1960, Santa Cruz gave 60 per cent of its vote to Kennedy, but polled a bare majority for Republican Paul Fannin for governor.

In one California and three Arizona counties, the 1960 census showed more than 25 per cent of the population to be American Indian. Two counties, Apache and Navajo in Arizona, contained absolute majorities of Indians. In none of these counties do the original inhabitants of North America play a significant role in politics or government. In Arizona, county election officers, mostly Democrats, reportedly avoid setting up polling places on Indian reservations. Few Indians are willing to make the long and sometimes difficult journey to the nearest town on election day. In 1962, Paul Jones, the Navajo tribal leader, announced plans to organize his fellow tribesmen politically and to run as a Republican for the state Senate from Navajo County. The path which he faced was a steep one: in the early sixties, not a single elected holder of public office in Arizona was an Indian.

ECONOMIC INTERESTS

The real substance of politics, it is often argued, is who gets the economic privileges and opportunities that are within the power of government to bestow. On the simplest level, this may mean political jobs, legal fees, highway contracts, insurance commissions, real estate purchases, government supply orders, and so forth. Many successful political organizations are operated on just this kind of nourishment. Far more important in the long run, however, are the attitudes taken by public authorities toward the aspirations and activities of the three major divisions of the economy: agriculture, business, and labor. Realizing this, the three giants are organized in all states to influence the decisions of government in their favor.

(Lesser divisions, like professional groups, consumers, and the underworld, are also organized, with more or less success, to protect their interests, and, when it serves their purposes, to lend support to one or more of the giants.)

Traditionally, agriculture and business have had far more effect on government at the state level than has the third member of the economic triumvirate, organized labor. This condition appears to be the natural consequence of the fact that organized labor can grow strong only after the economy has been developed by business enterprise. The attempt by labor in 1917 to gain control of the economically primitive society of Arizona was thus premature. The strike leaders rattling across the New Mexico state line in cattle cars had been defeated as much by a law of history as by the energy of Governor George W. P. Hunt.

As industrialization has progressed, however, labor has usually come into its own. By 1962, only in Virginia of the states studied was the influence of organized labor negligible. Despite increasing industrialization of the Old Dominion, union members during the fifties tended politically to be guided by their views on the race issue rather than by their economic attachments. Senator Byrd and many of his cohorts continued regularly to flay the CIO and its Political Action Committee. In Texas and Arizona, labor was waging uphill but increasingly effective campaigns to enlarge its influence with state government. About one-eighth of the members of the lower house of the Arizona legislature identified with labor, while in Texas labor was well represented in the legislative delegations from Houston, San Antonio, Fort Worth, and El Paso. In Nebraska, labor in 1958 took advantage of farmer disaffection with the Republicans to contribute to the election of the first Democratic governor in twenty years. Defeat of right-to-work laws in California and Ohio in 1958 demonstrated the power of labor in those states when challenged on an issue directly affecting the union movement. Labor in Pennsylvania, New York, and Massachusetts was, during the period studied, relatively safe from such frontal attacks. The experience of Michigan during the decade, on the other hand, demonstrated that an attempt to substitute labor domination for business domination of state government is likely to fail. So long as the national economy remains capitalist, business will have at its disposal resources to stalemate if not to defeat a government which is its avowed antagonist.

The relationship between labor and the Democratic party tends to be most intimate in those states passing from a rural or business dominated society to a more complex political structure. Labor, thus, is in the minority, even among Democrats, in Virginia, Arizona, and Texas. In Ohio and Nebraska, labor's strength is increasing, but it still must share power with other groups. Only in Michigan does labor appear to reign supreme within the Democratic party. In Pennsylvania, labor's importance in the party seems to be on the decline, partly as a result of the cordial treatment given to business by the administration of Governor David Lawrence. In the mature societies of Massachusetts and New York, labor has adjusted to a role of bargaining and negotiation within the general constellation of interest groups. In the fully developed system of collaborative politics, labor remains normally Democratic, but is not above striking de facto alliances with the Republicans. California, where labor was virtually bipartisan before 1958, presents a special case as a result of the right-to-work campaign of that year. Of necessity, labor employed the Democratic party as its instrument to repel the assault of militant business. Even so, development of a labor party on the model of Michigan seems unlikely in the complex society of California. Senator Thomas Kuchel, Republican, received considerable labor support in his campaign for re-election in 1962, while Governor Pat Brown, Democrat, maintains ties with many business leaders and groups.

Organized labor's impact at the polls remains uncertain except where it is directly challenged as on right-to-work. Of the 160 counties covered by the study in which more than 35 per cent of the work force was devoted to manufacturing (presumably the most highly unionized), 111 in 1960 voted for Richard Nixon and 90 had voted for the last Republican candidate for governor. These figures no doubt underestimate the effectiveness of labor, as they do not fairly represent the size of the labor vote in large cities. They do, however, suggest that many union members think last rather than first of the recommendations of their unions when casting their ballots.

While no longer exercising unchallenged dominance in most states, business continued during the fifties to play a prominent role in the decisions of all state governments. New tax laws in Michigan and Arizona were admittedly written by business lobbyists. Despite the right-to-work fiascoes of 1958, Democratic governors elected in Ohio and California that year hastened to conciliate business interests in their states. Legislatures of most states remained responsive to the wishes of the business community. No new income tax law, the *bête noire* of many businessmen, was enacted by any state during the 1950's. The share of the general tax burden borne by corporations was reduced by one-half in both New York and Massachusetts between 1948 and 1961. Ohio, Michigan, Nebraska, and Texas remained without state taxes on either personal or corporate income. With the support of both business and labor, Pennsylvania, Nebraska, and Ohio, among other states, established elaborate programs to attract new industry within their borders.

The influence of business is expressed both through the political power of individual business leaders and through the lobbying activities of groups like the Chamber of Commerce and the Manufacturers Association. Many businessmen are careful to remain on friendly terms with leaders of both political parties. In California, for example, millionaires like Ed Pauley and Howard Ahmanson can count on a friendly reception in Sacramento no matter which party is in power. Others, like some of the great oil tycoons of Texas and California, have devoted their fortunes with single-minded zeal to the promotion of conservative candidates only.

As patronage-based Republican organizations have proven increasingly ineffective in many states, business leaders have begun to assume responsibility for party strategy as well as for financial support. In the late forties, the large automobile manufacturers in Michigan launched a successful campaign to eliminate a corrupt element from the leadership of the state Republican party. During the fifties, under the pressure of repeated defeats by the Democrats, the party divided into two factions, supported, respectively, by General Motors, controlling the suburban organizations, and the Ford Motor Company, powerful in Detroit. In 1962, George Romney, former president of American Motors, assumed the leadership of a united party.

In Virginia, Richmond businessmen, entering politics directly for the first time as volunteers for Eisenhower in 1952, three times carried the state capital by majorities of more than 60 per cent for the Republican national ticket. (In state and local politics they remained Democrats, converting Richmond from a center of insurgent strength in 1949 to an Organization bulwark in 1961.) A group of Pennsylvania financiers, led by Phillip W. Sharples, set out after the 1960 election to reform the leadership of the Republican party in Philadelphia and the state. The 1962 gubernatorial candidacy of William Scranton was a direct consequence of this effort.

The new interest of businessmen in the day-to-day strategy of politics sometimes has had unhappy results: the business leaders who met at the Queen City Club in Cincinnati in 1958 might have done well to accept the advice of Ray Bliss and Senator John Bricker to abandon their right-to-work crusade. It springs, however, from a change of attitude among businessmen, as well as from the relative weakness of the Republican party. The earlier businessman in politics, like Joseph Grundy of Pennsylvania, regarded himself as primarily a defender of the business interest. Many contemporary businessmen turned politicians, like Nelson Rockefeller, Barry Goldwater, and George Romney, proceed on the belief that business owes the duty of leadership to the entire community. The danger that the businessman's view of the public interest will prove strikingly similar to the business interest is considerable. The gain to society in resourceful and efficient leadership, however, can be great.

Within the business community, single interest dominance of a state has become rare. The automobile manufacturers in Michigan come close to calling the shots for business in their state, but executives of such diverse interests as Dow Chemical Company and Gerber Baby Foods play important roles in state government and politics. The copper interests, particularly Phelps Dodge, once absolute masters of Arizona, have yielded place to the electric utilities as the state's most active lobby. In Pennsylvania, the Manufacturers Association shares its old supremacy with the Sharples group in Philadelphia and the Mellon interests in Pittsburgh. The petroleum industry in Texas has found its efforts matched by those of the Manufacturers Association and the Texas Life Convention (an association of insurance companies). The tightly organized business lobby in Ohio is ruled by a triumvirate composed of the Chamber of Commerce, the Manufacturers Association, and the Council of Retail Merchants. Electric utilities also are active in Ohio. Although sometimes at odds with each other, as in the conflict between the railroads and the steel companies in Ohio in 1951, the various business interests normally present a united front on most pieces of general legislation. Their influence is greatest with legislators elected from safe one-party districts, often located in rural areas. By their corporate nature, the business lobbies rarely are able to rise to the lofty view of the general public interest expressed by some individual business leaders.

Agriculture, once the most powerful segment of the economy in all states, retains influence out of proportion to its wealth and numbers almost everywhere. This is due in part to apportionment favoring rural counties in state legislatures, but largely to the force of tradition and the high moral position awarded the farmer in American culture. Actually, many rural areas by 1960 contained comparatively few farmers. In the Dutch crescent of Pennsylvania, seven of nine counties devoted more than 35 per cent of their work forces to manufacturing; none had as much as 20 per cent of their populations living on farms. In the rich agricultural country of central Ohio, only three of twenty-nine counties had more than 30 per cent of their populations living on farms; fourteen devoted more than 35 per cent of their work forces to manufacturing. Of California's twenty-five cow counties, only four reported more than 20 per cent of their populations living on farms.

Yet agriculture remains a formidable influence in all states studied except Massachusetts, where the farm population in 1960 was less than 1 per cent. In Arizona, with a farm population of 4 per cent, the farming and cattle people hold a virtual veto over all bills in the state legislature—possibly an echo of the long-past day when the state was tied almost exclusively to a cattle economy. Texas farmers (less than 8 per cent of the population) have succeeded in keeping most farm implements exempt from the state sales tax, obtaining tax refunds for gasoline used in tractors, and holding the cost of licenses for farm trucks to one-half the cost of licenses for ordinary trucks.

In Nebraska, where farmers and their families in 1960 constituted 21 per cent of the population, the farm vote is regarded by both parties as decisive. A drive against the gasoline tax by farmers, allied with petroleum and trucking interests, in 1950 resulted in reduction of the tax from six to five cents. When Governor Val Peterson, who had advocated increasing taxes for highway construction, was defeated in a bid for the United States Senate two years later, farmers were given the credit. Democratic gubernatorial victories in 1958 and 1960 were attributed to farmer dissatisfaction with Republican agricultural policies.

The farm vote in most states remains overwhelmingly conservative, or at least traditional. Of the sixty-six counties with farm populations over 20 per cent in Michigan, Ohio, Pennsylvania, New York, and California, sixty-four voted for Richard Nixon for president in 1960 (the two exceptions being Madera and Plumas Counties in California), and fifty-seven had voted for the last Republican candidate for governor. Of twenty-eight Nebraska counties more than half populated by farmers and their families, twenty-six voted for Nixon; only eighteen, however, voted in 1960 for the Republican candidate for governor, probably reflecting a degree of unrest among the farmers of the Great Plains. Of eighty-five counties with farm populations over 30 per cent in Texas and Virginia, all but thirty-two remained loyal to John Kennedy in 1960. In Virginia, only six of twenty-seven farm counties voted for Ted Dalton, Republican candidate for governor, in 1953. Only fourteen of fifty-eight Texas farm counties supported John Tower, Republican candidate for the United States Senate, in 1961. Not surprisingly, farmers, whose vested interest in the status quo is great, appear to support whichever party is traditionally dominant in their area.

The political impact of a fourth large economic group, the unemployed, is more ambiguous than is commonly imagined. In 1960, for instance, of 176 counties with serious unemployment (more than 7 per cent) in the states studied, 111 voted for Richard Nixon, who presumably was identified with current economic conditions. Democratic victories in 1958 undoubtedly were based in part on the economic recession that year. Yet, of the 19 California counties that registered gains of more than 20 per cent for the 1958 Democratic candidate for governor over his 1954 predecessor, only 7 were among the 26 counties in which unemployment was heaviest. The 16 Ohio counties which showed gains of more than 15 per cent for Democratic gubernatorial candidates from 1956 to 1958 included only 3 of the 19 counties with heaviest unemployment. In Pennsylvania and New York, the Republican showing for governor between 1954 and 1958 actually improved in 32 of the 50 heavy unemployment counties. Of the 17 constituencies that went Republican for governor in Virginia in 1957, 6 were among the 22 suffering with heavy unemployment.

There are several explanations for these apparent anomalies. For one thing, the unemployed may react against the party in power, regardless of its ideological coloration. Thus, Democratic administrations in Pennsylvania, New York, and Virginia may have been held responsible for continued unemployment in those states. (Also, in Pennsylvania and New York, many of the unemployed may have accepted the Republican argument that Democratic hostility to business was bad for the economy.) Mennen Williams in Michigan, likewise, did less well in 1958 than in either 1956 or 1954. Secondly, included in the total of heavy unemployment counties were 107 rural counties, where the political influences of tradition and sectionalism are presumably great. In nonagricultural regions of Pennsylvania, Michigan, and New York, continued unemployment has over the long run seriously undermined Republican strength. Finally, unemployment in great metropolitan areas like Detroit, Cleveland, Buffalo, and Pittsburgh may be relatively slight, yet very severely felt. The city dweller without a job has no farm to which to return. Often he owns neither land nor home. Used to many luxuries as well as necessities, he may have difficulty adjusting to straitened circumstances. Living largely on credit, he finds himself unable to pay the butcher, the baker, and the automobile dealer, thereby passing on his economic distress. A small increase in unemployment in metropolitan areas may thus produce a political reaction both powerful and swift. None of these factors is properly represented in a simple analysis by counties.

13

AREAS OF MANEUVER

B eside the great social and economic forces which affect the outcome of elections, there are certain other factors which candidates and parties are themselves able to manipulate with relative freedom. These factors compose the tools of the politician's trade. The skill with which they are wielded dictates the result of most campaigns in which other elements are more or less equal. They are: (1) money; (2) organization; (3) publicity; (4) personality; and (5) issues.

MONEY

No campaign for state office can succeed without sizable financial support. Just how sizable is difficult to estimate, due to the confusion, concealment, and outright dishonesty which almost universally characterize reporting of campaign expenses. State laws governing political expenditures usually do not limit the amounts spent directly by volunteer committees and the like. As a result, candidates themselves frequently do not know (and do not want to know) the total amounts that have been spent on their campaigns. In many states, laws requiring that campaign expenditures be reported are frequently ignored. "I have never heard of any penalty being invoked against candidates for failing to file campaign expenses," Roland Luedtke, Nebraska deputy secretary of state, told the *Lincoln Journal* in 1959. "It would be virtually impossible to get a conviction, because an official can regain good standing by filing at any time, even after the deadline."

A further complication in figuring election costs arises as a result of the different ways in which campaigns are financed in different states and by the two parties within the same state. Funds for Republican campaigns in New York, Pennsylvania, Massachusetts, Ohio, and Nebraska are channeled to a central campaign organization, which then spends money when and where it is needed for the entire state ticket. Even in these states, candidates usually set up their own funds in addition to the general party effort. In Massachusetts in 1960, for instance, John Volpe, Republican candidate for governor, reported expenditures of $443,000 beside the State Committee's outlay of $974,000. For Democratic campaigns in New York, Pennsylvania, and Ohio, most funds are raised and spent by local organizations. In Virginia, some funds are raised at the state level, but local organizations also take care of much of their own financing. Democrats in Massachusetts and Nebraska, and candidates of both parties in the other four states studied, usually handle most campaign expenditures through ad hoc committees set up for each campaign. In most Northern states, Democratic candidates are aided by fund-raising drives conducted by labor political action committees. Business and conservative groups likewise sometimes organize independent fund-raising efforts for Republicans and conservative Democrats.

Of the states studied, the cost of campaigning was apparently greatest in Pennsylvania. Total expenditures for both parties in the state campaign of 1958 (a gubernatorial year) were estimated at $6 million, with $4 million reported; in the 1960 presidential campaign estimated expenditures in the Keystone State rose to $10 million, of which about $6 million were recorded. In the 1958 campaign, Democrats reported a bit more than $2 million spent, while Republicans reported a bit less. Expenditures in 1960 were spread over a wide variety of committees, but again the Democrats and their labor auxiliaries, on the record, outspent the Republicans.

Other big spenders on political campaigns were New York, Massachusetts, Texas, and California, with the rank among them uncertain because of the differences in handling funds in the four states. The cost of electing a governor in New York was estimated at around $1.5 million. A similar sum was cited in Massachusetts, although many candidates were said to find it necessary to get along with smaller sums. Reported total expenditures in the Bay State totaled more than $3 million in 1958 and more than $4 million in 1960. In both years the Republican State Committee outspent the Democratic State Committee by about ten to one, at least partly because the various Democratic factions did not entrust funds to their State Committee. The cost of winning the Democratic primary for governor or senator in Texas, including the runoff, was placed at more than a million dollars in a close contest. In California, where fund-raising committees were set up for individual candidates for each state office, it was estimated that an adequately financed campaign for one candidate would cost $853,000.

The cost of campaigning in the other states studied was somewhat less, although on a per-capita basis cost appears to increase as population diminishes. The expense of waging a successful statewide campaign in Michigan was estimated at $500,000, with the candidate for governor needing at least $100,000 for direct expenses. Expenditures were spread through such a wide assortment of committees in Ohio that accurate estimate of the total cost of a campaign was deemed impossible. The Ohio Republican State Committee reported expenditures of $685,000 in 1960, $422,000 in 1958, and $762,000 in 1956 (governors were no longer elected in presidential years after 1956); its Democratic opposite spent $136,000 in 1960, $50,000 in 1958, and $86,000 in 1956. The wide difference between expenditures by the two parties was due to the fact that Republican funds were raised by a central committee, while the Democratic state organization had to be satisfied with whatever contributions the county organizations were willing to pass up to it.

Expenditures in Virginia were heavier in contested Democratic primaries than in general elections, but the proliferation of committees made it difficult to judge just how much was spent at either time. The Organization slate reported expenditures of $115,000 in the 1961 primary, while the insurgent ticket spent $75,000. In 1957, the year of the last serious Republican drive on the governorship, the Democratic candidate reported spending $49,000 in the general election to $43,000 for his Republican opponent. Since $75,000 was said to have been spent for bloc payments of poll taxes before one election in the Ninth Congressional District alone, these reported expenditures probably fell far below the actual outlay.

A Republican candidate for the United States Senate in Arizona in 1962 privately estimated that his campaign, without a primary contest, would cost $150,000. Total reported expenditures by gubernatorial candidates in Arizona in 1960 were $290,000, with the unsuccessful Democratic aspirant outspending the Republican incumbent by about $10,000. Interviews with Nebraska politicians and fund raisers by the *Lincoln Sunday Journal and Star* in 1960 produced the estimate that a total of $1,000,000 had been raised and spent by both parties in the state that year. The Republican State Committee reported raising $209,000, and its Democratic opposite declared income of $42,000—leaving a balance of $750,000 either reported at the local level or unrecorded. Such a relationship between reported and unreported funds was probably, in all states, more the rule than the exception.

The largest cost item for campaigning during the fifties was publicity. In New York, the necessary outlay for promotional activities of all kinds was estimated at between $750,000 and $1,000,000. Of this sum, 60 to 70 per cent would be spent on television (costing $4,500 for a five-minute program on one station in New York City —coverage of the entire state would run as high as $10,000). Purchase of a reasonable amount of billboard space cost $50,000, and one mailing of a campaign brochure to 20 per cent of the state's voters required expenditure of an additional $50,000. The rest of the promotional budget went for newspaper advertising, buttons, campaign literature, operation of the campaign headquarters, and miscellaneous items. In California, publicity expenses for one statewide candidate were estimated at $703,000. Distribution of this sum was, however, somewhat different. Only about one-third would be spent on television. More than one-fifth would go for newspaper advertising, and one-tenth for radio. The cost of billboard space rose to

$159,000. In addition to the direct cost of publicity, fees of from $20,000 to $50,000, for both primary and general elections, were paid to public relations experts who in the Golden State often served as professional campaign managers.

A much more expensive item in New York than in California was the amount paid for political organization. In the latter state, organization cost about $100,000. In New York, it was deemed necessary to spread between $300,000 and $500,000 across the state to local party organizations to help pay election day expenses. Even in New York, however, the amount spent directly at the polls on election day has in recent years declined considerably. In states like Pennsylvania, Virginia, and Arizona, where oldtime party organizations still flourish, outlays at the polls remain high. Sometimes, this takes the form of outright buying of votes ("a drink and a dollar" being the traditional purchase price in the Pennsylvania coal regions). More commonly, party workers are paid for transportation—the cost of hauling loads of voters in private automobiles to and from the polls.

Bloc payment of poll taxes is a major political expense in some parts of Texas and Virginia. In the Lone Star State, this practice long contributed to the power of political chieftains in Mexican-American counties. More recently, organized labor has reportedly expended large sums to get poll taxes paid for its potential urban supporters. Virginia's "Fightin' Ninth" has been the scene of many squabbles over bloc payment of poll taxes by both parties. These quarrels reached a climax in 1956 when a state court nullified the election of four Republicans to offices in Lee County on the ground that the Republican party had illegally paid poll taxes for hundreds of voters. The judge of the Lee County Circuit Court promptly filled the vacancies with four Democrats, including three defeated candidates from the preceding election. Ted Dalton told the Republican state convention a few weeks later: "It is a poor rule that won't work both ways . . . I have yet to hear of one single instance where a Democrat has been removed from office because he participated in, or was the beneficiary of, the payment of poll taxes of others than himself and family . . . To my certain knowledge most of the Democratic leaders of this state, including members of Congress, state officials, and county office holders by the hundreds, have year in and year out been paying the poll taxes of their supporters and party stalwarts."

Campaign funds are raised from a variety of sources, including economic interest groups like corporations and labor unions, wealthy contributors (the so-called "fat cats"), party jobholders and job-seekers, and ordinary voters who wish to assist a party or a candidate. Laws against contributions by corporations are evaded by paying executive salaries or legal fees out of which it is understood that political offerings will be made. Unions usually set up allegedly autonomous citizenship committees, which are supported by assessments and contributions from dues-paying members. Republicans undoubtedly receive more and larger gifts from wealthy contributors than do their opponents, but the Democrats, too, have their rich benefactors. In Pennsylvania, in 1960, for example, Republican candidates and committees received $60,000 from the Pew family of Philadelphia, $40,000 from the Mellon family of Pittsburgh, and $15,000 from the Pitcairn family of Philadelphia, while the Democrats received gifts of $11,000 from the Greenfield family, and $10,000 from the Mann family, both of Philadelphia.

Fund-raising dinners have become a major source of party funds, particularly for the Democrats. (The device was invented by Matthew McCloskey, former treasurer of the Democratic National Committee, in Philadelphia in 1934.) Called "pay as you yearn" dinners by one observer of national politics, the "$100-a-plate dinners," "Jefferson-Jackson Day banquets," "Lincoln Day dinners," and the like attract large numbers of hopeful candidates, political jobholders, lawyers and contractors doing business with state and local government, labor union delegations, and a sprinkling of ordinary citizens who enjoy the excitement of political affairs or wish to express identification with their party. The mammoth Philadelphia Democratic $100-a-plate dinners, held in that city's Convention Hall, have been known to raise more than $300,000. State committee dinners held by both New York party organizations in large Manhattan hotels usually net between $150,000 and $250,000. The Jefferson-Jackson Day dinner staged by Massachusetts Democrats in 1960 brought income of $33,-000 to the Democratic State Committee, with additional sums going to the National Committee and for a voter registration drive. In recent years, a trend has begun toward holding fund-raising dinners for individual candidates as well as for the collective party war chests. One of the most successful of these was the "Tribute to Jacob Javits," held in New York City in 1962, which not only raised funds for the New York senator's re-election campaign, but also demoralized the opposition by showing numerous Democrats and Liberals among the contributors.

No small share of the cost of campaigning must usually be borne by the candidates themselves. This fact has contributed to the tendency of big-time American politics to turn into a sport for millionaires. Of the seven candidates most prominently mentioned for the presidency in 1960, five possessed sizable private fortunes. While wealthy contributors are more common on the Republican side of the fence, wealthy candidates seem, if anything, more frequently Democratic. The Republican Rockefellers, Tafts, Scrantons, and Goldwaters appear outnumbered by the Democratic Roosevelts, Harrimans, Lehmans, Kennedys, Clarks, Johnsons, Shivers, and Symingtons. (This phenomenon springs partly from the fact that the Democrats, in most places the less wealthy party, have the greater need for well-to-do candidates; partly from the resentment that some men of inherited wealth appear to feel toward the new managerial class, which nowadays largely dominates the Republican party.)

Personal wealth is a less important asset for a candidate at the state than at the national level. Party organizations and economic interest groups are more prepared and better able to finance campaigns for control of state governments than to stand the cost of a run for the presidency. Nevertheless, the wealthy candidate maintains an undoubted advantage over his financially less fortunate rivals. Not only is he able to afford such expensive campaign aids as private airplanes and personal pollsters, but also he can to some degree remain independent of party managers and fund raisers.

Proposals that campaigns should be financed in part by the government no doubt have merit, though their implementation would encounter formidable administrative and practical difficulties. Strict enforcement of reporting laws, accompanied by removal of unrealistic legal limitations on campaign spending, would go far toward eliminating many of the current evils of political fund raising. Revision of tax laws to permit write-offs of political contributions also would encourage private citizens of limited means to give financial support to their parties, thus reducing the roles of unions, corporations, fat cats, and other big contributors. Inevitably, however, powerful economic interests will continue to be the major source of funds for both parties and candidates. The dangers of this system can at least be reduced if it is made a matter of public record who is giving what to whom.

ORGANIZATION

The organization—usually known by its detractors as the machine —is perhaps America's most important contribution to the practice of politics. Developed first by the Anti-Federalists, nurtured by their Democratic successors during the age of Jackson, and brought to perfection by the Republican master politicians of the late nineteenth century, the organization has provided means for democratic control within a tradition of governmental continuity. It has proven sufficiently flexible to register change in popular sentiment without recourse to violent revolution, sufficiently strong to permit reasonably stable government, and sufficiently broad to give basis for compromise of all but the most fundamental differences. Since World War II, the techniques of American party organization have been copied with much success in other nations of the Free World. At the same time, the organization, it is generally agreed, has played a declining role in the politics of the nation of its birth.

The professional organization, despite its huge success, has never enjoyed a very savory reputation in the United States. It has been linked with and sometimes blamed for the two great shortcomings of American democracy: corruption and mediocrity. Particularly at the state and city levels, the organization has too often proven the willing instrument for graft and organized crime. Its genius for compromise, at the national as well as at other levels of government, has too often elevated to power men barren of either ideas or ideals. Some of its attributes—like the spoils system of distributing government jobs—have placed an almost intolerable burden on the business of public administration.

The leaders of the Progressive movement, around the beginning of the twentieth century, became convinced that the professional political organization and the party system which it created were dangerous anachronisms. In many Western and Midwestern states, they succeeded in enacting laws which made it impossible for organizations to continue in the old way. Although their analysis may have been incomplete and their reforms sometimes misdirected, the Progressives undoubtedly did much to fumigate the structure of American politics and to prepare the way for much social and economic change.

Many liberals of the New Deal and subsequent periods did not share the antipathy of the Progressives for professional politicians. Pragmatism replaced idealism as the guiding philosophy of liberal opinion. The politician was recognized as a technician, useful for his ability to deliver necessary electoral majorities, and even sentimentalized as a sort of lovable old crook, humanizing the impersonal machinery of government. At the same time, the growing importance of the central government (which had been largely removed from the patronage system), the increasing prosperity of the private sector of the American economy, and the gradual loosening of old sectional and ethnic ties contributed to the further weakening of the party organization. After 1946, newspapers regularly announced the downfall of "the last of the oldtime machines." Despite these frequent interments, the political organization at present still survives, in almost classic form in several states, and even displays signs of revival in some areas where it had been thought to be extinct.

The most powerful association of professional politicians in the country is probably the Byrd Organization of Virginia. Dominating the Democratic party of the Old Dominion for more than fifty years and extending its control deep into the councils of the Republican party as well, the Organization (the only one in the country which habitually thinks of itself with a capital "O") has survived a decade of repeated challenge and remains supreme in all branches of Virginia government. Not surprisingly, the Byrd Organization is not a typical representative of its breed. Almost alone among organizations, it has acquired the trappings and the prestige of an institution. It has identified itself with the history of Virginia and shares the pride which many Virginians feel for all things Virginian. It represents a definite philosophy—conservative individualism—rather than the mere aspiration of its adherents to remain indefinitely at the public trough. Its leaders are superior in manners, if not in ability, to the coarser bosses of most state and local machines. For all that, the Organization has during the last decade felt itself forced to resort to the ugly weapon of race prejudice to maintain its power. In the state legislature, the key to its continued rule, it was under fire and in retreat before the Supreme Court decision banning segregation of public schools in 1954. For the moment, the race issue seems to have persuaded the majority of white Virginians to close ranks behind the Organization. The gubernatorial primary of 1961, however, revealed that many weak spots in the front supporting the Organization still exist.

More typical of the old-line machines are those which continue to operate, with varying degrees of efficiency, in states like Pennsylvania, Massachusetts, New York, Ohio, and Arizona. In all of these states, patronage remains an important element in politics. The ability to offer government jobs to its supporters is probably the essential characteristic of the classic political organization. Loyal armies of jobholders build the organization's following in the wards and precincts, tighten the bond between the state high command and its county leaders, provide kickbacks from their salaries to feed the organization's war chest, man the polls on election day, and, when necessary, risk prison sentences to produce the majorities needed to keep the organization in power. At the peak of its development, the organization is self-supporting and self-sufficient, beholden neither to economic interest group nor to ideological faction. It is an association of politicians who have used their combined skills to gain control of a valuable resource: the public treasury. For continued access to this resource, they are prepared to offer certain services, such as maintenance of schools, construction of highways, protection of various economic groups; their primary interest in government, however, is not much different from that of the wildcatter in his oil well—private profit. (An old politician in an upstate Pennsylvania county, learning that the opposition had adopted the slogan, "Give the Court House Back to the People," commented, "Let the people build their own court house. This one is ours, and we mean to hold onto it!")

The differences between Republican and Democratic machines

are likely to be noticeable but of no great significance. In the North, the Republican organization is likely to be a bit more conservative and the Democratic organization quite a bit more partial to the demands of organized labor; neither, however, willingly offends or alienates either business or labor. Democratic politicians in machine states tend, according to a national union leader, to play "dog-catcher politics"—based on patronage, not ideological or economic attachments. Businessmen make similar complaints about their Republican allies. In ethnic terms, Republican machine leaders as a group once tended to be Anglo-Saxon and Democratic machine leaders to be Irish. There were always, however, numerous exceptions, and in recent years a trend in organization leadership comparable to the balanced ticket trend in candidates has gone far toward wiping out ethnic distinctions. In many states, the Democratic machine is based on a powerful organization in one or two large cities, while the Republican machine maintains ties with numerous upstate county courthouse rings. (In Arizona and Texas, however, the Democrats control the courthouse rings and are less strong in the cities.) State patronage binds these local organizations into an effective state machine. (For instance, the Philadelphia Democratic organization, among the strongest in the country, depended until 1963 almost entirely on state rather than city patronage to keep its foot soldiers gainfully employed.)

Considerable variation exists among the organizations of the different states, depending on local laws and conditions. The Republicans operate well-disciplined organizations in Massachusetts, New York, and Ohio as do the Democrats in Pennsylvania and Arizona. The Democratic organization in Ohio, on the other hand, was during the fifties continually buffeted by rebellion and defeat. In the early sixties, Governor Michael DiSalle, with the aid of his able state chairman, William Coleman, attempted to build a cohesive organization. In the 1962 gubernatorial primary, however, DiSalle was opposed by an insurgent who received 45 per cent of the vote. A major weakness of the Ohio Democratic organization appears to be the continued autonomy of the Cleveland and other city machines. (While unwilling to submit to the state leadership, the Miller organization of Cleveland also has been unable to gain control of the state machine, as the Philadelphia Democratic organization did in Pennsylvania and as Tammany, for a time, did in New York.) The New York Democratic organization, after a period of strength under the leadership of Carmine DeSapio, was defeated by the Republicans and finally demolished by insurgent reformers. (Whether the reformers will develop their own organization—and whether it will differ significantly from the old Tammany crew—remains to be seen.) The Republican organization in Pennsylvania was beset by factionalism from 1950 to 1962. Although the factions usually lined up in two alliances, under vague ideological banners, there were in fact at least a half-dozen separate groups in the field, each prepared to strike a bargain with almost any of the others in the common quest for power. In Massachusetts, factionalism in the Democratic organization during the fifties virtually deteriorated into tribalism. Family and local chieftains led clans too numerous for classification in wild and chaotic contests for party control.

A new kind of volunteer organization began to develop during the 1950's, particularly in Michigan, New York, Texas, and California. The programmatic, participative political party built in Michigan by Neil Staebler and Mennen Williams was perhaps the model for this new variety of machine, based on principles rather than patronage. On the Democratic side, it usually has the labor movement and the local liberal "white-shoe outfit" (academics, social workers, socialites) at its core. Among the Republicans, the volunteer organizations have been active in national campaigns, but have been slow developing in state and local politics. This is partly because the existing Republican organizations as a rule have been more efficient than their Democratic opposites, partly because the Republican point of view has generally failed to arouse enthusiasm among intellectuals and young people who provide manpower for the liberal clubs, and partly because many conservatives seem unwilling to sacrifice doctrinal purity for political success. (A notable exception is Senator Goldwater, who in Arizona has been able to motivate an army of volunteer workers for his conservative philosophy.)

In some ways similar to the earlier Populists and Progressives and the splinter parties of New York and the South, the new volunteer organizations differ from most of their predecessors in that they usually seek to achieve their ends within the structures of the existing parties. (The New Deal liberals, who in this respect resembled the leaders of current ideological organizations, as a rule neglected state and local politics.) Whether the organization tradition will in the end capture the ideological movements (as to some extent seems to be happening in California) and whether, if the ideologues do succeed, American politics will lose much of its essential flexibility and spirit of consensus (as the hatreds which have entered some recent campaigns appear to suggest) are questions that remain to be answered.

The central problem, it would seem, is to find some way to preserve the great virtues of the old organizations, while eliminating the vices of patronage, favoritism, and corruption to which they all too obviously have pandered. If the professional organizations are finally destroyed, the viability of American democracy may perish with them; if their vices are permitted to continue, the growing demoralization of public life seems sure.

PUBLICITY

In a democratic system of government, the means by which politicians communicate with the electorate are of utmost importance. When populations pass fifteen million, as in New York and California, communication media (as indicated by the campaign budgets previously described) are bound to become a night-and-day concern to all persons holding or seeking public office.

Newspapers continue to be regarded by most state politicians as their best means for reaching the voters. Candidates may weather the editorial hostility of the newspapers of their states—Mennen Williams was six times elected governor of Michigan, despite the fact that he was regularly opposed by all of the state's leading daily newspapers (Michigan has only one traditionally Democratic daily, *The Marshall Evening Chronicle,* published in a city with a population of 7,000), and John Tower carried Dallas in the 1961 runoff by almost 13,000 votes against the opposition of both the *Dallas Morning News* and *Dallas Times Herald.* Coverage in the news columns, however, appears indispensable. This, with few exceptions, newspapers of all political leanings grant with reasonable fairness to all major candidates. Although placement of stories, choice of photographs, and outright bias of reporting in some papers are used to promote particular candidates or parties, the days when a newspaper was partisan "from the weather report on the front page to the last obituary on the back" are largely past. The current danger, rather, is that in striving for objectivity, much political reporting has become flat. A few liberal newspapers, like *The Texas Observer* and the *Guardian* (Pennsylvania), strive to keep the ideological pot boiling. Informed commentary on state politics from a personal point of view is confined in most states, however, to a few reporters writing daily or weekly columns in the metropolitan papers.

Newspapers intervene directly in politics by promoting both issues and candidates from time to time. The doctrine of interposition, under which segregationists all over the South sought to nullify the Supreme Court decision ordering integration of public schools, was first proposed by James Jackson Kilpatrick, editor of the *Richmond News Leader*. Feuding with Texas Attorney General Will Wilson in 1960, the *Houston Post* campaigned vigorously for Wilson's opponent, Waggoner Carr, speaker of the state House of Representatives. Although Carr led in the first round primary, he was ultimately defeated in the runoff by Wilson. Two years later the *Post* again took up the cudgels on Carr's behalf, and he was nominated and elected attorney general. The *Boston Globe* in 1959 launched a campaign for a constitutional convention to reduce the size of the Massachusetts legislature, strengthen the governorship, and extend the merit system to county employees. Although the constitutional convention was opposed by most members of the legislature, considerable popular support appeared to be developing for the proposal.

During the 1950's, television received a larger and larger share of the advertising dollar expended by political candidates and parties. A pleasing television personality replaced a good speaking voice as the most indispensable quality for a candidate. Governor Williams, Senator Tower, Governor Pyle of Arizona, and Senator Clark of Pennsylvania were among the many who relied heavily on electronic media to get their message to the voters. Despite its increasing revenues from politics, television made little effort, at the state level, to undertake the responsibility for covering political news. In Michigan, for instance, no electronic medium gave daily coverage of state government news before 1959; after that, only the Lansing stations provided such service. There have been no reported cases of newspapers reducing their coverage of candidates who prefer to place the majority of their advertising with television.

Publicity, inevitably, has become a specialty for professional experts in politics. Many candidates and political leaders have themselves a highly developed instinct for attracting and holding the attention of the news media. Most, however, have felt the need to employ press secretaries, public relations advisors, or directors of information. In many states, including some of the largest, these press assistants are former journalists who have deserted the capitol press room for more lucrative berths in the governor's office or party headquarters. At the end of a campaign or an administration, they may return with relieved hearts to the more congenial tasks of reporting. A few press assistants are intense militants, deeply committed to promotion of their party's programs and candidates.

A growing role in politics has been played by professional public relations firms, whose personnel are normally drawn from the traditions of advertising rather than of reporting. In the East, South, and Middle West, the activities of these firms still are usually confined to preparing advertising for the various media, supervising direct mail operations, and producing radio and television programs. In the Far West, particularly California, they have tended to take over entire campaigns. The rise of the political public relations agency in California has been due not only to the weakness of party organizations, but also to the frequency with which referenda on issues are placed on the ballot. Public relations firms have been able to extract sizable fees from economic groups interested in supporting or opposing such issues as right-to-work, changes in the tax structure, and old age pensions, as well as from individual candidates, each of whom feels it necessary to conduct a personal publicity campaign. Pioneered in the early forties by Whitaker and Baxter, who handled Earl Warren's first campaign for governor, the political public relations trade was divided among at least ten major firms by 1962. These firms often accept responsibility for the fund-raising and organizational duties assigned to party leaders in most other states. The public relations system has the virtue of reducing the dependence of candidates on venal politicians and political machines; it has the serious fault of over-emphasizing the importance of political packaging at the expense of program and substance. (In California and other Western states, there is more than a suspicion that some referenda are generated by publicity firms who hope later to profit by their promotion.)

The influence of the political public relations advisor seems to be increasing across the nation. In New York, for example, while the Republicans continue to alternate between two general advertising agencies, the Democrats usually employ Lloyd Whitebrook, a specialist in political publicity. In Pennsylvania, William Keisling, a twenty-six year old publicist, was among the principal directors of William Scranton's successful campaign for governor in 1962. For better or worse, the future appears to provide a rich prospect for the buildup boys with a flare for politics.

PERSONALITY

The widely held belief that the right kind of advertising can put over almost any candidate or issue was supported during the fifties by the public relations experts themselves and also by liberals seeking some explanation for the continued popularity of Dwight Eisenhower. This unlikely concert of opinion for a time drowned out the obvious fact that while publicity may enhance the appeal of an attractive candidate, it cannot be successful with men or notions which are inherently repellent to a majority of the electorate. Eisenhower's hold on the public imagination was based, quite simply, on the trust and confidence which his character inspired in the hearts of most ordinary men and women. Public relations techniques perhaps promoted but by no means created these sentiments. Their secret, rather, was locked within the mysterious element of human nature known as personality. Whether Eisenhower reminded the mass of voters of their father, their coach, George Washington, or their dormant longing for a legitimate monarch, he succeeded by his smile, his wave, his manner of speech, or some other quality in persuading them that as long as he was president, the country was in good hands.

Personality, of course, has been important to politics since men made their first rudimentary attempts at social organization. The magic ability to inspire popular loyalty has always been counted among the necessary qualifications for leadership. As party organizations grew weaker and ancient economic and ethnic conflicts less intense during the fifties, personality became the essential factor in deciding many close elections.

What were the qualities possessed in common by Mennen Williams, Barry Goldwater, Joseph Clark, and Nelson Rockefeller, to name four who either upset political traditions or bucked electoral landslides? They were, first of all, attractive men—handsome, articulate, clean cut. They did not, in the popular view, look like politicians. There was little in any of their manners to suggest the atmosphere of smoke-filled room or party caucus, which many voters had evidently come to distrust. Second, they seemed dissatisfied with the status quo. Whether they wished to move toward untrammeled individualism, toward world peace through world law, or in some other direction, they appeared ready and anxious for political change. Third, their public personalities were warm without being inflammatory—somewhere between the coolness of Robert Taft, Sr., and the raking heat of Huey Long. Fourth, they were—or gave the impression of being—men of principle. In contrast with the pragmatic type of political leader that had been common since the New Deal, they were unblushing idealists (different though their ideals might be). Some of them were in fact expert political horsetraders, and all had been guilty at one time or another of inconsistency and compromise; they succeeded nevertheless in conveying an image of personal dedication to absolute goals. (The attraction of idealistic personalities in politics has seemed to increase proportionately as the actual policies of American government have become yearly more tentative and finite.) Last, they were participants in a common culture of relative sophistication. Goldwater displayed little desire to associate himself with the "revolt against civilization" which had seemed to engage the conservative camp during the heyday of Senator Joseph McCarthy. Clark and Williams occasionally spoke in the rhetoric of the radical left, but both enjoyed the pleasures and shared many of the attitudes of the social establishment. Rockefeller, above all, was the model of catholic taste and temperament. Extremism—not to be confused with idealism—became one of the cardinal political sins of the time. The day of the radical demagogue was either past or not yet arrived. Successful politicians could easily be found during the decade who displayed few or none of the qualities common to these four men; their shared characteristics (which also fit, to some degree, both Presidents Eisenhower and Kennedy) provide, however, an initial guide to the personality factors apparently attractive to voters from about 1955 to 1962.

Tied to the increasing emphasis on personality has been the growing use of public opinion polls. Valuable in discovering how the public is reacting to particular issues, as well as in predicting the popularity of candidates, the polls have won particularly wide acceptance among the political leaders of New York and California. Members of the Kennedy family, during their various campaigns, also have relied heavily on the findings of public opinion researchers. In 1962, Governor DiSalle of Ohio reportedly reversed his decision not to seek a second term after hearing the results of a favorable poll. The Philadelphia Democratic organization after 1953 employed a full-time pollster (who resigned in 1962 when the Pennsylvania Democrats slated Richardson Dilworth for governor, despite the pollster's findings that Dilworth was unpopular in Philadelphia). Whatever the accuracy of the polls, their influence on political strategy has undoubtedly become immense.

One interesting finding of the polls has been that popular judgments of political personalities are usually based on remarkably scant information. In the opinion of one pollster, at least, these judgments are almost always correct—the bungler is known as a bungler, the crook as a crook, the fighter as a fighter. Whether or not these swift characterizations form adequate basis for a reasoned approach to politics, their impact will undoubtedly continue to determine the outcome of many elections.

ISSUES

According to the theoretical ideal of political democracy, candidates and parties appear before the electorate with varying approaches to the problems and responsibilities of government. The public chooses among these approaches and elects to office those persons and groups whose programs win its approval. The actual role of issues in American politics is, needless to say, not nearly so simple. In reality, any or all of the forces discussed in the last two sections may far outweigh the importance of issues in any given election. Nevertheless, the program which a party presents may decisively influence the small but sometimes crucial minority of wavering voters. In any case, the issues are likely to create poles of attraction around which, in the long run, other factors tend to arrange themselves.

Issues in state campaigns have in recent years, outside of the South, generally been of two kinds: economic liberalism versus economic conservatism, and administrative reform versus administrative experience. The two groups of issues are not necessarily related. Thus, Richard Nixon could in 1962 promise to clean up "the mess in Sacramento" and pursue a relatively conservative line on economic matters; while in Pennsylvania and Michigan, Democrats were flying the banners of both liberalism and experience.

The "ins" are, of necessity, committed to arguing the value of tested experience. The "outs," on the other hand, may hesitate to take up the issue of reform, sometimes fearing to find their own hands dirty and sometimes hoping to secure for themselves the potential rewards available under the existing system. (Only a very rare bird can match the performance of Mayor Robert Wagner of New York City, who in 1961 successfully sought re-election as the candidate of both experience *and* reform.)

Economic conservatives usually attract the support of business, while liberals can count on backing from large segments of organized labor. (Labor, in many states, makes its message unmistakably clear, issuing lists of key votes in the state legislature, on which legislators are recorded as either right or wrong.) Farm groups usually line up with conservatives, although in some states, like Nebraska, troubles in the farm economy may move some segments of agriculture into the liberal camp.

A third category of issues, dealing with racial discrimination, frequently divides politicians into camps similar to those formed by economic liberalism and conservatism. Despite the sincere dedication of many economic conservatives to civil rights progress, the economic impact of the race problem, particularly in such areas as housing, is likely to lead politicians normally allied with business to a moderate position. In the South, economic liberals have sometimes been among the most ardent segregationists. At least in Virginia and Texas, however, there has been a considerable tendency in recent years for economic liberals to take the locally more liberal position on civil rights.

A fourth group of issues, involving the relations between church and state, has been treated with great diffidence by almost all politicians. No set of issues is more potentially disruptive to the current alignments in American politics. Much of the leadership, as well as the rank and file, of organized labor, for instance, take leave of doctrinaire liberals on such issues as Sunday closing laws. The powerful influence of the Roman Catholic Church has during the past decade begun to shift in favor of a more intimate relationship between religion and government. The possibility of an alliance between urban Catholics and rural Protestants is a nightmare to most liberal leaders. At the same time, many economic conservatives among both Yankees and Jews uncompromisingly oppose any lowering of the barrier between church and state. The problem, long dormant except for occasional blue-law controversies, has recently begun to attract increased attention in the political arena.

Party discipline on issues in state legislatures is, as a rule, much stronger than in the federal Congress. This is particularly true in Eastern and Great Lakes states. In the 1961 session of the Pennsylvania Senate, for example, of thirty-one key votes listed by the AFL-CIO, the twenty-five Democrats (not counting absentees) voted unanimously on twenty-one, while the twenty-five Republicans were unanimous on fourteen. More than 80 per cent of the Democrats voted together on all but one issue, while the Republicans were at least 80 per cent united on eighteen of thirty-one roll calls. (The superior Democratic cohesion was no doubt due in large part to the facts that the Democrats held the governorship and had succeeded in organizing the Senate. In prior sessions, the Republicans were similarly united.) In the same year in the Pennsylvania House of Representatives, the majority Democrats voted unanimously on twenty-three of thirty-seven key roll calls and were at least 80 per cent united on all but one; the minority Republicans were at least 80 per cent united on twenty-one of thirty-seven roll calls. The AFL-CIO report for Massachusetts in 1961 showed the fourteen Republicans in the Senate unanimous on ten of twelve key roll calls; the twenty-six Democrats were unanimous on only three roll calls, but were at least 80 per cent united on all but one. Both Republicans and Democrats were at least 80 per cent united on five of six key roll calls in the Massachusetts House of Representatives. Of seven votes in the 1961 session of the Ohio Senate analyzed by the AFL-CIO, Republicans voted unanimously on all seven while the minority Democrats opposed them unanimously on all but one. (The exception, involving a change in the workmen's compensation law opposed by organized labor, was supported by only two of eighteen Democrats.) In the Ohio House of Representatives, both Republicans and Democrats were better than 90 per cent united on seven of eight key roll calls.

In states where Republican legislators have been few or non-existent, such as Virginia, Texas, and Arizona, party divisions are replaced by relatively loose coalitions of conservatives and liberals. The same is true of Nebraska, where the nonpartisan Senate has a tendency to fragment into small blocs, some of which contain only a single member. Before the advent of the Brown administration in California, party lines tended to be almost without meaning. This situation changed somewhat after 1958, but party discipline still does not approach that of the states in which party organization is traditionally strong. Of thirty-nine key roll calls in the 1959 California General Assembly selected by the AFL-CIO, the forty-six Democrats voted unanimously on four and the thirty-three Republicans on only two. The Democrats were at least 80 per cent united on twenty-eight key roll calls, but the Republicans achieved 80 per cent cohesion on only twenty-one of thirty-nine crucial votes. Three of the four important tax proposals submitted by Governor Brown were opposed by more than 25 per cent of the Democratic legislators.

Groups formed to develop issues, like Americans for Democratic Action (ADA) and Americans for Constitutional Action (ACA), have had relatively little influence on state politics. The most powerful ideological group (as distinguished from party organizations and identifiable economic groups) of the 1950's was probably the liberal California Democratic Council, which succeeded in taking over a large part of the machinery of the Democratic party in the Golden State. Democrats of Texas, under various titles, served as a rallying force for liberals in the Lone Star State. ADA was influential in Pennsylvania, chiefly through its ties with the leaders of the Philadelphia reform movement, and active in Massachusetts and Ohio. Nebraska Constitutional Conservatives, affiliated with ACA, was in the early sixties regarded with respectful attention in the Cornhusker State. The Ohio Information Committee, seeking to preserve the "free, competitive, private enterprise system in Ohio," was working on ambitious plans for a statewide precinct-based organization in 1962. In Virginia, Defenders of State Sovereignty and Individual Liberties acted during the fifties as spokesman for last-ditch defenders of segregation. Nonpartisan groups, like the Citizens Union of New York City, Citizens for Michigan, and the League of Women Voters, have served to focus issues in some states. Chapters of the American Civil Liberties Union, the National Association for the Advancement of Colored People, the Urban League, and other specialized groups carry on the fights at the state level for their respective causes.

The impact of scholars and intellectuals on state politics during the fifties was surprisingly slight. Only the Liberal party of New York consistently included persons of academic background in its top councils. The mutual distrust which has existed between the majority of intellectuals and the leadership of the Republican party since the New Deal period is still in force in most areas in the middle sixties. On the other hand, the national alliance between intellectuals and the Democrats has had little carry over at the state or local levels. Most of the Harvard faculty members who flocked to the support of John Kennedy regarded the Democratic party of Massachusetts with unconcealed aversion. The lack of influence of intellectuals in state government and politics seems partly due to the resistance of state political leaders and partly to the fact that many of the intellectuals themselves have lost (or never had) faith in the states as effective instruments of government.

EPILOGUE
STATES IN CRISIS

Politics is not, after all, a game. Although the most successful politicians no doubt find in it a kind of sporting pleasure, its results and its essential nature are extremely serious. Through politics not only is the distribution of the world's wealth largely managed, but also the moral potential of mankind is either thwarted or fulfilled. (Even a completely free economy owes its freedom to the political constitution under which it operates; and the most individualistic moralist must acknowledge the involvement of society in his conduct.)

The problems, the tribulations, the opportunities for future development of state governments are of utmost importance to every American because the American political system has, to a great extent, been based and constructed on the fact of the existence of the states. If the states should fail to meet the challenges that are being put to them during the seventh decade of the twentieth century, the only alternatives, short of chaos, would be an enormous expansion of the resources and authority of local government or acceleration of the present trend toward complete assumption of governmental responsibility by the national government. The former, while offering some promise in such fields as urban development and regional planning, would hardly provide adequate means to cope with the more fundamental political and economic realities of the age of automation, mass culture, and population explosion. The latter, while to some degree a military and economic necessity, would, carried to its logical extreme, almost surely undermine if not destroy the political freedom, regional diversity, and social and economic flexibility which have thus far characterized the American system.

The problems of the states, as they have emerged in the foregoing chapters, may be categorized under three major headings: (1) constitutional obsolescence, (2) lack of financial resources, and (3) possible loss of political legitimacy.

State constitutions (by which is meant the organic governmental systems of the states, as well as the written documents which more commonly are so designated) have all too frequently created paralyzed executives, malapportioned legislatures, partisan judiciaries, and political parties representative of little beyond a common thirst for patronage and plunder. Constitutional revision in Michigan and determined efforts in that direction which are currently underway in such states as Pennsylvania and Massachusetts give some evidence that the states possess the internal energy necessary to achieve a measure of self reform. Entrance of the federal courts into the area of legislative apportionment, while still uncertain in its ultimate effect, has already produced a healthy redistribution of seats in a score of state legislatures. Appearance of effective citizen organizations with ideological objectives in such states as California, Texas, Michigan, and New York have introduced new meaning into the sometimes purposeless competition between the parties. Civil service extension in even so notorious a stronghold of the spoils system as Pennsylvania proves, indeed, that almost anything is possible. Although the states, even under current conditions, enjoy certain constitutional advantages over their federal rival—superior party cohesion, a more manageable scope of activities, fewer and less restrictive legislative roadblocks and rituals—there can be no doubt that continued vast efforts at reform are essential if the states are to remain (or become) effective instruments of government.

Even with the best will in the world, the states would still be faced with extremely grave financial difficulties. Actually, as shown in Figure 11, the states have demonstrated an almost phenomenal willingness since 1950 to increase taxation in order to meet the increased demand for services. (Comparison among the individual states in this respect is misleading, since the distribution of responsibilities between state and local governments varies from state to state. In Arizona, for example, 59 per cent of total state and local government direct expenditures in 1960 were made by the state, while in New York the comparable figure was only 44 per cent.) Increased taxation has been reflected in greatly increased state services—total state expenditures for both education and highways

Figure 11. Total Per-Capita State Taxes, 1950 and 1961

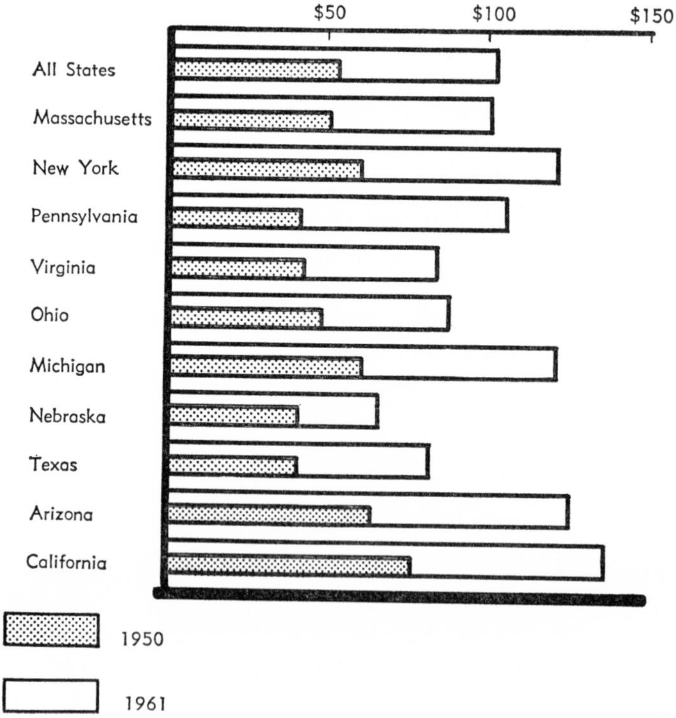

1950

1961

(the two largest items in most state budgets) almost tripled between 1950 and 1961, welfare expenditures increased more than 50 per cent, and expenditures for health and hospitals more than doubled.

There is little reason to believe that the demand for increased state expenditures has in any way achieved a plateau in the middle 1960's. Rather, the rising cost of public education, pressure on the states to aid their cities in problems like mass transit and urban renewal, and participation by the states in the federal Kerr-Mills medical-aid program, to name only three major items, point to an increasing rate of growth for the size of state outlays. At the same time, sources of additional revenue are becoming more and more difficult for state administrations to uncover. Resistance to state invasion of the income tax field is stiffening wherever this form of levy has so far been avoided. Taxes on business are held in effective check in most states by the heated competition for new and expanding industry. Soak-the-rich devices, like the graduated inheritance tax, are also discouraged by their supposed effect on businessmen seeking new locations for investment. The sales tax continues its majestic march toward 5 per cent (achieved in 1963 by Pennsylvania, with food, clothing, industrial machinery, and many other items exempted) —beyond which both politicians and economists shudder to calculate its effects. Incidental excise taxes have in many cases reached or are approaching their points of diminishing return.

Attempting to find relief from their financial difficulties, states have in recent years turned increasingly to the federal government for at least partial support for their programs and have utilized the device of long-term borrowing to expand their supplies of capital. The federal contribution to total state revenues rose from 12 per cent in 1942 to 16 per cent in 1950 and to 20 per cent in 1961. Total state debt was almost four times as large in 1961 as in 1950, although annual borrowing did not increase as rapidly as either total state revenues or expenditures (60 per cent for borrowing, as compared to 150 per cent for revenues and 130 per cent for expenditures).

Increased financial reliance by the states on the federal government has within it obvious perils, both for the states and for the federal system. For one thing, financial dependence rarely if ever forms an enduring basis for institutional freedom. As the states receive more of their income from Washington, they will inevitably fall increasingly under the surveillance and control of the central government bureacracy. For another, the nature of the federal union makes it unlikely that federal funds will be distributed among the states in a manner entirely efficient or equitable. Should the federal government expend its funds according to varying need, offering more support to relatively poor Virginia than to rich New York; or to match the state's own effort in given fields, serving generous California more handsomely than frugal Ohio? Or should it return funds in rough equation to the rate at which they are gathered, supporting, say, Nebraska in proportion to the federal taxes collected only from Nebraskans? And are not the political realities of the United States Senate and the power of Southern committee chairmen in Congress bound to influence the way in which the federal effort is distributed? In 1961, as a matter of fact, federal contributions per capita to state governments ranged from $132.37 in Alaska to $18.07 in New Jersey. Federal contributions per capita to the ten states studied and the share which these amounts formed of total revenue are shown in Figure 12.

Borrowing, on the other hand, provides the states with a fiscal tool over which they may maintain more direct control. Its utilization has thus far been limited, due partly to constitutional ceilings on debt in many states and partly to the deep-seated American preference for pay as you go rather than borrowing as a means for financing the operations of government. In the middle sixties, fiscal conservatism among the great mass of voters—including many who favor broad expansion of state services—seems likely to prevent any enormous enlargement of borrowing in the immediate future. Overlapping majorities of Americans appear, particularly at the levels of state and local government, to subscribe to *both* the social philosophy of G. Mennen Williams and the economic policies of Harry Flood Byrd. Whether the so-called new federalists—like Governors Rockefeller, Romney, and Scranton—can implement the former within the limits set by the latter remains uncertain.

Perhaps most fundamental of all the problems confronting the states is that of political legitimacy. Do the states, after all, have any real basis for continued existence? Do they inspire loyalty and respect in the hearts of their citizens? Are they political anachronisms, like the Turkish and Austro-Hungarian Empires in the years immediately preceding World War I, or are they vitally related to the social and economic realities of the present day? In short, would any one care (beside armies of politicians and a few sentimentalists) if they were to perish? Would any large group suffer if they were to be superseded by rationally planned administrative departments of a thoroughly centralized national government?

Political legitimacy is the product of both history and geography, of both economic and social facts. The historical legitimacy of the

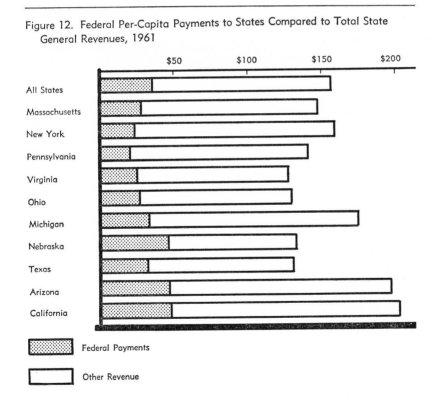

Figure 12. Federal Per-Capita Payments to States Compared to Total State General Revenues, 1961

states, while firmly rooted in the federal constitution and in more than two centuries of experience, is increasingly threatened by the migratory habits of so much of the modern middle-class. History, as the object of felt commitment, is viewed more and more in national terms. Frequent movement, in search of economic opportunity, new associations, lower inheritance taxes, seems to have, if anything, a strengthening effect on the national identification and patriotism of most citizens; even local identification—through the churches, the PTA, the chamber of commerce, the service clubs, the local newspaper—may at least temporarily be re-enforced; but state loyalty is undoubtedly subjected by repeated migration to an eroding effect which is both steady and inevitable.

Geographically, legitimacy is strongest in most states in the interior counties and weakest in border areas, particularly if these areas fall within the sphere of influence of out-of-state cities. (Southwestern Nebraska, for example, looks more toward Denver, Colorado, than toward Lincoln or Omaha. Many residents of the suburban counties south of Washington, D.C., make no secret of their hostility toward the Commonwealth of Virginia. The state of New Jersey, divided between the attractive forces of New York City and Philadelphia, appears to enjoy a minimum of legitimacy—partial explanation, perhaps, for the extreme intransigence with which Jerseyites have traditionally resisted state taxes.) Legitimacy also grows weak in geographically isolated areas, like the Texas Panhandle and Michigan's Northern Peninsula. The situation in metropolitan areas is somewhat mixed. Many city dwellers, particularly New Yorkers, appear to feel little sense of identification with their states. Bostonians, on the other hand, seem to identify quite strongly with Massachusetts (there is a tendency, in fact, among some Bostonians to feel that their city *is* Massachusetts); similar sentiments are felt among Richmonders toward Virginia, among Houstonians and Dallasites toward Texas, and among Angelinos toward at least Southern California.

Geography, on the whole, appears to strengthen the legitimacy of state government. The locality is too small and the federal union is too large to comprehend the problems of the regional groupings which compose the social and economic structure of the continent.

But are the states, as now established, capable of commanding the human resources of these regions? It has been charged that the states place metropolitan areas at the political mercy of their hinterlands and that some states artificially combine two or more essentially dissimilar regions (like the Philadelphia and Pittsburgh regions of Pennsylvania, or Northern and Southern California). Both of these charges are to some extent valid, but neither provides reason for abandoning the institutional values available in the states. The future of cities, as Lewis Mumford has pointed out, must lie in the redistribution of many of their functions—and many of their people —to the hinterlands. Thus, the unit of the state, rather than the unit of the city or even the unit of the metropolitan area, appears to possess the greatest potentiality for future governmental utility as well as for political legitimacy. The most urgent (and least understood) task confronting state politicians is to manage the extension of social and economic opportunities now available mainly in cities to the great hinterlands of region states. Any attempt to redraw state boundaries to fit the patterns of alleged natural regions would be bound to destroy that very cement of historical and social legitimacy which will be indispensable to the states in this task—while at the same time failing inevitably to match except momentarily the swiftly changing patterns of a dynamic economy.

The fact that the states can and should continue to play an invaluable social role is, of course, no guarantee that they will survive. The constitutional, financial, and, one may say, existential problems which they face are, as has been shown, formidable. Political systems at least equally valid, from the city states of ancient Greece to the ethnic nations of Eastern Europe created at the end of the World War I, have perished long before accomplishing missions no less significant. The question which remains unanswered is whether the states have within themselves the political vitality to solve the problems which history has set them. The recent political histories of ten states reviewed in these pages may provide some clue to the answer to this question, but no such answer can or should pretend to be definitive.

The future of the states depends finally on their people—how much their people want them, how firmly their people will guard their honor, how devotedly their people will work and sacrifice for their success. And the people, as has been said, are a great mystery —as inscrutable as oceans, as filled with possibilities as the morning sun.